Dedication

To the memory of my parents: Matthew, who valued education highly and made many sacrifices to ensure mine, and Bridget (neé Rochford), who passed on to me a great love of reading in my formative years.

To my wife and children also, with thanks for all their encouragement and support.

Dyslexia
An introductory guide

Second Edition

JIM DOYLE

Consultant in Dyslexia
PROFESSOR MARGARET SNOWLING
University of York

W
WHURR PUBLISHERS
LONDON AND PHILADELPHIA

First published 2002 by
Whurr Publishers Ltd
19b Compton Terrace, London N1 2UN, England and
325 Chestnut Street, Philadelphia PA 19106, USA

British Library Cataloguing in Publication Data

A catalogue record for this book is available from the British
Library.

ISBN 1 86156 309 4

Printed and bound in the UK by Athenaeum Press Limited,
Gateshead, Tyne & Wear.

Contents

Acknowledgements **vii**

Chapter 1 **1**

The measurement of reading

Chapter 2 **14**

Reading difficulties explained

Chapter 3 **26**

The influence of intelligence

Chapter 4 **43**

The importance of mental age

Chapter 5 **53**

The teaching of reading

Chapter 6 **71**

The learning of reading

Chapter 7 **82**

Dyslexia examined

Chapter 8 **96**

The dyslexic child

Chapter 9 **110**

Assessment of the dyslexic child

Chapter 10   **141**

Possible causes (I) Biological bases

Chapter 11   **164**

Possible causes (II) Phonological awareness

Chapter 12   **181**

Help for the dyslexic

Chapter 13   **195**

Advice for parents

Chapter 14   **212**

Other issues and questions

Chapter 15   **223**

Useful information

Chapter 16   **233**

A brief history of dyslexia

Appendices   **240**
Glossary   **247**
Bibliography   **267**
Index   **269**

Acknowledgements

Thanks are due to:

- Dr Kathleen Henry (former course tutor at the University of Manchester) for inspiring my initial interest in dyslexia
- Ms Julia Evans (formerly a teacher at an LEA Specific Learning Difficulties Unit) for much information and advice during 11 years of working together
- John Wilkins (educational psychologist, friend and colleague) for imparting so much of his knowledge in discussions and debates
- John Maguire (formerly a pupil at St Xaviers College, Liverpool) for his assistance when the first drafts of the illustrations were being prepared
- Professor Margaret Snowling (Department of Psychology, University of York) for much-valued advice and criticism of the initial text
- the staff at Whurr Publishers for their consideration and support.

For this second edition my thanks are also due to:

- Matthew Doyle for his artistic expertise in preparing the illustrations used
- Mrs Joan (Jean) Doyle for her typing and word-processing skills in preparing the draft version.

Notes

For ease of expression throughout the book I have referred to the child as 'he' and the teacher as 'she'. No sexism is intended by this. In each case the words 'he or she' are understood.

In early July 1995, after the main body of the text was set, the Department for Education (DFE) became the Department for Education and Employment (DFEE). This in turn, in June 2001, became the Department for Education and Skills (DfES).

Chapter 1
The measurement of reading

A dyslexic child has difficulty with learning to read. He is also likely to have other associated difficulties, such as poor spelling, slow or immature handwriting, or an inability to deal with numbers, but the reading difficulty is the principal reason that makes him a cause for concern in the first place.

The question then arises as to exactly why a teacher or parent should suspect a child of being dyslexic. In fact, we can leave dyslexia to one side for a moment and ask why a particular child should ever be considered to be a poor reader for any reason. To find an answer to any of these questions we need to know what the basic facts are regarding learning to read:

- What is a good reader?
- What is an average reader?
- Is there any means of distinguishing between them?
- If so, what is it?
- How is a poor reader identified?
- Is a dyslexic child the same as any other poor reader or is it possible that dyslexia is different in nature from other types of reading difficulty?

There *are* answers to these questions, but they need to be fully explained. They can be understood only by setting the explanations into the general background, which relates to such matters as the everyday teaching of reading, the differences that arise between children when they are learning to read and how the differences can be measured.

The teaching of reading

Each year millions of children in Britain attend school and are taught reading by hundreds of thousands of teachers. This is a practice that has applied for more than 120 years and has proved, by and large, to be a successful one. Success can be claimed as most children leave school able to read at a level that allows them to cope quite adequately with the demands of life in present-day society.

The fact that *every* school leaver is not fully literate is very much to be regretted and is a situation that everyone would like to see corrected. But the positive side of the picture is quite remarkable. The fact is that most children in Britain do learn to read despite there being many differences and difficulties to be found within the child population generally and despite the fact that there are a number of approaches to reading in general use. The rate of success in reading is independent of size of school and also of where the school is located. Village schools, those in suburbs and ones in inner cities all produce literate children with more or less equal rates of success.

What happens in the case of most children is that they start to learn to read at about the age of 5, having worked for some time at building up their pre-reading skills. After this they acquire more reading skills and steadily become more proficient over a period of about four years by which time, at the age of about 9, they are fully literate. By 'fully literate' we mean that they can decipher print accurately and make sense of what is written by being able to 'decode' the text of a book or newspaper. However, after the age of 9, children must continue to read increasingly more difficult types of writing if they are to enlarge their vocabularies and build on the skills they have acquired. This process is illustrated in Figure 1.1.

Comparing one age group of the child population with another, it is only to be expected that the 9-year-olds are able to read better than the 8-year-olds who, in turn, read better than 7-year-olds and so on down the age groups. Also, the 7-year-olds of today will in a year's time be able to read as well as today's 8-year-olds. In two years from now they will be reading as competently as today's 9-year-olds and so on into the future.

It is important to be able to measure how well a child can read so that an accurate and unbiased assessment of the child's progress may be made. This is best done by using reading tests and we now need to consider these and the manner in which they are used.

The measurement of reading progress

Over the years, a large number of reading tests have been designed and developed. These will show some variety when compared one to

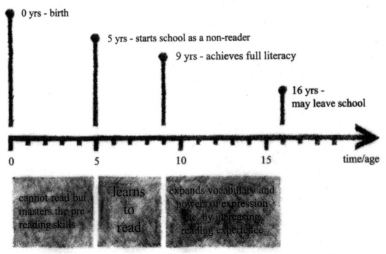

Figure 1.1 Stages in reading development (ages refer to the average child).

another. Many reading tests have been designed to be given to a whole group of children, such as a class, at the same time; others are meant to be given to an individual. Some consist of a list of single words, others consist of sentences each with a word missing, which needs to be supplied or chosen from a group of possibilities.

The simplest and most straightforward reading tests are the word lists. Each of these tests consists of a number of words, which need to be read in a certain order. At the start the words are short, common and easily pronounced, but they gradually become longer, less common and irregular. The Schonell graded word reading test is a good example. The test starts off with words such as 'tree', 'little' and 'book' and progresses to 'ineradicable, 'fictitious' and 'idiosyncrasy'. (A few of the many reading tests that are available to teachers and others are shown in Figure 1.2.)

For a reading test to be of any real value it needs to be properly designed, checked and standardized, otherwise the results will have little meaning. A person or team designing a word-list type of reading test should start by drawing up a list of words which they assume will be suitable to determine the reading progress of children between the ages of 5 and 14. A perfectly designed test is one that is easy enough for most 5-year-olds to make a start on, yet still difficult enough for some 14-year-olds not to be able to complete. In addition, it needs to distinguish each of the age groups in between; that is, children aged 12 should do better than those aged 11, who in turn will do better than the 10- and 9-year-olds, etc. What they must avoid is producing a reading test that is so easy that many children

Figure 1.2 A few of the many reading tests available.

(even the youngest age groups) obtain high scores, so difficult that very few children (even the older ones) can achieve any success or so badly designed in between the two extremes that children of different ages all score the same and cannot be distinguished.

Needless to say, a properly designed reading test is a sensitive, and therefore quite accurate, measuring device and to achieve these qualities the designers will need to invest some work in it. Therefore, the initial word list drawn up by the design team will need to be tested out in one or more pilot studies with one or more groups of children. The pilot study should identify any words that are too easy, those that are too difficult and also whether any particular words have been included 'out of order', i.e. either too high up or too low down the list. A word which is found in practice to be read very easily, but which has been placed between two more difficult words, will need to be placed somewhere more suitable. Eventually, the team will produce a word list that is an improvement on what was first drawn up, because the errors will have been corrected, but it will still need to be standardized. It is not sufficient simply to have a list of suitable words arranged in order of difficulty and which is capable of being used on children from 5 to 14 years of age. You also need to know how many words a given child should be expected to read correctly. For instance, if the list consists of 100 words, what scores would you expect from an 8-year-old and an 11-year-old?

To obtain this information the test must be given to more children, and this time larger numbers will need to be used than in the pilot studies. Ideally, the test should be given to the whole population of schoolchildren, but because there are several million in the British Isles this would not be very easy to do, so groups of children are used instead.

The ideal would be to standardize the test on a large number of groups each containing a large number of children, but in most cases this is not possible and the test design team is forced to settle for something less. However, they do have a great deal of information about the nation's schoolchildren and can make use of this in selecting their groups. What they will aim for is to standardize the test on a group of children who will be, as far as possible, a 'scale model' of the total population of schoolchildren. The group should have the same proportion of inner-city children, children from ethnic minority backgrounds, children from each of the social groups, etc., as in the overall population. Provided this is done, the results will be accurate to within a very small margin of error and the test can be standardised accordingly, e.g. children aged 5 score 5, those aged 6 score 12, those aged 7 score 18, etc.

It cannot be emphasized too strongly just how important the process of standardization is as part of test design. It is not much help to a teacher or parent to know only that John, aged 8, was given a reading test and was able to read 35 words correctly. What needs to be asked is whether his score is a good, average or poor achievement for a child of his age. If most other children of John's age score only 20 then he is doing well, but if they are scoring 50 the picture is a very different one.

The Schonnell Test mentioned above was revised in 1971 by being standardized on 10 000 children in Salford, Greater Manchester. It was found that the average 7-year-old could read 15 words, 8-year-old 30 words, and so on. (This particular test consists of 100 words and is capable of measuring the reading ages of children from below 6 to above 12 years.)

The pattern of children's reading scores

We now need to examine the picture that is produced when a properly designed and well-standardized reading test is used on a large numbers of children. Imagine there is such a test, which we will call the 'Smith and Jones' Reading Test, and the Department for Education and Skills (DfES) decides to use it to assess the reading ability of the country's 7-year-olds. There could be many good reasons for carrying out such a survey. The DfES might want to see how well today's 7-year-olds compare with those of last year, or five years or even 10 years ago. It might want the information to use as a basis for comparing future 7-year-olds in the years to come.

Whatever the reason, the survey should ideally include all 7-year-olds, but as there are more than 700 000 of them, the DfES would probably consider this to be too large a number to organize and that only a proportion should be used. It could be agreed that 100 000 would be sufficient to provide the information required and this number settled on. Of the 700 000 children due to reach the age of 7 during the year planned for the survey, it could be arranged for the 100 000 required to be chosen completely at random by computer and for each of these children to be tested in school within a week of their birthday. At the end of the year there would then be information available on 100 000 children who represented one seventh or so of the country's 7-year-olds and who should be exactly like the total population of 700 000 in every other respect. There should be the same proportions of girls and boys, of city dwellers and those from rural areas, of children from ethnic minority backgrounds, etc.

The result obtained from each child would be a number representing how many words from the 'Smith and Jones' Reading Test he or she was able to read. Obviously, 100 000 results is a large amount of information to cope with and make sense of. Decisions would need to be made on how best to record it all.

Listing the results

The simplest way would be to draw up a list of the names of the 100 000 children with the number of words correctly read by each child recorded next to his or her name. This would produce a large document, e.g. if it were possible to put details of 100 children on each page it could be bound into a booklet of about 1000 pages.

Tabling the results

A better way to present the results would be to ignore the details of individual children and instead count them in groups. For instance, a count could be made of the number of children who were not able to read any words, the number who could read just one word, two words and so on down the list until the greatest number of words read was reached. (In our example this is 30.) It is not necessary to know the names of the children involved, so listing all the names individually would result in a large quantity of irrelevant information. Counting the number of children able to read each given number of words would summarize all the important details on a single sheet of paper and make this information available at a glance.

This has been done in Table 1.1. Essentially there are five columns of figures. The first is a list of the number of words read and runs from 0 to 30. The second column lists the number of children able to read each given number of words. The third column tells us the same as column 2 but gives the number as a percentage of the total. Columns 4 and 5 are very useful as they show how many children can read any given number of words or fewer. (Column 4 gives the information as a number and column 5 gives it as a percentage.)

Looking at the table, we see from the top line that only 129 children of the total number tested were not able to read any words at all (0) and this comparatively small number was only one tenth of 1% of the population tested (0.1%).

We can also see that 964 children (or 1% of the total) were able to read five words. However, the number of children who could read five or fewer words was 2522 (2.5%). The figure of 2522 is obtained by adding those who read 0 words (129) to those read one (151) to those who read two (242), three (402), four (634) and five (964). Hence 129 + 151 + 242 + 402 + 634 + 964 = 2522 (2.5%). The number 2522 is the *cumulative total* of children reading five words or fewer.

The most important point to be appreciated from the results of this imaginary survey is that despite the fact that all the children were of the same age they did not all produce the same results. In fact, a very wide range of results is seen, with a few children not able to read at all yet some others able to proceed to as many as 30 words.

Table 1.1 'Smith and Jones' Reading Test: results obtained from children aged 7.0 years (total children 100 000)

1 Words read	2 Children	3 (% of total)	4 Cumulative total of children	5 Cumulative % of children
0	129	0.1	129	0.1
1	151	0.2	280	0.3
2	242	0.2	522	0.5
3	402	0.4	924	0.9
4	634	0.6	1558	1.5
5	964	1.0	2522	2.5
6	1419	1.4	3941	3.9
7	2018	2.0	5959	6.0
8	2760	2.7	8719	8.7
9	3702	3.7	12421	12.4
10	4672	4.7	17093	17.1
11	5688	5.7	22781	22.8
12	6824	6.8	29605	29.6
13	7734	7.7	37339	37.3
14	8330	8.3	45669	45.7
15	8662	8.7	54331	54.3
16	8321	8.3	62653	62.7

the table continues

30	88	0.1	100000	100

However, the most important thing this survey tells us is that for 7-year-olds the ability to read 15 words on this particular reading list has significance. Why this is so can be understood from column 5. As can be seen, 14 words or fewer can be read by about 46% of the population, which is less than half. By the same token, *more than half* of the population (54%) can read 15 words or more and so the 'expected' or 'normal' score for 7-year-olds on this reading test is 15. At any stage in a child's education it is to be expected that he will perform at the same level as most other children of the same age and so a score of 15 or more will be expected from any 7-year-old who is given this test. We should add that this is what will be expected *provided that all other things in the child's life are equal.* Often they are not equal, however, and we will be considering this later in the book.

Graphing the results

A third way of presenting the results so they may be analysed accurately would be to use the data from columns 1 and 2 in the table to draw a graph. The number of words read (0 to 30, from column 1) would be listed along the horizontal axis of the graph and the number of children would be listed up the vertical axis of the graph. This would best run from 0 to 9000 to accommodate the actual range of 129-8662 (from column 2).

The graph is shown in Figure 1.3a. If we scan across it from left to right we see that it is a curve, with a high point in the middle, and it falls away in a regular manner on either side, one half of the graph being a 'mirror image' of the other.

The score of 15 is all-important because:

- the peak of the graph is directly above it, showing that 15 is the most 'popular' score as more children obtain that exact score than any other
- more than half of all the children tested scored 15 or above
- most children are grouped around the score of 15 and so are in a fairly close range of it. There are far fewer at the extreme ends of the graph in the 'low score' and 'high score' ranges.

Because a score of 15 on our 'Smith and Jones' Reading Test has proved to be so significant in the case of 7-year-olds, it is perfectly in order for teachers, parents and others to regard this score as a READING AGE OF EXACTLY 7 YEARS 0 MONTHS, and this is what is done to make results more meaningful. To say that 7-year-old John has had his reading ability tested and he scored 15 tells us very little. To say that he proved to have a reading age of 7;0 tells us a great deal, as a comparison can now be made between John and other children in the country of the same age. It is only with *this* information (a reading age) that we are able to judge how well or badly he can read.

Testing other age groups

So far in our imaginary reading survey we have concentrated on a single age group: 7-year-olds. But much can be learned by testing other age groups and making a comparison. If the same procedure that was carried out on 7-year-olds was also applied to the country's 8-year-olds, and the resulting graph was drawn on the same axes as that of the 7-year-olds, it would look like Figure 1.3b.

The graph relating to the 8-year-olds is identical in shape to that of the 7-year-olds but lies to the right of it, the 'peak' for the older children being at the 25-word level, which is 10 greater than that for the younger ones.

This should not be a surprise. The 8-year-olds, having had an extra year at school, will naturally be able to read more words than the 7-year-olds. Just as a score of 15 represents a reading age of 7;0 years, so a score of 25 represents a reading age of 8;0 years. Further-

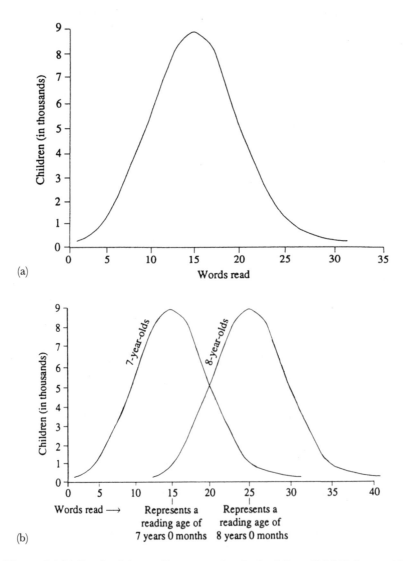

Figure 1.3 (a) Graph of the reading test results obtained from 100 000 7-year-olds; (b) Graph comparing the reading abilities of 7- and 8-year-olds.

more, the two groups of children are found to overlap in their reading abilities to a certain extent, with the more able younger children being as competent at reading as are the less able older ones.

It is not hard to appreciate that if the process were to be continued with 9-, 10- and 11-year-olds, then a series of curves would result, with each successive curve lying to the right of that of the age group immediately below it and overlapping those on either side. The number of words read corresponding to each reading age can be identified from the peaks of each age group's curve, as shown in Figure 1.4.

The horizontal axis of this graph can also be viewed as a ladder lying on its side, with the rungs numbered in order from the foot (which lies at the left-hand end of the axis) to the top (at the right-hand end). Particular rungs are then marked to represent reading ages, e.g. rung 15 is reading age 7;0, as in our 'Smith and Jones' Reading Test. When the ladder is set upright, a child undergoing a reading test can be thought of as 'climbing' the ladder and it can then be seen just how 'high' he is able to climb. Each marked rung shows the height that most children of that age group are able to reach. For example, most 9-year-olds will reach the 9 years rung (number 35 in our example) but some will not be able to achieve this, just as some others will be able to 'climb' even higher. This is shown in Figure 1.5.

Summary

We began this chapter by saying that it is important for all concerned with dyslexia to have a clear idea in their minds as to how a dyslexic child can be identified.

We are now in a position to answer many of the questions we asked:

- *What is a good reader?* We now know that a child who is considered to

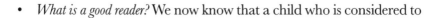

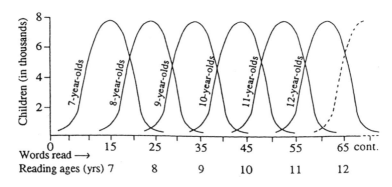

Figure 1.4 Graph comparing the reading abilities of consecutive age groups.

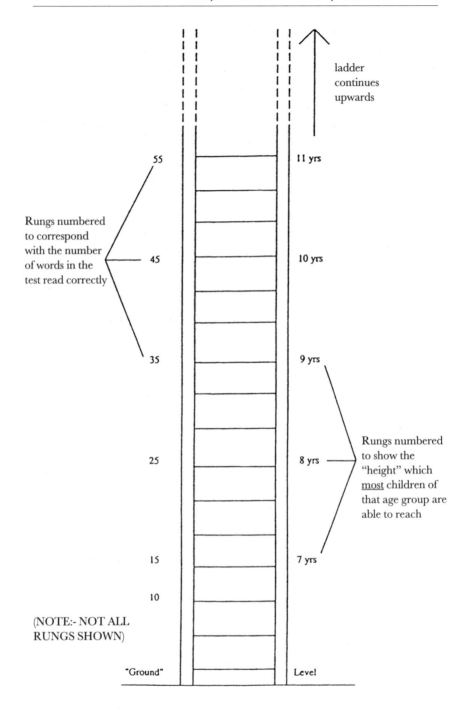

Figure 1.5 Diagram to illustrate how a reading test may be viewed as a 'ladder' a child can 'climb'.

be a good reader is able to read *better* than most children of the same age as himself. The child will obtain a 'high' mark on reading test, which in turn shows that he has a 'high' reading age.

- *What is an average reader?* One who is capable of reading at the *same* level as most children of his age.
- *Is there any means of distinguishing between them?* A reading test that has been properly designed and accurately standardized on samples of the particular population of children for which it was intended will distinguish between a good and an average reader.
- *How is a poor reader identified?* From the score obtained on a reading test of the type described. (Before we proceed to the last question it will be appreciated that the important task of identifying children with reading difficulties is something that can be undertaken in an efficient and unbiased manner using an appropriate reading test. Consequently teachers, parents and others do not need to rely on their own impressions, hunches or suspicions, which can often be quite misleading. Any worries about a child's reading ability should be settled at the earliest opportunity by the use of a test.)
- *Is a dyslexic child the same as any other poor reader or is it possible that dyslexia is different in nature from other types of reading difficulty?* Nothing we have covered so far can provide an answer to this question. The information we need in order to answer this question is dealt with in the following chapters.

Now that we know something about how reading progress is measured, we can go on in Chapter 2 to discuss what factors influence a child's reading progress, the various difficulties that can arise and the manner in which they operate.

Chapter 2
Reading difficulties explained

The single most important piece of information covered in Chapter 1 is that *not all school-age children have the same reading ability* but show quite wide variation. Although most children are within the average range, a certain percentage (say 15–20%) are below average and a similar percentage above.

This is common knowledge of course, and hardly needs to be stated, but it does not answer the burning question of *why* this should be so. Why can't all children show the same progress in reading? What are the reasons for it? Can we detect them? Can anything be done to help matters? These questions are very important in our attempts to understand dyslexia. If a group of children - a school full, say - do not all have the same level of competence in reading, then logically there can be only one expla-nation: *there are factors involved that produce differences.* These factors must be:

either (a) causing the reading ability of some children to be *better* than that of others;

or   (b) causing it to be *worse* in some than in others;

or   (c) causing *both effects*, i.e. causing the reading ability to be better than average in some children but worse than aver-age in others.

We now need to examine every part of a child's present make-up, history and social background that could possibly affect his read-ing ability in one direction or the other. But before we do that it might be helpful to mention some factors that do not affect reading ability so they may be eliminated to prevent possible future confusion.

Location of school

Neither the general nor the particular location of a school should prevent children from learning to read adequately. Children in all parts of Britain are found to master the skill. England, Scotland, Wales and the Isle of Man all produce literate children. Schools are located in a wide variety of geographical settings: in highland communities, on small islands, as part of pit villages, big cities and towns. However, although full literacy can be achieved by a child in any of these settings, there are some differences with respect to *average* results.

Social class

A child's ability to read does not depend directly on his parents' occupation(s) or his family's level of income. Good, average and poor readers are found in all social groupings. However, *general* differences are to be found, with children from higher social groupings tending to produce better results than those from lower social groupings.

Gender

Boys and girls are both capable of achieving full literacy, but do display differences in the process. Generally speaking, girls learn to read at a faster rate than do boys so that within any particular year group the reading ability of the girls will be somewhat better, on average, than that of the boys.

None of these three factors has a profound influence on the ability to read, any more than does height, weight, eye colour or blood group. There are other aspects of children's development that are mistakenly considered by some to cause difficulties with reading but location of school, social class and gender are the ones most commonly placed in this category.

Factors that influence reading

And now to examine those factors that definitely *do* have a part to play in the way a child's reading skills develop. Figure 2.1 lists 20 factors in alphabetical order, and includes all the influences that are commonly considered to play a part by people working in education. (However, it is not claimed to be an exhaustive list; over time other influences could well be discovered.)

When primary school teachers attend courses on the teaching of reading they are often asked to produce their own lists of the factors

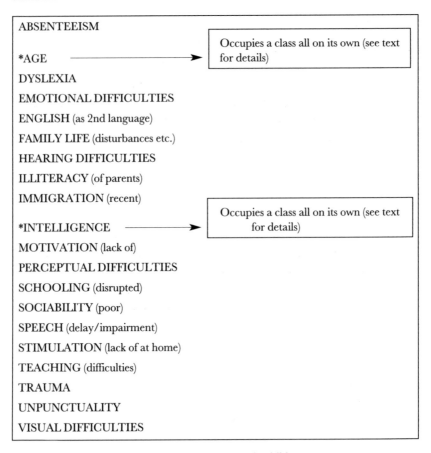

Figure 2.1 Factors that can affect reading progress in children.

they consider to be causes of reading difficulties. Figure 2.1 has been produced by putting a number of these lists together, so we can be reassured that we are not dealing with unreal, high-flown theory but rather down-to-earth, basic facts. Real teachers who are working every day in the nation's schools are able, from long experience, to identify what applies and what does not. Their opinions are confirmed by others in the education system who work with children.

Our list can be analysed in a number of ways, each of which provides useful information. It would be useful for us to know, for instance:

- What influence each has on a child's reading progress: positive, neutral or negative?
- Whether a particular factor influences all children or only some.
- Where the difficulties are to be found: within the child? Within the home background? Within the school?

- Which agencies should be consulted? And which can provide support?
- How soon after onset can any particular difficulty be detected?
- How serious an effect is there likely to be on the child's reading ability: mild/moderate/severe?
- How long-lasting is the effect likely to be: short-term/medium-term/long-term?

We shall consider the first of these classifications as, at this stage at least, it is the most informative. We need to be clear that as a first step towards understanding children's reading difficulties we are considering *any influence at all* that has a bearing on their reading progress. We are just as interested in anything capable of improving reading ability as we are in anything that has a negative effect. Once we are familiar with all possible factors we can look more closely at those that delay reading progress.

Types of influence

When we divide the list into the types of influence on children's reading we find that there are three distinct categories:

- age
- intelligence
- the other 18.

Age

Age occupies a class on its own. It relates positively to reading progress, with an increase in age leading to an increase in reading ability - 10-year-olds are able to read better than 9-year-olds who, in turn, can read better than 8-year-olds, etc. Age is unique, as it is the only one of the 20 factors listed that:

- affects every child *and*
- does so to the same degree, year on year.

When comparing one child with another it is to be expected that an older child will be able to read better than a younger child. Many comparisons of one child with another can be made in a meaningful way only if the children are of the same age, thereby removing the age factor. (This will be covered in more detail later in the book.)

Intelligence

Intelligence also occupies a class on its own, being different from age and also from the other 18 factors. Intelligence is unique because it is the only one of the 20 factors that:

- affects all children *and*
- can relate to reading ability in three different ways. It can relate positively (by being above average and contributing to a high reading age), in a neutral way (by being of average range and so producing an average reading age) or negatively (by being below average and contributing to a low reading age).

The other 18

The other 18 can all be grouped together into one category as they all have two characteristics in common:

- Each relates in a negative manner to a child's reading ability, causing it to be lower than it would otherwise be.
- Each affects only a small proportion of the total population of children.

The results are summarized in Table 2.1. We can see from the table that all three possible types of influence are at work.

Table 2.1 Influences that can affect reading progress in children

		Type of influence (summary)		
		Positive	Neutral	Negative
		Age	—	—
Proportion of children affected	All	·······················Intelligence···		
		High	Average	Low
	Some	—	—	Absenteeism etc. ↓ Visual difficulties (18 in total)

Analysing the problems of poor reading

So far in this chapter we have learned that:

- there are at least 20 factors at work in a child's make-up, history and social background that can influence his reading ability
- these 20 fall into three distinct groupings
- between them, they can act in three different ways on the child's reading.

All this makes for a rather complex picture, so when we come to consider an individual child we need to pick our way very carefully through the details of the case as we know them in order to give an accurate analysis of his difficulties. In the first place, it is easy to make the mistake of not making proper allowance for age. It is not unknown for parents to be worried about the reading progress of their 7-year-old child because he is not reading as well as his 9-year-old sister. This demonstrates a *real difference* in reading ability between two children, but does not automatically mean that there is any kind of *difficulty*. It is quite possible that each child is reading at an average level for this or her age group and that neither child is experiencing any difficulty. It is reasonable to suppose that when the younger brother attains the present age of his older sister he will be able to read as well as she is doing now. A difference is *not* a difficulty if it can be accounted for by age.

But of course even within a group of children of the same age there are poor readers and when they are considered they are found to fall into two groups:

- Those whose reading level is capable of being higher than it is at present but is prevented from being so by a particular difficulty (or combination of difficulties), which will be found in the group of 18 in the bottom right-hand box of Table 2.1. Each of these affects only a small proportion of children but always delays their reading progress.
- Those children who do not have any particular difficulties but are still not able to read as well as most other children of their own age. These children show a *difference* between themselves and others in their age bracket because unfortunately they do not have the basic ability to perform at a better rate than they are doing.

These two groups of poor readers are the products of two different types of influence that act on the general population of schoolchildren. This is only to be expected. Having removed age from the analysis at the beginning of the process by considering and comparing only children of the same age, we are left with intelligence and the group of 18. The effects of the latter produce the group of children with reading ages lower than they ought to be, and the effects of intelligence (low, in these cases) produce the children who are at the bottom end of the scale.

The child with a reading difficulty caused by one of the 18 factors is understood to be capable of achieving more, and consequently will make progress in reading once the factor involved is identified and cured/corrected/remediated/improved/prevented. The concept is that the child has a certain level of potential which the particular factor is presently preventing him from attaining (visual difficulties, hearing impairment and absenteeism are good examples).

The child who displays no detectable difficulties whatsoever but still achieves below average is considered to have a lower level of potential than the others but to be reading to the limit it allows. This type of child is usually found to be performing at a similar low level in most other areas of schoolwork, therefore confirming the overall picture.

Where difficulties arise

When the 20 factors known to influence a child's reading progress are grouped according to where they originate, it is seen that there are only three sources: the child himself, the home background and the school. The child accounts for 10 of the factors, the home for another nine and the school for just one. Table 2.2 shows which factors can be grouped under which headings. We will now mention each one briefly, with the exceptions of age, intelligence and dyslexia. The first two have already been discussed and dyslexia is covered in detail in Chapter 7.

- *Absenteeism*: No child will make progress in reading unless he is in school available to be taught. Generally speaking, the greater the absenteeism the less progress will be made.
- *Emotional difficulties*: The extremely sensitive or insecure child will be such that his emotional state acts as a barrier to learning. Sensitive handling will be required on the part of the school and in extreme cases outside opinion may be necessary.

Table 2.2 Where reading influences originate

Within child	Within family	Within school
Age	Absenteeism	Teaching (difficulties)
Dyslexia	English (2nd language)	
Emotional difficulties	Family life (disturbed)	
Hearing	Illiteracy (of parents)	
Intelligence	Immigration (recent)	
Motivation	Schooling (disrupted)	
Perception	Stimulation (poor at home)	
Sociability	Trauma	
Speech	Unpunctuality	
Vision		

- *English as a second language*: When this is the situation in a family, a child who is learning to read is likely to be at a disadvantage. Many such families lack the background knowledge of English that the other children in the class have, and reading could take longer to get established.
- *Disturbances to family life*: Unfortunately some children are in families that do not have a settled existence. Frequent changes of address during the early years of schooling, particularly when the child has to change schools, can result in underachievement. Even when a change of school does not feature, disturbances that cause a child to often have a broken night's sleep or to spend time away from home with relatives can contribute to reading progress being less than it should.
- *Hearing*: A child may have imperfect hearing in one or both ears and the degree of hearing difficulty can show wide variation. Any hearing problem will result in difficulties at school, particularly in relation to reading, so early detection is vital. Much can be done to remedy hearing difficulties.
- *Illiteracy of parents*: Any young school-age child will be at a big disadvantage if his parents cannot read. Much encouragement in reading comes from the home. The child whose parents cannot read him stories or help with his reading aloud is bound to be hindered in his attempts to progress.
- *Immigration (recent)*: The young child who has recently arrived in the UK from a different culture - particularly one where a different language is spoken - will need some time to adapt to the new culture in general and school life in particular.
- *Motivation*: Most children are keen to read, but a small proportion lack this drive. This could be for a number of reasons, often quite

complex, and will normally need investigation if the school's attempts to encourage the child do not succeed.

- *Perception*: In certain cases a child can have adequate eyesight and hearing and yet not always be able to make proper sense of what he is looking at or listening to. For example, a child may interpret a letter of the alphabet as facing the opposite way to what it actually is. Perceptional difficulties can lead to reading difficulties and justify further investigation.
- *Schooling (disrupted)*: In an ideal world each child would attend just one primary school where he would be happy and would achieve. Happily most children are in this category, but a proportion have the continuity of their primary education disrupted by having to change schools, sometimes more than once. This can have an adverse effect on a child's progress while he is settling into a different school and classroom routine as well as adapting to a different teacher.
- *Sociability*: Some children display a poor ability to socialize with others and settle into the school routine. At one extreme are the withdrawn, shy, under-reactive children, and at the other are the boisterous, outgoing, aggressive types. All children need a settling-in period, but if a particular child shows difficulties for a prolonged period then additional support is likely to be required.
- *Speech*: Any difficulties with speech will affect a child's reading progress. Speech may be delayed, immature or have some kind of defect such as a stammer or stutter. In reading, any child not able to pronounce a word properly will be disadvantaged and is likely to experience a delay in the development of his reading skills. In moderate or severe cases a speech therapist's opinion should be sought.
- *Stimulation (poor at home)*: Unfortunately some children are from homes where there is little intellectual stimulation for them. Conversation is lacking, and books, stimulating toys and other materials are in short supply or non-existent. Any child from such a home will undoubtedly find it more difficult to cope with reading and other school work, as a smooth start often depends on the child's experiences and variety of stimulation in the pre-school years.
- *Teaching (difficulties)*: On occasions, a class in a primary school can be unfortunate enough to experience a change of teacher part way through the school year. Sometimes, if the regular class teacher is absent on a long-term basis, the class can be taught by a succession of supply teachers, depending on the exact circum-

stances under which the school operates. Such a state of affairs is to be avoided if at all possible as the pupil's progress is quite likely to suffer as a result.

- *Trauma*: If a child suffers an accident or experiences the death of a close relative, there can be a period of time afterwards, often quite lengthy, in which school progress will suffer. All possible allowances will need to be made for such a child but any ground lost should eventually be made up.
- *Unpunctuality*: Any child regularly late for school, even though putting in a full attendance, is likely to be missing out on opportunities to develop his reading skills. In all such cases, the education welfare officer for the school should take action, and certain families may need support to encourage regular school attendance by their child.
- *Vision*: Some children have difficulties related to vision, but fortunately most of these are not serious and can easily be corrected once detected. The problem may be long-sightedness, short-sightedness, astigmatism, lack of acuity in one or both eyes or a squint (strabismus) in one or both eyes. Early detection is important, as good vision is essential for reading progress.

Support agencies

Fortunately we have a society where there are numerous agencies available to assist children with a wide range of difficulties. Sometimes these agencies may be undermanned, under-resourced and overworked, but at least they exist and may be called on when a child is found to have reading difficulties. Table 2.3 shows the particular professional personnel that can be called on to advise and support in the case of each of the difficulties we have described in this chapter. The three main agencies involved are the local education authority (LEA), the area health authority (AHA) and social services (SS), but others also contribute. The range of services available will vary from one part of the country to another and the exact title used will, in some cases, be different from those used here, but most, if not all, should be available wherever a child in difficulties might live.

Although it is possible to analyse the difficulties in other ways, those we have covered here are the most productive and informative. It would be useful to have additional information, such as the degree to which a child can be affected and how readily each type of problem can be detected, but questions such as these are difficult to answer with any degree of accuracy, so no further analyses will be attempted here. Another complicating factor is that it is possible for a child to experience a number of difficulties at the same time, and in those cases the effects are likely to be more marked and the remedies more difficult to put into practice.

Table 2.3 showing supportive professionals and their employing bodies

	LEA					AHA		SS	OTHER	
	EP	EWO	SpT	PSP	Sch	CMO	SpTh	SoWk	CG	LC
Absenteeism	–	●	–	–	–	–	–	–	–	–
Emotional difficulties	●	–	–	–	–	–	–	–	–	–
English (2nd language)	–	–	●	●	–	–	–	–	●	●
Family Life (disrupted)	–	–	–	●	–	–	–	●	–	–
Hearing	–	–	–	–	–	●	–	–	–	–
Illiteracy (of parents)	–	–	–	●	–	–	–	–	●	●
Immigration (recent)	–	–	–	–	–	–	–	●	●	–
Motivation	●	–	–	–	–	–	–	–	–	–
Perception	●	–	–	–	–	–	–	–	–	–
Schooling (disrupted)	–	●	–	●	–	–	–	●	–	–
Sociability	●	–	–	–	–	–	–	–	–	–
Speech (difficulties)	●	–	–	–	–	–	●	–	–	–
Stimulation (poor at home)	–	–	–	●	●	–	–	●	–	–
Teaching (difficulties)	–	–	–	–	●	–	–	–	–	–
Trauma	●	–	–	●	–	–	–	●	–	–
Unpunctuality	–	●	–	–	–	–	–	●	–	–
Vision	–	–	–	–	–	●	–	–	–	–

EP	= educational psychologist	EWO	= educational welfare officer
SpT	= specialist teacher	PSP	= parental support project
Sch	= school	CMO	= clinical medical officer
SpTh	= speech therapist	SoWk	= social worker
CG	= community groups	LC	= local college

Summary

To summarise the chapter:

- A child's progress in reading is affected by two universal influences: age and intelligence. These are so described because they affect *all* children. Progress may also be affected by one or more other influences related to *either* the child, *or* the home/social background, *or* the school. These affect only some children. Dyslexia is one of these other influences and is dealt with fully in this book.
- Intelligence is a significant influence on reading because it can contribute a great deal to a child being able to read *better* than most others of his age, as well as having the opposite effect.

- We need to be aware of the difference between a child who cannot read as well as others in his age group due to the influence of intelligence, and a child who cannot read as well as he should due to other reasons, such as those shown in Table 2.3. These two groups have, over time, been given various descriptions by different bodies in order to distinguish between them. We shall refer to the former group as *slow learners* and to the latter as children with *specific difficulties*.

Chapter 3
The influence of
intelligence

Intelligence plays a large part in our lives and particularly in how we learn. This applies irrespective of whether the learning takes place informally (i.e. picking things up as we go along, which is how we gain a great deal of our knowledge of the world and how it operates) or formally (i.e. by being taught in school or workshops, etc.).

The intelligence a child possesses will govern many aspects of the manner and ease by which he acquires new knowledge and masters new skills, such as learning to read, etc. When trying to diagnose a child's learning difficulties, one of the most important and relevant pieces of information that needs to be established is just how intelligent the child is. Sensible and accurate interpretations of much of the other information acquired about the child will only be possible when carried out against a background knowledge of his intelligence level.

The idea of intelligence is well known to us in the everyday sense of the word - it means clever, brainy, quick-witted, fast on the uptake, etc. We judge a person to be very intelligent, average or 'slow' on the basis of what they say and do, and often by what they achieve in life. Intelligence itself cannot be seen, only the products of intelligence, and these are very diverse. The world acknowledges that it takes a reasonable level of intelligence to compose a piece of music, write a novel, plan a battle, design a building, write a computer program, manage a firm, navigate an aeroplane and so on. All of these activities are the products of intelligent minds, and parents and teachers judge a child to be intelligent or not by comparing him with other children in the family or at school.

Because intelligence is so important in life generally, as well as in employment and general education, it has been studied in depth for many years and a great body of knowledge has been built up.

However, many of the findings have been challenged or contra-dicted, and the situation is far from clear-cut.

Some knowledge of how intelligence has been studied down the years may help in understanding the situation.

- In 1921, 14 experts were asked to describe what they considered intelligence to be. The result of this was 14 different descriptions. However, there was a general agreement that intelligence involves:
  - the capacity to learn from experience, and
  - the ability to adapt to the surrounding environment.
- In 1927, it was proposed by Spearman that intelligence consists of two parts, or factors, one being a *general* factor and the other a *specific* factor. He proposed that there is only one general factor but many different specific factors. General ability is what we use when performing mental tasks of all kinds, and has been described as 'mental energy'. However, a specific ability is required for just one kind of mental task. Because of this it is possible for a person to be good at verbal skills (such as reading, writing and expressing them-selves fluently in speech) and mathematics, but to have little, if any, musical ability and hence be quite poor when it comes to learning to play a musical instrument.
- In 1938, Thurstone argued that intelligence consists of a number of primary mental abilities, which include verbal comprehension, word fluency, numbers, spatial visualization, perceptual speed, memory and reasoning.
- In 1967, Guilford proposed that intelligence is made up of 120 elementary abilities.
- In 1971, Vernon proposed that intelligence can be described as comprising abilities at varying levels of generality. At the highest level is *general ability* (as proposed by Spearman), at the next level are *major group factors* (such as verbal/educational ability and prac-tical/mechanical ability), below these are *minor group factors* and finally there are *specific factors* (as also proposed by Spearman).
- More recent work has attempted to prove that the different descriptions and definitions proposed in the past can be reduced to the same thing. A number of information-processing psycholo-gists have sought to understand general intelligence in terms of elementary components (or processes) used in the solution of vari-ous kinds of problems. They distinguish *meta-components* (used for planning), *acquisition components* (used in learning), *retention compo-nents* (used in remembering), *transfer components* (used in the transfer

of knowledge from one task to another and *performance components* (used in problem solving).

This information-processing view of intelligence seems to unify what were formally a number of differing views regarding the nature of intelligence. However, a number of important questions relating to intelligence remain unanswered. Three of these are:

- How accurately can intelligence tests predict the performance of people in the real world?
- Is intelligence largely inherited (as has been claimed by some) or is it largely, or even exclusively, determined by environment, as has been claimed by others?

One important fact that must be kept in mind when attempting to understand intelligence is that it is not a single, isolated entity (such as a person's height or weight) but a collection of abilities, each one usually being the ability to reason in a particular way. Everybody has all of these abilities, but not all of them to the same level. For example, a person might be brilliant at maths and doing jigsaws but only moderate at writing a story and may have almost no ability to paint a picture or play a musical instrument.

Not only is there variation within each person but there is also very wide variation between one person and another. A very intelligent person is one who has high abilities overall, an average person is one with moderate levels across the ability range and a slow learner has a low level of abilities overall. However, that is not to say that a highly intelligent person is very good at everything. He may have only a moderate, or even a poor, ability in one or two areas of achievement, but when *all* abilities are considered, he will be found to have a high overall level of achievement.

Intelligence can be better understood if we compare it with something such as athleticism. We all know what an athletic person is and can recognize one when we see one. We also know how such a person differs from a non-athletic person. Nevertheless, the concept is still vague rather than exact. If we consider a pentathlete, such a person needs to be very good at five different athletic activities. But it is possible for a number of people to take part in a pentathlon and for the overall winner not to be the best at anything, as the following simple example shows.

Imagine that six people compete in a pentathlon. Table 3.1 shows their positions in each of the five events and their overall position.

Remember that in this example the competitor with the *lowest* total score is the winner, because first place = 1 point, second place = 2 points, and so on, therefore the best possible score, for winning all five events, is $5 \times 1 = 5$. The worst possible score, for five sixth places, $5 \times 6 = 30$. It can be seen from the table that competitor A is the winner (and hence the most 'athletic' of the six who competed) yet did not come first in any of the events. He is the winner because he was sufficiently good overall to beat the other five overall. Each of the other five competitors was excellent at one event and proved it by coming first in that event, but their results in the other events were more varied. Their average level of performance, and hence their overall result, was below that of competitor A.

In the same way, the child who is considered to be 'top of the class' need not be the best in the class at every subject taught. Likewise a highly intelligent person need not be excellent at everything and in fact might be quite poor at a few things, while a person considered to be average or even generally slow could well have one or two intellectual strengths, e.g. mental arithmetic.

The assessment of intelligence

For the best part of a century, psychologists and others have been engaged in producing intelligence tests. A great many have been designed and produced for a number of different purposes - some for administering to whole groups at once, others for administering to one person at a time, some intended for adults and others for use with children. Over time, the process has become more refined and sophisticated. Some of the older ones have not withstood the test of time and been discarded, while others have been periodically revised and updated. Occasionally a new test is produced, although, as will be explained later, they now tend to be called scales.

Table 3.1 Places gained by six competitors (A–F) in pentathlon

	COMPETITORS					
EVENT	A	B	C	D	E	F
Riding	2	1st	6	4	5	3
Duelling	3	4	1st	5	6	2
Shooting	3	4	5	6	2	1st
Swimming	2	5	3	4	1st	6
Running	2	4	6	1st	5	3
Total of places	12	18	21	20	19	15
Overall position	1st	3	6	5	4	2

The tests (or scales) attempt to assess an individual's potential to engage in useful behaviour, i.e. intelligent *activity*, rather than intelligence itself. Although there are many definitions of intelligence, most of the tests attempt to obtain an accurate picture of it by measuring a person's *mental abilities* or current *intellectual capacities*.

The amount of agreement between experts on what it is that an intelligence test actually assesses is far greater than many people realize. An intelligence test is essentially a test of deductive reasoning and many psychologists prefer to call is a test of 'reasoning' rather than of 'intelligence'. More specific phrases are generally used, such as 'verbal reasoning', 'numerical reasoning', 'perceptual reasoning', etc. When a person's intelligence is measured by an intelligence test, the result needs to be given in some unit of measurement. This measure is called the *intelligence quotient* (IQ), and we shall now see just what the numbers given mean.

The IQ

There are a number of ways in which the results of an intelligence test can be expressed, but the IQ is the one most often used and is certainly the one best understood by the general population. However, improvements in test design mean that nowadays a lot more information is obtained about a child (or adult) during the course of testing than can be conveyed by one single number. In fact, the question is often raised as to just what use an IQ figure is on its own. This is a valid and important question, because not only does the IQ not tell us everything about a child's intellectual ability, but under certain circumstances it may actually be misleading. How this can be so should become clear during the course of the chapter.

The manner in which intelligence tests are designed and the means by which the IQ is derived from the test results are, in theory, logical and quite easy to understand. Any of the tests used consist of a number of items that are ranged in order from those considered to be very easy to those considered to be very difficult. The order of items is such that the difficulty increases in an orderly and gradual manner from one item to the next. (When we say 'item' we usually mean a question to be answered, an explanation to be given, a calculation to be made or a task to be completed.) The items chosen will not have been assembled in an haphazard manner. They will usually have been selected from a much larger number because they have been proven to be most appropriate. The order in which they are arranged will also have been arrived at after much preliminary work in the form of 'pilot' studies.

In the case of tests designed for use with children, two things are assumed. One is that any given child will be able to perform better in the same test as he gets older. (The 7-year-old child tested today will be able successfully to complete an even greater number of items in one year's time and more still a year after that.) The other is that any two children of the same age who are tested at the same time will achieve the *same* score if they are of *equal ability*. By the same token, if they are of *unequal* ability then they will obtain *different* scores, the more intelligent child scoring more highly than the less intelligent one. If the test does *not* distinguish between children of different levels of intelligence, then it does not serve the purpose for which it was designed and will need to be abandoned.

Any properly designed test intended for use with children will have been piloted using large numbers of children spread throughout the age range for which the test is designed, e.g. 7 to 16 years. A pilot study can confirm that the basic design of the test is sound and is also used to check and cross-check the accuracy of the results obtained. Once the pilot study has been completed successfully, it should be known exactly what score an average 7-year-old, as well as an average child aged, say, 8;6 or 12;3, will obtain.

Just like the reading test described in Chapter 1, an intelligence test can be viewed as a fairly long ladder, with each rung marked as the natural stopping point for a normal child of a given age (see Figure 1.5). In the case of a child aged 8, he would be expected to 'climb the ladder' (so to speak) to the rung marked '8 years', which would be higher than the '7 years' rung but below the '9 years' rung. What will be found in practice is that half the 8-year-olds will be at or below this rung with the other half at or above it. Slower 8-year-olds will not be able to climb as far as the '8 years' rung, but the brighter ones will be able to climb above it. Some 8-year-olds will be on the '9 years' rung, a smaller number on the '10 years' rung and a very few even higher. Similarly, some will occupy the '7 years' rung, a few the '6 years' rung and a very few will be below this. The whole population of 8-year-olds will, if tested, be found to be spread across a range with the '8 years' rung marking the *average* stopping place for them.

Talking about rungs on ladders is all very well, but it is not the easiest or the clearest way in which to give information about a child's intellectual abilities. The easiest way is to use a scale of *numbers*. The system that has been used since the earliest days of intelligence testing has been to let the number 100 stand for average intelligence, with lower numbers (down to 50 or below) indicating lower intelligence and higher numbers (up to 150 or greater) indicating higher intelligence.

In fact, the scale is sometimes divided into sections, and descriptions may also be used to make the IQ scores more meaningful. One scale ranges from 70 to 130 and has the divisions and descriptions as follows:

- 130 and above = exceptionally high
- 120–129 = high
- 110–119 = high average
- 90–109 = average
- 80–89 = low average
- 70–79 = low
- below 70 = exceptionally low.

If the IQ scores of the population are plotted as a graph, the result is Figure 3.1. As can be seen, the average IQ for the population is 100. Most individuals lie between 85 and 115 (marked by dotted lines), and this is known as the normal range. In fact, 68% of the total lies between these two IQ scores, leaving 16% at the bottom end (below average) and the same percentage at the top. When a child is tested, his score is compared with the average score for children of his age, which will indicate whether he is average, above average or below average.

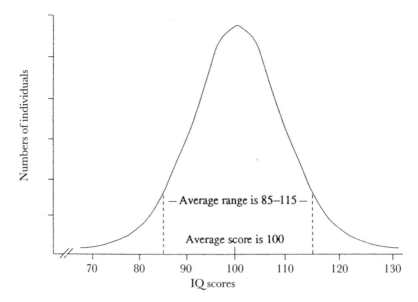

Figure 3.1 IQ scores of the UK population.

All of the above could be applied quite simply, if intelligence was known to be a *single* entity, such as a person's height or weight. It would be easy to assess a child by asking him a number of questions of increasing difficulty, finding out where the 'ceiling' of his ability was and then consulting a table to see how his score compared with those of most other children of the same age. In other words, his single 'raw' score could be converted into a single 'scaled' score, which would indicate his IQ.

Unfortunately, things are not quite that simple, because, as was made clear earlier, intelligence is *not* considered to be a single ability but a *collection* of abilities (just as athleticism is a collection of abilities relating to a number of sporting events not just one).

Therefore, to obtain an accurate picture of a child's intelligence it is necessary to test a number of the child's separate intellectual abilities and to see not only how they average out across the whole range but also what sort of a pattern or 'profile' they make.

The intelligence tests produced in recent years, and which are in general use by educational psychologists and others, all fit in with this basic design. Present-day intelligence tests are really collections of mini-tests (or subtests, to give them their correct name), each of which assesses something different about the child's ability to reason, solve problems, manipulate concepts, etc.

The question arises as to just what abilities an intelligence test should be designed to assess. After all, people possess a wide range of abilities (Guilford claimed that intelligence is made up of 120 different mental abilities) and it would be impossible to test all of them. The number of abilities chosen should be reasonably small, so that the test does not require too much equipment (for easy transportation from school to school, etc.) and can be administered within a reasonable period of time (one hour seems to be the most common time allotted).

The abilities tested tend to be selected by the test designers on the basis of those which best represent general intelligence, as it is thought that these:

- generate the greatest amount information about a child's mental capacity
- act as useful tools in the field of educational assessment
- help to appraise learning and other disabilities
- can be used to predict future school performance accurately.

The Wechsler Intelligence Scale for Children (WISC)

The Wechsler Intelligence Scale for Children (WISC) is probably the most commonly used of all the tests/scales available to educational psychologists, and is certainly very popular with them. It is a well-established scale with a design that is very helpful in assessing children's learning difficulties. It has undergone a number of revisions since it was first produced. It is designed to be used with children aged from 7 to 16 years of age and thus covers almost the entire age range of the school population in the British Isles. There are companion scales to the WISC - a downward extension (the WPPSI) and upward extension (the WAIS) - which enable younger and older pupils to be assessed if necessary.

This is probably a good point at which to explain why the word 'test' is no longer officially used and has been replaced by 'scale'. A test is something that a person either passes or fails. (The driving test is a good example of this.) With intelligence testing, however, it is not a question of 'pass' or 'fail', but simply a question of obtaining a measure, and so the WISC and other similar instruments should be regarded as a scale or measure by which the child is compared with others of the same age. It is more like a ruler or a pair of bathroom scales. However, despite these changes the expression 'intelligence test' is very much a part of everyday speech and will be used in this book from time to time.

To return to our description of the WISC, which has been designed and organized to measure general intelligence. The WISC consists of a number of subtests, and the particular subtests used were selected on the basis of two concepts:

- that intelligence is an overall or global entity which is multi-determined and multi-factored, rather than an independent, uniquely defined trait
- that no one particular ability is of any very great importance compared with any other.

The subtests are divided into two groups:

- the verbal subtests
- the performance subtests.

It is possible for a psychologist to administer to a child:

- the verbal subtests only and hence derive a verbal IQ

- the performance subtests only and hence derive a performance IQ
- both sets of subtests and hence derive a full-scale IQ.

The verbal scale

This consists of six subtests, but normally only five are administered to the child because the results from five are adequate to produce a reliable verbal IQ. The sixth subtest is available to the psychologist as a supplementary subtest, to be used in the event of one of the others being spoiled. However, it can also be administered in order to yield useful information in its own right. The verbal subtests are:

- Information
- Similarities
- Arithmetic
- Vocabulary
- Comprehension
- Digit span (the supplementary subtest).

The performance scale

This consists of seven subtests, only five of which are usually administered. The subtests are:

- Picture completion
- Picture arrangement
- Block design
- Object assembly
- Coding
- Symbol search (the optional subtest)
- Mazes (the supplementary subtest).

The scaled scores that children can obtain on the subtests range from 1 to 19, the average score of each being 10, and most scores are grouped around this from 8 to 12. The following example should help to clarify this.

Table 3.2 shows the scores obtained by an imaginary average child (whom we shall call child A). A graph plotted from his scores (Figure 3.2) gives us an instant picture or profile of child A's intelligence. (The WISC-3/UK test form on which the child's results are

Table 3.2 WISC scores of child A

VERBAL		PERFORMANCE	
Information	11	Picture completion	12
Similarities	8	Picture arrangement	10
Arithmetic	10	Block design	8
Vocabulary	9	Object assembly	9
Comprehension	10	Coding	11

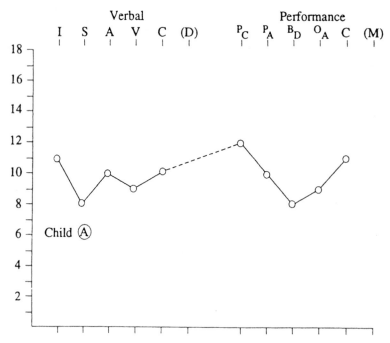

Figure 3.2 WISC scores of average ability (child A).

written is provided with a grid for this very purpose.). A number of features can be noted:

- The verbal scores add up to 48, which converts (by means of a special set of tables) into a verbal IQ of 97.
- The performance scores add up to 50 and convert into a performance IQ of 100.
- The totals of the verbal tests (48) and performance tests (50) add together to make 98, which can be converted into a full-scale IQ of 98.
- Child A is, therefore, of average overall ability as he lies within the IQ range of 85 to 115. What is more, he is only two points away from the mean of 100.

- The full-scale or overall IQ of 98 was obtained by combining a verbal IQ of 97 and a performance IQ of 100. These two IQs (97 and 100) are very similar, the difference being only three points. This is the situation for most children. A difference of just a few points is quite common and large differences are quite rare. For example, a difference of 12 points between verbal and performance IQs is found only five times in a hundred by chance alone. If there is a difference of 12 points within an individual child there are only five chances in 100 that the difference has occurred by chance alone and 95 chances in 100 that something has *caused* it. Differences larger than 12 are found in ever-smaller percentages of children, with very large differences being very rare indeed.
- The five verbal scores are tightly 'banded' together - the lowest is 8 and the highest 11, a separation of only three points. Because of this, the profile of the verbal scale section of the graph is quite 'flat' or 'even', with no extremes, i.e. no very high 'peaks' or very deep 'valleys'.
- The same applies to the performance items.

We can now compare these findings with those of another child - one of low ability, whom we shall call child L. His scores are given in Table 3.3, and the graph produced from these scores is shown in Figure 3.3.

Table 3.3 WISC scores and IQs of child L

Verbal scores	6, 7, 7, 8, 9 Total = 37	*Verbal IQ = 85*
Performance scores	6, 6, 7, 8, 8 Total = 35	*Performance IQ = 80*
		Full-scale IQ = 80

As can be seen, the verbal scores and the performance scores are all low - even the highest (9) is below the population average of 10. The verbal scores total only 37, which converts to a verbal IQ of 85, compared with a population average of 100. The performance scores total 35, and a performance IQ of 80. The verbal and performance score totals (37 and 35) add together to produce 72, which converts to a full-scale IQ of 80. A score of 80 or below applies to the least-gifted 9% of the total population.

However, each set of scores is, once again, quite tightly 'banded' (between 6 and 9 and 6 and 8 for the verbal and performance scores respectively). There are no large variations, which is the case with the majority of children, whether they are of high, average or low intelligence. With child L, the *general* picture is very similar to that of child A, except that his scores lie lower down the scale.

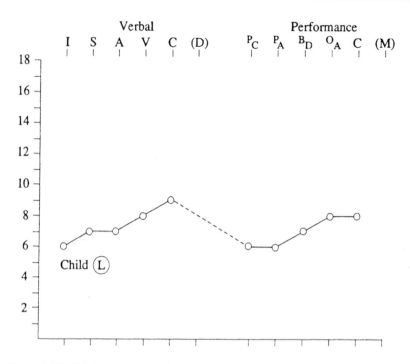

Figure 3.3 WISC scores of low ability (child L).

The final part of the overall picture is obtained by considering a child of high ability - child H. The scores for this child are given in Table 3.4.

Table 3.4 WISC scores and IQs of child H

Verbal scores	13, 14, 12,13,14 Total = 66	*Verbal IQ = 119*
Performance scores	15,12,13,14,12 Total = 66	*Performance IQ = 122*
		Full-scale IQ = 122

When we analyse these figures we see that the same picture emerges as for child A and child L, except that the graph plotted from his results will lie higher up the scale. We can see this for ourselves by looking at Figure 3.4, in which the results for all three children are plotted on the same axes or framework.

The line plotted from the results of the child of high ability lies above that of the average child, which is, in turn, above that of the child of low ability. All three are quite 'flat', i.e. they show only a small range in the spread of scores.

When educational psychologists assess children, they are particularly interested in children who are different from the majority. The graph of a child's WISC scores can show two types of difference. The

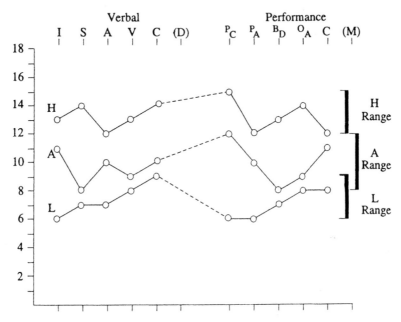

Figure 3.4 High, average and low ability children displayed together for comparison.

first is for the verbal and performance scores to be at different levels, either the verbal being at a high level and the performance at a low level, or vice versa. In such cases, further investigation is needed to find an explanation for this variation in the two types of performance, but is unlikely to be related to dyslexia.

The other type of difference is for the graph to show a wide range of scores, producing quite marked 'peaks' and 'valleys', rather than the more usual 'flat' appearance. Many people consider this second type of graph to be an indication of dyslexia, particularly if certain of the subtests are at the low points. The particular subtests concerned are Information, Arithmetic, Digit span and Coding. If the initial letters of these are rearranged they form the word 'acid', which, in the circumstances, is thought by many to be very appropriate as it allows them to talk about the 'Acid' tests that can indicate dyslexia. However, recent research has shown that only about 4% of children diagnosed as dyslexic demonstrate a definite 'acid' profile in their WISC scores. This type of graph shape or profile is shown in Figure 3.5.

Before we end this chapter a word of explanation about the WISC is required. The WISC has existed in three forms: that is to say the original version has been updated twice. The information in this chapter is based on the WISC-3/UK latest version, which became available in 1992 (the UK stands for the fact that norms

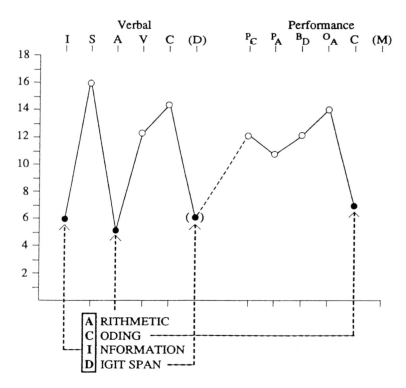

Figure 3.5 A profile of a dyslexic child (note the 'ACID' tests).

which have been obtained from the UK population are used with children tested in the UK).

WISC factors

In addition to the three IQs (verbal, performance and full-scale), four further scores can be calculated. These are each factor-based and produce an index score. They are verbal comprehension (VCI), perceptual organization (POI), freedom from distractibility (FDI) and processing speed (PSI). These factor-based scales have a mean of 100 and a standard deviation of 15, just as do the IQs. Many workers find them useful in interpreting WISC results.

Over time, the WISC-3/UK has replaced earlier versions and parents are likely to find that this is the test (or scale) being used by educational psychologists and quoted in their reports.

British Abilities Scales (BAS)

We have devoted a significant amount of space to the WISC, but it is not the only test in use. A second test, the British Abilities Scales

(BAS), is of more recent design and has enjoyed increasing use since its introduction.

The BAS covers a wide age range (from 2 years 6 months to 17 years 11 months) and consists of 22 subtests. However, all except one of these subtests are intended to be administered to certain age groups only, so no child would be assessed on all 22. In fact, the whole test is subdivided into an 'Early years' battery of subtests (intended for children aged 2 years 6 months to 5 years 11 months) and a 'School age' battery (intended for those aged 6 years 0 months to 17 years 11 months). At the lower end of the 'Early years' age range six subtests are administered, increasing to 12 at the upper end. There are 15 subtests intended for use throughout the 'School age' range.

The initial research that produced the BAS started as long ago as 1965 and it has been a continuous process since. The first edition of the BAS was published in 1979, with a revised edition (the BAS-R) in 1983. A US version known as the Differential Ability Scales (DAS) was produced in 1990.

The current version of the BAS (the BAS-II) was published in 1996. The scores obtained can be interpreted at three different levels. For instance, the scores obtained for the subtests Word definitions and Verbal similarities can be interpreted individually (i.e. they can each be compared with the scores produced by an average ability child of the same age). They can also be clustered to produce a score for verbal ability, which is a less specific (and hence more general) ability. Verbal ability can itself be clustered with two other more general abilities (non-verbal reasoning ability and spatial ability) to produce a third (and even less specific/more general) ability, general conceptual ability (GCA). GCA is a measure of a single general cognitive factor, which on its own cannot explain all human abilities but which nevertheless underlies all mental tasks.

The BAS-II does not produce an IQ, despite the fact that the original BAS and BAS-R did. The term intelligence has also been abandoned, and the GCA is given instead. The BAS-II test designers consider this to be very much a refinement of the assessment process. They point out that the term 'intelligence' is subject to numerous definitions - 'a word with so many meanings that finally it has none' - and also that widespread misunderstandings have resulted. They argue that the GCA produced by the BAS-II is a purer, more homogeneous and therefore more interpretable measure than an IQ produced by a WISC-3/UK.

Now that we have discussed the important role played by intelligence, we need to find out how it is related to mental age, as this plays a large part in the diagnosis of dyslexia. Mental age is explained in Chapter 4.

Chapter 4
The importance of mental age

The first three chapters covered some of the issues we must be familiar with and are likely to encounter in connection with dyslexia. We now know that we need to be able to measure a child's reading ability accurately and objectively. We also know that reading ability is measured in terms of reading age and that a child's reading age can be determined only by the use of a well-designed and accurately standardized reading test. We have dealt with the fact that any group of similarly aged children will show variations in reading age (assuming that the group has not been previously selected on the basis of reading age). Half will be average or above average and half average or below. Because of this, it can be difficult, if not impossible, to decide whether a particular child is dyslexic unless we can prove in some way that:

- the child is reading less well than he should
- his difficulty is due to dyslexia and not some other reason.

The mere fact that the child is reading less well than other children of the same age is not on its own a sufficient reason to suspect that dyslexia is present. In the first place, he could be of low intelligence and so belong to the group of generally slow learners - the bottom 15% or so. Second, as will become clear, it is possible for a child to have an average reading age and still be affected by dyslexia. There will be good grounds for suspecting dyslexia is part of the picture only if it can be shown that he is basically capable of achieving better and would be doing so if he were not dyslexic. At this point we are left with an all-important question:

> Is there any way we can calculate how well a child can be *expected* to read - as opposed to how well he actually does read - and, if so, how can this be done?

43

Fortunately we can do this by making use of the idea of a person's mental age, which can be calculated quite simply. What mental age is, the reason why we can use it and the way in which it is calculated can be understood if we first compare the intelligence test scores produced by a group of children with the reading ages they have achieved.

Let us take as an example a large group of 10-year-olds. We need to consider thousands rather than hundreds and we need to choose them on a completely random basis, not by any kind of deliberate selective process. In short, we want our group to be truly representative of the whole population of 10-year-olds in the country, to be in effect a 'scale model' of the total. (We have selected 10-year-olds as it makes the calculations that need to be done easier, but what we say applies equally well to any group of school-age children.)

When the IQs of the group are shown in graph form, the result is as in Figure 4.1. When the same 10-year-olds have their reading progress tested and their reading ages are shown as a graph the result is as in Figure 4.2.

As can be seen, the graphs are identical in shape. Our large group of children have been assessed on two aspects of their development - intelligence and reading ability - and have produced overall results in one which match the overall results of the other. The children have been found to be a mixture of low, average and high intelligence, and they are also a mixture of poor, average and good readers.

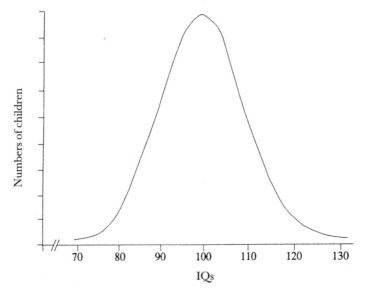

Figure 4.1 IQ scores of 10-year-olds.

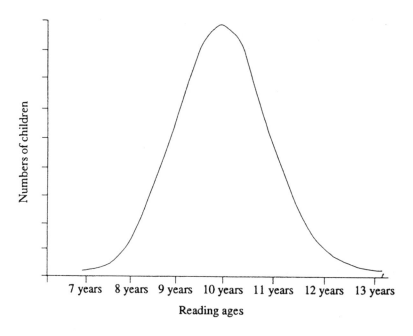

Figure 4.2 Reading ages of 10-year-olds.

Because there is such a close match between the *overall* results, it is tempting to assume that there is individual matching - a situation of very close correlation. That is to say, we are tempted to think that the children who have high intelligence are the same ones who have the good reading ages, that average IQ is linked with average reading ability and low IQ with poor reading. But this is an assumption, which at this stage, we are not allowed to make, tempting though it might be. We need *proof*, and without it can go no further because, in fact, the graphs produced when intelligence and reading age are measured in large numbers of children are exactly the same shape as those produced for *many other* aspects of human development. Graphs of this shape are common and the shape itself is known as 'the normal curve'.

Height and weight are two other aspects of development that would produce the same shape of graph if they were measured in a sufficiently large number of children. Therefore if, instead of intelligence, the height of each 10-year-old had been measured and a graph drawn, we would have found it to be of similar shape to that produced by intelligence. We then would have had a situation where the graphs of height and reading age for the large group of 10-year-olds matched one another. However, that would not entitle us to assume that tall children were better readers than average height children nor that average height ones were better than shorter ones. No correlation between height and reading ability has ever been shown.

Further investigation and information is required. However, when we do this for intelligence and reading age we are rewarded, because our assumption turns out to be true. Generally speaking, children with higher IQs tend to be better readers and consequently attain higher reading ages than do other children of the same age. However, the correlation is not a perfect one, for various reasons. In the first place, although intelligence features largely in determining reading ability, it is not the only factor involved and therefore it is possible to have a group of children of the same age and intelligence level who show some variety in their reading abilities. Likewise, children of the same chronological age and also the same reading age will be found to exhibit a range of IQs that will not be very tightly banded together. A second factor that needs to be taken into account is the fact that no intelligence test is a perfect instrument and cannot possibly measure intellectual ability with the same accuracy that a ruler can measure of person's height or a pair of bathroom scales an individual's weight. In the world of education, psychology and intelligence testing, we rarely, if ever, encounter perfect measuring instruments.

These limitations notwithstanding, there is a correlation of some significance between intelligence level and reading age, such that children of whatever intelligence level tend to have reading ages at about the same level whether it be high, average or low. These findings might be obvious and, some might say, quite predictable, but that is not the point. Carrying out correlation measures means we have been able to move past the point of guesswork and now have the knowledge we need to move forward with some degree of certainty.

The situation can be illustrated as in Figure 4.3. In the majority of cases, therefore, intelligence is a good *predictor* of reading age. It can be, and is, used as a means of calculating what any particular child's reading age should be. When we compare intelligence with reading we need to remember that intelligence, as we refer to it, is a *general* ability but that reading is a highly *specific* skill.

Because of the nature of intelligence we find that it acts as a good predictor of how well a child should be performing in school subjects generally - or at least those with an academic content, in which success depends on the ability to remember, discover relationships, perform calculations and benefit from past experiences, etc.

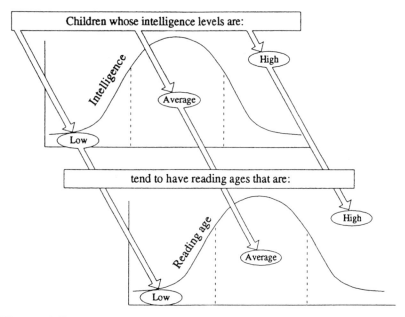

Figure 4.3 The relationship between intelligence and reading age.

What teachers and others working with children have come to find useful is the concept that each child possesses a certain *mental age*. A child's mental age can be calculated from his intelligence level and can then be used to predict his reading age.

The idea on which mental age is based is that any child of average intelligence has a mental age that is equal to his chronological age. If his intelligence is higher than average then his mental age will be greater than his chronological age, and naturally it follows that if the child is of low intelligence his mental age will be lower than his chronological age.

Mental age can be thought of as a measure of how much the child's general mental abilities have been able to develop during his lifetime. Although it is adequate for certain purposes to know that a child is of average, high or low ability, in other circumstances this is not accurate enough. Often it is necessary to know more than in which particular one of these three categories the child happens to fall.

It is possible for a child to be described as 'average' and for that child to have an IQ as low as 85, which means that he is more able than only 17% of the population. It is also possible for another child to be described as 'average' and for this one to have an IQ as high as 115, which makes him more able than 83% of the population. The term 'average' therefore covers a wide range of abilities and to have two such different children as the ones just described both called 'average' can lead to confusion.

Mental age is a vast improvement on this system as it is an *exact* measure and is given in years and months, in just the same way as a child's chronological age. To calculate mental age (MA), all that needs to be known are a child's age and IQ. The calculation is quite simple - the chronological age (CA) and IQ are multiplied together then divided by 100:

$$MA = \frac{(CA \times IQ)}{100}.$$

For example, in the case of a child who is aged exactly 10 years (CA = 10) and whose IQ is 80, his mental age will be 8 years:

$$MA = \frac{(10 \times 80)}{100} \qquad MA = \frac{800}{100} \qquad MA = 8 \text{ years.}$$

In exactly the same way, a child aged 10 with an IQ of 125 will have a mental age of $12\frac{1}{2}$ years:

$$MA = \frac{(10 \times 125)}{100} \qquad MA = 12\frac{1}{2} \text{ years (or 12;6).}$$

In the case of the first child, because his IQ is 80 (which is 20 below the average of 100) it is considered that throughout each year of his life he has been able to learn at a slower rate than normal - at 80% or 4/5 of the normal rate, in fact. Hence at the age of 10 years, it is considered that he has been able to gain only the same amount of general knowledge and learning experience as an average 8-year-old, and so this is his mental age.

The second child, on the other hand, has been sufficiently intelligent to be able to learn at about one and a quarter times (or 125%) the normal rate and so at the age of 10 he has acquired the same amount of knowledge, experience and understanding as an average child aged 12;6.

Having moved from the position of knowing the child's age and IQ to calculating his mental age, how do we move from there to finding his expected reading age (RA)? Quite simply, mental age and expected reading age can normally be expected to have about the same value. Whatever mental age a child has, his reading age can be expected to match it, although in many cases the match will not be absolutely exact. A child with a mental age of 8 years should be able to read at the 8 years level (as well as perform at the 8 years level in other tasks and skills). Someone with a mental age of 11 years should also have a reading age of 11 years. The whole procedure can be summarized as:

$$\frac{(CA \times IQ)}{100} \quad \text{will give } \textit{mental age, } \text{which is the same as } \textit{expected reading age.}$$

For a group of children who are all of the same age, it is possible to link IQ, mental age and expected reading age by means of a simple diagram. All three are inter-connected in a straightforward and easily understood manner. Each can be represented by a 'ladder', and the three ladders can be set side by side. In the case of any given child, once his position on the first ladder is located, then his position on the other two is more or less determined by a simple move side-ways, staying at approximately the same height whichever 'ladder' the child is on. This is shown in Figure 4.4. Once again we have chosen the age of 10 as an example to make the calculations easier, but the same rules apply whatever the child's age.

We are now in a position to appreciate exactly what information is needed before it can be said with any certainty that a child could possibly be dyslexic - let alone definitely is so. A dyslexic child must always have an *actual* reading age that is *lower* than his *expected* reading age. It is not sufficient to suspect dyslexia merely on the basis of a child having a below-average reading age, because such a child could be of low intelligence and hence unable to produce any better results. This is a case of a *general* learning difficulty and such a child is described as a slow learner, as we have made clear earlier.

Where dyslexia is concerned we are dealing with a *specific* learn-ing difficulty. The child's expected reading age can be calculated from his general level of intelligence, and for dyslexia to be a possi-bility his actual reading age must be found to be below this. What we are doing, in fact, is comparing the child who is suspected of being dyslexic with all other children who are of the *same age and of the same level of intelligence*. In other words, we are comparing him with all other children of the *same mental age*. If his reading age is less than it should be on this basis then we have a specific difficulties reader, not a slow learner and it is *possible* that dyslexia is the reason for the deficit. Such a deficit is a prerequisite for a diagnosis of dyslexia, but is not in itself confirmation of such - as the deficit could be caused by another factor (or factors).

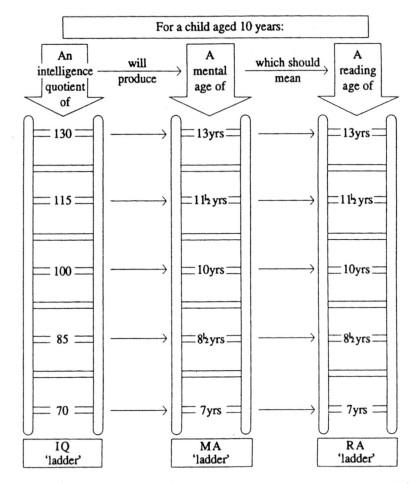

Figure 4.4 Conversion of IQ and chronological age into mental age and expected reading age.

When a shortfall between expected and actual reading age is discovered, we are only at the first stage of a possible diagnosis of dyslexia. It is possible for a depressed reading age to be accounted for by visual difficulties, hearing problems or indeed any of the many possible causes listed in Chapter 3. It is only when these can be discounted as possible causes that we can claim that dyslexia or specific learning difficulties are the likely explanation.

Summary

1. When a child's reading age is below average it is possible for this to be due to one of two reasons - being a slow learner or having a specific difficulty.

2. Without further investigation it is not possible to know to which of these two very different categories the child belongs. A slow learner has difficulties because of a lack of basic ability to do any better. Half of all children will be below average, but it is usually the worst 17% or so that are considered to be general slow learners. A child with specific difficulties does possess the basic ability to read better but is being held back by one or more influences. Dyslexic children are part of this group but not all specific difficulties readers are dyslexic, as a child's poor reading ability could be due to other reasons.

3. The way to investigate whether a child is a slow learner or has specific difficulties is to calculate what his *expected* reading age is and compare this with his *actual* reading age.

4. The expected reading age will be about the same as the mental age, which can be calculated from the child's exact chronological age and his IQ.

5. Once the expected reading age and actual reading age are known, any shortfall or discrepancy can be identified.

6. Such a discrepancy is only an indication that dyslexia *could* be the cause. Further investigation will then be required to exclude other possible causes. The procedure is summarized in Figure 4.5.

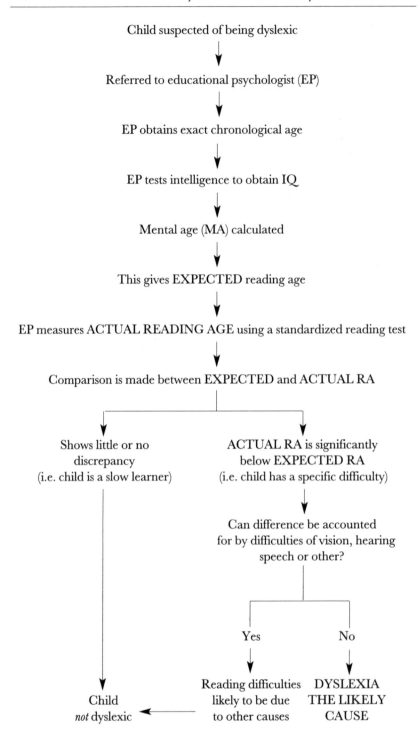

Figure 4.5 Steps in the investigation of suspected dyslexia.

Chapter 5
The teaching of reading

Reading involves the bringing together and mastery of a number of skills. It is preceded by the development of speech which is, in turn, just one of many forms of communication, all of which are made possible through and generated by man's intelligence. We can represent this in a simple diagram (see Figure 5.1).

Although the use of language is a natural attribute of man, the ability to read is an acquired skill. In fact, it represents the acquisition of a number of subskills (most of them quite complex) and involves the essential knack of learning to bring them all together and use them in an automatic, almost effortless manner.

The manner in which children learn to read is still largely a mystery to us, but the skills they need to master and the knowledge they need to acquire is quite well known and easily described. What children experience in the various stages through which they must

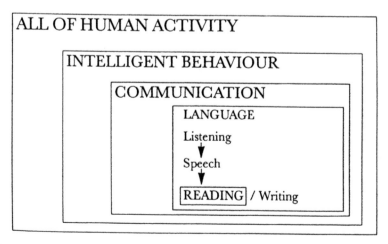

Figure 5.1 Reading in the context of general human activity.

pass, from being quite illiterate to fully literate, has been recorded in detail, but exactly how it is done is still largely unknown. We do not understand the neuropsychology involved but we do know that, for most children, all they require is the opportunity and the proper encouragement right at the start and in the early stages.

In learning to read, children enter a world that is new to them and full of rules, which are often quite arbitrary and sometimes completely contradictory. It is stating the obvious, of course, to say that in our society children learn to read mainly from books. When still quite young, they need to know that books contain words and so are important for reading. They also need to know that books open at the right-hand side and have a 'spine' on the left, that they consist of sheets of paper called pages, and that each page has a top, bottom, left side and right side.

Children need to know that the marks (usually coloured black) on the pages (usually coloured white) are the print and that the print tell the story. They must learn that the print is set out in straight lines and that these lines, in our culture, are arranged from the top of the page to the bottom, with each individual line running from left to right and hence needing to be read that way. Reading a line of print the way we do, moving our eyes steadily from left to right in small jerky movements is, in fact, a quite unnatural way of looking at anything. Normally our eyes do not move in this way. (Some cultures read lines of writing from right to left, others write in columns of letters down the page.)

As the learning process continues, children must master the fact that a line of print consists of words, and that each word is made up of a collection of letters in a certain order, with white spaces left between each word:

asdoingitthatwaymakesitmucheasiertoreadandunderstand.

There will also be small spaces between the letters that make up each word. This applies not only to print in books:

but also when we do handwriting like this

although not when we are using this
style, usually known as "double writing"

All this, of course, is only the beginning. The 26 letters of the alphabet, of which all of our written words are composed, can each be found in two sizes:

- *CAPITAL* (also known as UPPER-CASE) size and
- *small* (also known as lower-case) size.

What is more confusing is that although eight of the letters are identical in both capital and small form (Cc - Oo - Ss - Uu - Vv - Ww - Xx - Zz) the majority are quite different (Aa - Bb - Dd - Ee, etc). A few letters can appear in more than one printed shapes when in the lower-case form (for example a, ɑ - g, ɡ - q, ɋ). The confusion continues when the child who is beginning to read has to learn to differentiate between pairs of letters that are mirror images of each other, or virtually so (bd - pq - mw - un). He also needs to be sufficiently alert not to confuse the small L (written as l) with the capital i (written as I).

Most children are building up their number skills at the same time as they are learning to read, and this can cause a lot of confusion. The *number* 0, which we call 'nought' or 'zero', can be confused with the *letter* O. Similarly, the number 1 (one) can be confused with the lower-case L (l) or the capital i (I); 2 and 5 can be confused with the letter S; 6 with the letters b or d; and 9 with the letters g, p or q.

The teaching of reading in schools

Reading has been taught in the British Isles in a widespread, regular and systematic manner for well over 120 years - since the Forster Education Act of 1870, in fact. Literacy has been intricately bound up with the education of the masses from this time on, but before this the situation was very mixed. The rich could afford to hire private tutors for their children, who went on to public schools and then university. The middle classes sent their children to 'Dame' schools, where they were taught mainly reading and bible study. The work of a few philanthropists produced some experimental schools for a very limited number of poor children, but the vast majority of the poor were given no education and hence remained illiterate.

From 1870 onwards, all children *could* have an education, but school attendance was poor because children were kept out to earn money instead. Attendance was not made legally compulsory for another decade, with the introduction of the 'School Board' or school attendance officers in 1880, and the system of 'payment by results'. The curriculum at this time consisted mainly of the three Rs. It was not until 1918, that the school leaving age was raised to 14, and not until 1946 that it was raised to 15 years.

One effect of the introduction of state education was that large numbers of children were brought together for a lengthy period of time. This enabled observations to be made and much useful information gathered about how children learn, styles of learning, patterns of learning characteristics, types of difficulties, etc. It also provided the opportunity to observe different teaching techniques. As a result, knowledge about the learning and teaching of Reading, wRiting and aRithmetic (the three Rs) grew extensively.

The teaching of reading has undergone a process of great change during the period of 130 or more years that all children in the British Isles have been required to attend school and hence be taught. Most of the changes have been brought about by advances in knowledge relating to how children learn, the various factors concerned with learning (such as motivation, attention, memory, etc.) and the processes involved in child development. As a result there has been an increase in the awareness of types of difficulty that are likely to arise in a child attempting to master the skill of reading.

Teaching styles vary tremendously and the conditions under which children are taught can also vary a great deal, but throughout the past 120 or so years teaching approaches have tended to follow a certain pattern.

Originally a child was taught to read using just one book, and this tended to be the Bible. Over time, various teachers who were also writers produced sets of reading books, graded from simple through to more complex. Today most children are taught using reading schemes, which tend to be produced under the name of the publishing company rather than individual writers. Well-known names in this branch of publishing are Ginn 360 and Ladybird. (We shall be saying more about reading schemes later on.) At the moment, it is true to say that there is no one single correct or perfect way to teach a child to read. A method one teacher finds successful will not work for another teacher. Also, the same teacher encountering two different classes of children will find that what works well with the first class will not be as successful with the second. This is because the process of learning to read is a complex mixture of the skills, talents, abilities and personality factors that we referred to earlier. What usually happens is that a teacher works by bringing together her knowledge of the individual children and of the various techniques of teaching (including the strengths and weaknesses of each technique).

Whenever the techniques of teaching reading are described they are usually divided into two main methods which are:

- the 'whole' method (or 'look-and-say' approach)
- the phonic method (or 'sounding-out' approach).

At certain stages in the history of education some methods have gained a special prominence for a period of time, usually some time after the theories on which they were based were first put forward. Teachers tend to be conservative in their approaches and hence unlikely to change techniques at short notice.

It is more usual for teachers to adopt a new approach gradually, trying it out to begin with and then using it more and more, slowly dropping the method they were using previously. One writer has described this as a 'grafting-on' process. As a result, most teachers do not use entirely a 'whole' method nor entirely a 'phonic' method, but generally a mixture of both.

Whole-word methods

The story method

Some reading schemes were based on repetition and memorization of stories and, as is only to be expected, were later criticized for teaching children to learn the contents of a book by heart rather than by reading. However, despite its limitations, children did learn to read using this method and so it had at least some factors in its favour. The children enjoyed the rhythm and repetition involved, and teachers do still use this method for material such as nursery rhymes, as do parents in the home.

Word patterns

This was a method of teaching reading by getting the child to look on each word as a particular shape or pattern or 'word envelope' as in Figure 5.2, rather than as a number of letters placed in a certain order. Interest grew after Helen Davidson published research in 1931 and the method was strongly associated with Gates, an American. Using this method, children could reach a stage where they were able to read sentences without realizing that words were made up of letters.

The later stages of Davidson's work were used far more than the earlier ones and the look-and-say method developed as a result, but in a form where actual words are used right from the beginning. The words are taught using pictures, flash cards, etc. The method became very popular in the 1940s and many schools dropped the 'phonic drill' technique that they had used previously. Many authorities on the teaching of reading since then have recommended that the look-and-say approach should be used exclusively in the early stages of reading growth.

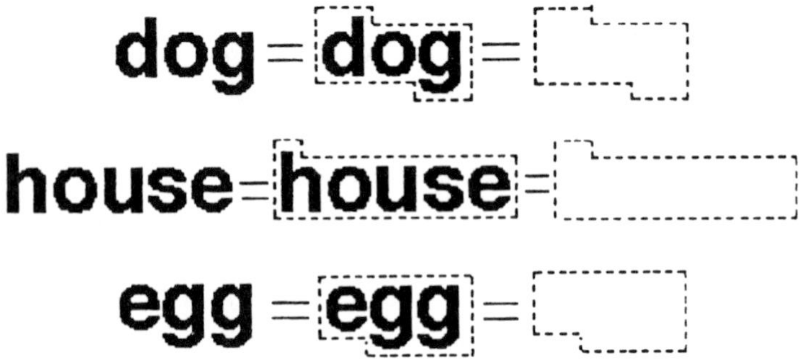

dog = dog = [ ]

house = house = [ ]

egg = egg = [ ]

Figure 5.2 Some 'word envelopes'.

Kinaesthetic method

In 1921, Fernand and Kelly formulated the kinaesthetic method in the US. As schools taught reading using predominantly visual and auditory approaches, Fernand investigated whether the sense of touch could be used to teach reading to children who had previously failed.

In this method, the child traced over a word that had been written in cursive (i.e. 'double') writing on a piece of card, and the word was spoken aloud by the teacher as the tracing commenced. The tracing was repeated until the child could say the word from memory. The child learned many words this way, and then had to try and write the words and, later still, sentences. This method was a great success with certain children, but a complete failure with others. However, the approach did emphasize the importance of introducing writing at the same time as reading, and also highlighted the importance of establishing good 'left-to-right' orientation in children learning to read.

The sentence method

This became popular in 1929, when Jagger (a London inspector of schools) published his book *The Sentence Method of Teaching Reading*, but the idea had been around since the end of the nineteenth century.

In this method, children are shown a picture and the teacher and children discuss it. The children compose their own sentences and certain of these are selected and written beneath the picture. When a child can read the sentence fluently with the picture present, he is then asked to try to match it with an identical sentence and then read it *without* the picture as a guide. When a number of sentences have become very familiar to the child he can then be expected to recognize individual words from them. At a later stage books are introduced.

This method has much to recommend it as it is a child-centred approach, with the child providing his own reading matter from his own personal experiences and so reading only sentences he himself has composed. Reading is thereby meaningful and is contained within the child's own language ability.

Phonic methods

Alphabetic method

In this method, the child was taught to recognize each letter of the alphabet in turn by its name. With each new word the child met, he had to read out the name of each letter in the word and then say the word itself. (For example, the word 'hat' would produce the response 'aitch-ay-tee-hat'). It was thought that by working in this way the child would look so carefully at the printed word that he would not only learn to read but to spell also.

The alphabetic method was criticized quite strongly. Although the child received a great deal of practice in letter recognition and left-to-right movement of the eye along each letter and line of print, the fluency of reading was held back. Nor was the child given any help in working out how a printed word was pronounced. However, the alphabetic method did achieve demands for a reform of the spelling system.

Diacritical marks

The 26 symbols we know as the letters of the alphabet have been replaced at different times and by different people in an attempt to make the process of leaning to read easier.

Gattegno used 41 colours in his scheme, entitled 'Words in Colour'. The Initial Teaching Alphabet (ITA) used 44 symbols, whereas the diacritical system (designed by Richard and Maria Edgeworth in 1798) used 73 different symbols. Marks were used to indicate the different sounds of a letter. The obvious criticism of this system was that it was more difficult for a child to learn 73 symbols than 26, and the amount of decoding the child would have had to do would have been excessive. Other, similar systems have been designed over the years, but there has never been a great following for any of them.

The work of Nellie Dale

Nellie Dale is often credited with having invented the phonic method of teaching reading. However, what she produced was a combination of certain earlier experiences with two new ideas of her own. The first of these was her insistence on ear, hand and eye training. The second was the use of colour as an aid (early on in the teaching process) to the recognition of the sound value of letters, e.g. red print for vowels and yellow print for silent letters. Only four colours were used, and they were introduced one at a time. However, in common with all other systems, Ms Dale's method had its limitations.

The phonic approach, which had originally dominated the education system, started to be challenged, first by the look-and-say and later by the sentence methods, and during the 1930s and 1940s it was relegated to second favourite.

The two main systems have long been in competition with one another and the results of research are far from clear-cut. Children learn to read at different speeds and also perhaps in different ways, however slight, from one individual to another, depending on each child's abilities, skills, interests and degree of motivation.

Although most teachers claim to follow either one or the other method, in practice, the situation tends not to be clear-cut. Those teachers who favour the look-and-say method believe that children learn to read more easily if they are presented repeatedly with a set number of words so that they eventually learn to recognize each one of them. This provides them with what is known as a basic 'sight vocabulary', which will continue to grow and from which they will learn the basic rules by which the 'code' of reading is 'cracked'.

Those teachers who favour the phonic approach hold that children are best taught to read by first learning how to break down a printed word into its component sounds (known as *phonemes*) and then building up the phonemes into the complete sound of the word. For example, the child sounds out the printed word 'cat' as 'kerr-ah-tuh' and these three sounds are then blended together to make the sound of the spoken word 'cat'. In the same way, 'sun' is broken down to 'sss-uh-neh', to be blended into 'sun'. With practice, the process becomes quicker and smoother.

Irrespective of whether the look-and-say or the phonic approach is used, almost all teachers use many of the same techniques and aids to literacy. In the past, much teaching of reading was achieved by means of set drills and exercises, but in recent years reading has come to be considered as only one aspect of a language programme, and hence *meaningful* reading is considered to be the all-important goal to be achieved.

Children are found to master reading (and writing) most effectively if it is allowed to develop from their natural interests and activities. Pre-reading skills will first be established by encouraging the young child in the activities of listening, speaking, reading and writing. This will involve just about every mentally stimulating activity you can think of:

- telling stories
- looking at pictures
- saying rhymes and jingles
- singing songs
- watching suitable television programmes
- listening to the radio
- playing with sand/water/Plasticine, etc.
- dressing-up
- acting out a play
- using desktop games such as dominoes, draughts, snakes and ladders, etc.
- playing card games such as 'snap'
- sorting objects by size, shape, colour, etc.
- doing jigsaws
- playing with construction toys
- playing on large apparatus such as the see-saw, swings, monkey-ladder, slide, climbing frame, etc.

All these activities will encourage children to listen carefully, to note the details of things, to remember them and also to talk about them.

The activity of reading proper is introduced by such means as picture books and comics, road signs, flash cards, labels, notices, charts and other display material, as well as the book corner of the classroom. Early on, children make books for themselves.

Writing is introduced at the same time as reading using activities such as:

- scribbling
- finger painting
- brush painting
- pattern making
- drawing a story in pictures
- tracing pictures
- tracing letters
- drawing lines by dot-to-dot

- drawing circles and lines (the basic shapes and marks that go to make up lower-case letters), etc.

The intention behind the use of such teaching techniques is to develop skills such as *recognition*, *recall* and *discrimination*. For instance, the letter 'a' needs to be *recognized* whenever it is found in print. It may be found on its own (*a* pen), in a short word (h*a*t) or in a longer word (thous*a*nd). The sound the letter 'a' makes needs to be *recalled* accurately on each occasion it appears. In reading, it is vital for the child to be able to *discriminate* between one letter and another: 'a' is similar in appearance to c, e, o and u, as each of them is small and rounded in appearance. Discrimination is particularly important in the case of those letters that have other letters as their mirror images and can thereby be even more easily confused (b and d, m and w, u and n, p and q).

The first word a teacher introduces to a child is usually the child's own name. Most teachers then start to build on the child's immediate environment and interests and label the items found in the classroom, e.g. 'table', 'chair', 'window', 'bookcase', 'door', etc. Notices may also be displayed, e.g. OPEN, CLOSED, DANGER, and phrases and sentences can be put up around the classroom walls, taking care not to put up too many at any one time. The days of the week, the words used to describe the weather and the names of the children in the class are quite common collections used. Figure 5.3 shows the key words that every child needs to learn.

To help them work with words, children can be given a number of letters of the alphabet and a stock of common words written on small cards or tiles (as in the game Scrabble). Alphabets consisting of the actual letters cut out from thick card or plywood are also available.

Many teachers use the system where each child is involved with three books at any one time. One is the book the child is using for the formal task of learning to read, the second is a story book from which the teacher reads a story to the whole class each day, and the third is one the child has chosen for himself from the selection in the reading corner. This third book often goes home with the child and is used for reading to (or with) the child in the evenings. Each of the three books is exchanged for another one of the same type when appropriate.

At this point it is useful to explain reading schemes in more detail, in case their nature and purpose is not fully appreciated. A reading scheme is a set of books specially designed to teach reading. The vocabulary they use is strictly controlled so that new words are introduced at a gradual rate, while the earlier words are repeated suffi-

a and he I in is it of that the to was	all as at be but are for had have him his not one said so they we with you
	about an back been before big by call came can come could did do down first from get go has her if into just like little look made make me more much must my no new now off only or our other out over right see she some their them then there this two when up want went were what where which who will your old

This area represents 19,900 other words but there is not sufficient space to print them

The average adult uses around 20,000 different words, some more frequently than others, This chart shows how often we use the commonest of them. The box in the top left hand corner contains only 12 words, but these make up one quarter (25%) of what we read and write. These 12, added to the next 20, make up about one third (33%) of the overall words met with in ordinary reading. One hundred words (12+20+68) go to make up half of the total and so the other half consists of about 19,900 words but we are not able to show these here.

Figure 5.3 The key words of the English language.

ciently often for the child to learn them properly. The first books in the set usually contain only a few words, but they are well illustrated with many attractive, colourful pictures. Increasingly, schemes are designed based on research findings. Research has shown that about 100 words make up almost half of those in common use. In other words, very many stories can be told and ideas expressed using a comparatively small number of the many thousands of words available to us in the English language (see Figure 5.3).

Although many children are able to learn to read from books alone, reading schemes usually have a great deal of supporting material to help the teacher in her task, to provide variety in the work and to support the slower-learning child. Hence it is quite common to find word books, wall pictures, colouring books, flash cards, tracing books, work sheets, picture dictionaries, etc., all linked to a particular reading scheme being used the classroom. As the child progresses, more and more words are introduced, and the total number of words used is usually between one and two thousand.

A few other points need to be made before we move on.

Surveys have shown that most schools use a number of different reading schemes, with teachers generally being flexible in their approach and prepared to move from one scheme to another to ensure that each child is using the most suitable book from all the schemes available.

As indicated above, there is no clear-cut case that can be made in favour of either the look-and-say or the phonic approach, and many teachers use both in their work. Typically, a teacher will start off with the look-and-say method by building up a sight vocabulary, after which the technique of breaking down a word into the sounds of each of the component letters (or groups of letters) will be introduced. Gradually the child will build up his own skills by practice. With most children, the two approaches are found to dovetail together quite naturally.

Since 1985, there has been a growing movement in support of the 'apprenticeship approach' or the 'real books' method, which we will now spend some time describing to provide a comprehensive overview of the whole field.

The 'real books' method or 'apprenticeship approach' to reading

The supporters of this method say that two aspects need to be considered when evaluating the effectiveness of any approach to reading. These are the *quantity* of what is taught and the *quality*. (Everything in this section reflects the views of the supporters of the method.)

Most schemes teach children to read quite competently in so far as children can look at a piece of writing and make out accurately what it says (the *quantity* aspect). However, many of these children fail to develop a proper love of reading (the *quality* aspect) and so read only reluctantly - often stumbling through a piece of reading almost without realizing that it is supposed to make sense. It is claimed that many children exhibit no type of reaction to the books they read and apparently gain no enjoyment from being able to read or from the stories in the books they have read. The supporters of the real books approach claim that the present system of teaching reading produces too many children who can cope with reading but who are not *readers*, as they choose to avoid the task of reading if at all possible.

Because of this observation it is claimed that somewhere along the line there is a failure and that the failure lies in the approach adopted by most teachers. It is argued that the child is best taught by treating him as if he were an apprentice to a craftsman. The teacher and child should get together (as a craftsman would with an apprentice) and be closely involved with books and all that is associated with them (in a similar manner to tools and 'tricks of the trade'). It is held that reading and writing will best be acquired in the same way that the child acquired spoken language. A child learns to talk by being surrounded by speech. He becomes familiar with it, pays attention to it, works out its meaning and eventually starts to use it. The child learns to speak in an environment where there is nobody making any special effort to teach him. For this reason apprenticeship approach supporters believe it is unnatural to teach reading in a formal manner by introducing words in a set, regulated and controlled sequence. They believe effort should be concentrated not on getting children to use a series of small skills in a fluent manner but rather on *obtaining meaning* from the printed word.

Another of their firmly held beliefs is that the *type of book* the child is offered to read is vitally important. Books are regarded as falling into two categories: *organic* and *inorganic*.

Organic books are the only ones worth using with a child as they relate to a child's own emotions, needs and interests. They are written with the sole objective of telling a story and conveying a certain message or meaning. They are the books that children will naturally and automatically be attracted to and from which they will best learn to read. These books will sound well when read aloud. In short, they are *real books*.

Inorganic books, by contrast, are imposed on the child from outside and so are meaningless to him and will hold little attraction. Books *designed to teach reading formally* fall into this category. They sound very artificial, and contain phrases and sentences that real people never say in real-life situations. These inorganic books do not, therefore, encourage any proper love of, or even regard for, reading and are to be discouraged. The following is an example from one of these inorganic - and hence 'unreal' - books:

Go Tim
Go up

Go up Tim
Go up, up, up.

The writer is attempting to make the child familiar with two short
words and one short proper name by presenting them repeatedly,
but in so doing ends up producing a rather artificial style of language
which is unlikely to be encountered in real life. Also, it does not read
aloud very well. Compare this with the first few sentences from a
'real' book:

The hour was late,
Mr Bear was tired,
Mrs Bear was tired,
and
Baby Bear was tired,
so they all went to bed.
Mrs Bear fell asleep,
Mr Bear didn't.

This writer has produced something interesting, which 'flows' well
and which sounds attractive when read aloud. It uses far more
natural language and will probably catch the child's attention and
imagination quite easily.

Any teacher using the apprenticeship/real books approach will
make sure the child has a wide choice of 'real' books and will help
him choose one. The teacher will then read with him and generally
help him become familiar with the story in the book. In time, the
child will be able to read more and more of each book by himself,
getting to know where various words and sentences occur on the
page, feeling and saying the right parts of the story or rhyme, etc. In
short, the child is invited to behave as a reader. During the process
the teacher will act to ensure that the child is never made to feel a
failure or to think there is any element of competition in what is
happening.

It is not the purpose of this chapter to take sides in the long-
running look-and-say versus phonic issue, or to enter into the debate
as to whether it is better to abandon both of these in favour of the real
books approach. Rather this chapter is intended to describe what
children need to learn in the process of becoming literate and also to
describe some of the many skills the child needs to acquire when
learning to read. In addition, it is intended to convey some idea of the
methods teachers use to establish first the proper pre-reading skills
and then to get the children started on the process of reading itself. It

aims to get the message across that there is no one particular approach to reading that is successful, and that the teaching of reading is a constantly changing process with new ideas and approaches constantly being introduced and evaluated. They will then either be incorporated into the methods already in use or discarded.

The National Literacy Strategy

In 1996, the DfEE set up the National Literacy Project with the aim of raising standards of literacy in primary schools. Part of the approach was that there should be a 'Literacy Hour' for primary children each day.

The National Literacy Strategy (NLS) was developed from this, and produced *Framework for Teaching*, a handbook for schools detailing what should be taught during the Literacy Hour. It set out objectives, term by term from reception to year 6 (formerly fourth year or 'top' juniors), and so covers the entire primary phase of education, ie key stage 1 and key stage 2, formerly known as the 'infant' and 'junior' stages of education.

Framework for Teaching is a full and detailed document, 119 pages in length. It is bound to be regarded by all those who use it as a valuable resource. There are four sections. The first introduces the NLS concepts and aims, describes the main structure of the Framework, details the Literacy Hour and makes suggestions as to how the teacher can best plan for the work required.

Section 2 sets out the termly objectives, Section 3 consists of seven appendices and Section 4 gives additional guidance.

The Framework organises the teaching objectives at three different levels: word, sentence and text. It includes a wide range of reading and ensures that pupils cover a similar range of writing. Independent reading and writing is aimed for at an early stage and during key stage 1 the teaching of phonics, spelling and handwriting, together with other word-level skills, are emphasized.

The Literacy Hour is structured to provide 40 minutes of whole-class work and 20 minutes of either group or independent work. The whole-class work breaks down into 15 minutes devoted to shared text work (a balance of reading and writing) followed by a further 15 of focused word work then, after the 20 minutes of group or independent work (used for independent reading, writing or word sentence work), a final 10 minutes devoted to reviewing, reflecting, consolidating teaching points and presenting work covered in the lesson.

The Literacy Hour is considered by the DfES to be the means by which the contents of the Framework are taught.

Reception year work at the *word* level focuses on phonological awareness, phonics and spelling. Details include rhyme, rhyming patterns, invented words, grapheme-phoneme correspondences, the identification of initial sounds in words, the identification of initial and dominant phonemes in spoken words, being able to write them, alphabetic knowledge and phonic knowledge.

At the *sentence* level, grammatical awareness is the main objective and at the *text* level, the aims of teaching are related to the understanding of print (in both reading and writing), reading comprehension and composition.

Section 2 of the Framework continues by setting out in great detail the work to be covered in each term of each of the key stage 1 and key stage 2 years. What is more, the work is broken down into word-level, sentence-level and text-level items - a total of 57 separate 'blocks of information'. It is all extremely detailed, quite coherent, logical, well structured and clearly organized.

Section 3 lists a set of 153 words, 45 of which are high-frequency words to be achieved as 'sight recognition' words through reception to year 2. The remaining 108 words are to be learned between years 1 and 2. The children are also expected to master other key words relating to topics such as the days of the week, months of the year, etc.

A second word list is also provided. This consists of 119 words which are to be taught during years 4 and 5, with special emphasis placed on the children's ability to spell them accurately.

The specific phonics to be covered are set out as is a summary of the range of work for each term, a technical vocabulary list and a glossary of the terms used in the Framework.

In Section 4 there is advice as to how the Literacy Hour is to be taught in mixed-year classes, with children of reception age, with children who have English as an additional language (EAL) and with children with special educational needs. (This final piece of advice was added six months after the Framework was first published).

The Framework, which was launched in schools in September 1998, is based heavily on a phonics approach, but incorporates the look-and-say and the real books/apprenticeship approaches in parts as well. This reinforces the point made earlier in the chapter that there is not just one single approach to reading that is successful. However, a full and reliable evaluation is still awaited.

Before the end of the chapter it is worth making a couple of points to restore the balance. In the first place, we must never lose sight of the fact that the teaching of reading is very much a success story, in so far as most children leave school having achieved a satisfactory standard of literacy. Most teachers manage to teach reading quite successfully to most of the children they encounter. This holds true across a whole range of factors and is not related to any particular method(s) of teaching, or to whether the children come from high- or low-income groups, or to whether their schools are located in inner cities, leafy suburbs or rural areas.

Although some people leave school illiterate or with poor literacy skills, they tend to be very much in a minority. They are a cause for concern and a proportion of them are the subject of this book because of the special nature of their difficulties. Overall, however, the teaching of reading is, and for many generations has been, largely a success story.

A second point to be made is that the average child takes four years to learn to read adequately. A child unable to read is considered by those involved in education to have a reading age of 5;0 years, because in theory no child starts to learn to read until they go to school and 5 years is the legal starting age. Likewise, a child is considered to have reached an acceptable level of literacy if he has attained a reading age of 9;0 years. This is the reading age of an *average* child aged 9. Once a reading age of 9;0 years is attained then it is considered that the child has mastered all of the reading skills required for independent reading and that he can function adequately in society as regards reading requirements.

As time progresses, it is expected that these children (with a reading age of 9;0 years) will continue to read and will progress through stories and other types of writing that contain ever-more demanding vocabulary levels, i.e. longer, less common and more specialized words as well as more technical expressions, etc. In short, it is expected that once a child has learned the basic skill of reading he will go on to become more and more proficient by using this basic skill to his maximum potential. An average child of 16 should have a reading age of 16, but the increase in reading age from about 9 to 16 will be a product of *greater experience* acquired during those seven years, and not a continuation of the learning process. For them the basic rules of reading have been absorbed and the mechanisms of reading have been well practised. These pupils do not need to be given any further teaching as such, as there are no new reading skills for them to learn. However, they need to continue with practice in their reading by moving through increasingly demanding texts.

What needs to be borne in mind is that reading is a skill that is not usually acquired quickly or easily. It is a gradual process and a lengthy one. Children learn to talk and walk in far less time than they take to learn to read. They can learn to ride a bicycle, to swim, to ice skate, to roller skate and to do so many other things in life far faster than they can become literate. The process is a complex one with no short cuts available and no 'magic wands' that can be waved to improve matters. Learning to read requires hard work, concentration and dedication on the part of most children and these efforts need to be kept up for a considerable period of time. Even when a child is highly motivated to learn and is prepared to rise to the challenge, the effort required is still quite considerable.

A dyslexic child does not respond to the teaching of reading in the way that most children do. The next chapter looks at various factors involved in learning to read, and we then turn to the theme of dyslexia and start to examine where a dyslexic child's difficulties might lie.

Chapter 6
The learning of reading

Precisely how children learn to read - the exact mechanism by which they gradually and almost imperceptively change from being complete non-readers to fully literate young people - is still not fully understood. This is despite the fact that the number of children being taught to read worldwide has been increasing for several generations, to the extent that more than half the world's population is now literate. And also despite the fact that much time, effort and money is spent every year on research throughout the world, usually in university departments.

It would be a mistake, however, to assume that little or nothing is known about the process of learning to read; quite the contrary. The decades of research, particularly that carried out in the past few decades, have produced much invaluable information and consequently we are now far closer to understanding the process than we were a generation or two ago. But there is still some considerable distance to travel.

Any serious attempt to explain the process involved must describe exactly what form any improvement or acquisition of a new skill takes, and also what causes the actual acquisition. It is vital to know what prompts these changes if we are to be able to help pupils who have difficulties learning to read. Needless to say, describing what new skill has been acquired is a much easier process than explaining what has brought about the skills' acquisition.

Two theories of particular interest are those produced by Marsh (in 1980) and Frith (in 1985). Marsh felt that any changes brought about in relation to a child's attempts to master reading must be heavily influenced by the particular stage of intellectual development the child has reached.

It goes without saying that a person's intellect changes dramatically over time, as it both grows and develops. The changes are particularly pronounced in the early years as the child learns about the world and what is in it, how the countless features relate together, and what the processes are that are at work collectively and which make the world what it is. Should such intellectual growth and development, which occurs in parallel to physical growth and development, not take place, then intellectually we would not progress beyond the level of newborn infants.

Marsh based his theory on the findings of Piaget (1896-1980), who was a Swiss psychologist, but preferred to describe himself as a genetic epistemologist. Piaget spent most of his working life studying the intellectual, social and emotional development of the individual. He described this aspect of a young person's development as falling into four main stages, each of which could be further subdivided. Piaget's stages of development are known as:

1. sensor-motor (from birth to 2 years)
2. pre-operations (from 2 to 7 years)
3. concrete operations (from 8 to 12 years)
4. formal operations (from 12 to 18 years).

Piaget's second stage (pre-operations) is divided into the preconceptual substage (2-4 years) and the intuitive substage (4-7 years). His third stage (concrete operations) is subdivided simply into early and late stages.

When the average child begins primary school, he has already passed through the entire first stage of development and the early part of the second stage. The skill of reading is acquired during the latter part of Piaget's second stage (i.e. the intuitive substage, which lasts from 4 to 7 years) and the early part of the third stage (early concrete operations which lasts from 8 to about 10 years).

Marsh maintains that reading develops in four stages. In stage 1, children learn by 'rote associations', recognizing a word by its shape and/or the pattern of letters which combine to form it. In stage 2, the child begins to use the context in which the word appears and also begins to spot similarities between new words and ones that are already familiar. In stage 3, the child starts to analyse each new word into the basic sounds which, when correctly blended, produce the correct pronunciation of that word. Stage 4 is characterized by the child's ability to continue the stage 3 process of word analysis or decoding, but at a higher and more sophisticated level. The child will be aware that the letter 'c' is pronounced /s/ when it is followed by 'i', 'e' or 'y'. It is at this stage that children begin to make proper analogies when they read, i.e. on encountering the word 'faugh', the child would pronounce it as 'faff' because he is familiar with the word 'laugh', which is, of course, pronounced 'laff'.

Marsh's theory of reading development has much to recommend it, and the developmental stages described accord well with Piaget's theory of intellectual development. However, further data gathered since Marsh produced his theory have demonstrated that the theory has certain weaknesses insofar as it does not deal with certain aspects of the development of reading. We do not need to know what these are at this point. Suffice to say that the theory produced by Frith built on Marsh's theory and incorporated more recent findings.

Frith believes that the mastery of reading can be described as passing through just three phases. She calls these logographic, alphabetic and orthographic, all of which sound quite forbidding, but which can be explained relatively simply. Frith's theory also accounts for the development of the skill of writing as well as of reading, so it is doubly useful. Here, however, we will concentrate on reading.

Logographic phase

In this early phase, reading is visually based. Words encountered are remembered according to visual features and partial cues. Logographic readers have learned the relationship between particular written and particular spoken words and hence can read only familiar words. Reading is inaccurate and it becomes more difficult to recognize words as more are learned. At this stage, children do not possess the skills required to decipher novel, unfamiliar words. Eventually, the child builds up his reading skills, as well as the desire to write - and hence spell - and so moves on to the next stage.

Alphabetic phase

In this phase, the child starts to develop an awareness of the relationship between individual printed letters (or set sequences of letters) and the corresponding speech sounds, and this is particularly assisted by the child's attempts to spell when writing. The ability to deal with unfamiliar words increases and the child eventually progresses to the orthographic phase.

Orthographic phase

In this final phase, reading and spelling continue to develop by means of successfully combining the different types of knowledge acquired in the two earlier phases. The child also has the ability to take into account a number of different aspects of what he is reading at the same time. When reading in the orthographic phase, the child can not only relate the letters (or patterns of letters) within a word to the appropriate sounds, but can do it while also appreciating the syntax (sentence construction rules) and the semantics (meaning) involved. In this stage, children begin to recognize 'strings' of letters and they are able to combine and recombine these strings (and the sounds they represent) to produce an almost unlimited number of words.

Frith's proposed scheme has much to recommend it, but still does not account for all the known facts about how children acquire their reading and writing skills.

Both Marsh and Frith claim that when children first start to read they do so using a logographic method and then move on to an alphabetic method. Further research has proved this claim to be justifiable. However, the other aspects of their theories can be criticized, based on findings related to topics such as phonological awareness and knowledge of rhyme and alliteration, all of which are covered in detail later in the book.

The process of learning to read can be viewed from a number of different angles. There are many inter-related factors that come into play at different times, some of which combine to produce various effects that can be studied using well-designed research methods.

One area that repays study are the overall factors involved in reading (or being unable to master reading) properly. We can better understand the process if we know what these broad factors are, and the manner in which they inter-relate.

When a pupil is learning to read it is possible to separate these many, complex and inter-related factors into two groups:

- those within the pupil
- those within the environment.

It is possible to further divide the 'within-pupil' factors into three levels:

- the biological
- the cognitive
- the behavioural.

It is obvious that the environment is capable of affecting the pupil and his attempts to learn to read at all three levels.

Biological factors

These include vision, hearing, speech, relevant areas of the brain and general brain functioning.

Cognitive factors

These include phonological skills and deficits, the ability to relate graphemes (writing) to phonemes (the sounds involved), visual perception (difficulties), auditory perception (difficulties), motor control (deficits), short-term auditory memory (difficulties) and metacognitive strategies (lack of). Learning style is a cognitive factor, as is metacognition (described below).

Behavioural factors

These include difficulties with areas such as alphabetic skills, reading, phonological awareness (dealt with more fully in Chapter 11), naming memory, naming speed, motion detection, time estimation, balance, spelling, reading comprehension and listening. The *use* of metacognitive strategies is a behavioural factor.

Those factors *outside* of the pupil (and hence within the *environment*) include teaching, poor teacher-pupil relationships, medication, absences, socio-emotional problems, etc. These sets of factors can be represented diagrammatically as shown in Figure 6.1.

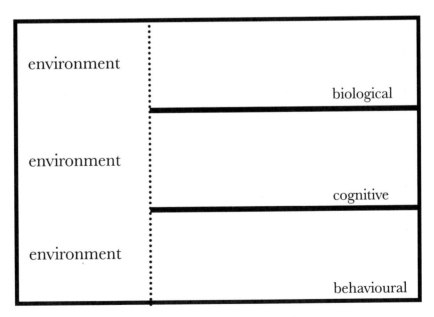

Figure 6.1 External and internal influences on reading ability.

If dyslexia is viewed as a developmental disorder, then some type of brain abnormality (a biological-level disorder) produces a difficulty with phonological processing (a cognitive-level deficit), the evidence for which is manifested as difficulty with reading, spelling, etc. (signs at the behavioural level). This can be represented simply, as in Figure 6.2.

This is a means of differentiating dyslexic children from non-dyslexic children even in potentially confusing cases. A dyslexic child might not show up as a poor reader if he has had excellent remedial help - although the dyslexia is undoubtedly present, its effects have been overcome by environmental factors. Similarly another child might be a poor reader because of problems in the environment (e.g. poor pupil-teacher relationships) and not because of any factors of a remotely dyslexic nature.

Yet another interesting, and possibly fruitful, area of great interest to psychologists and educational researchers in recent years has been that of the different styles of learning. We do not all learn in the same manner and it is in the interests of children and educators generally to learn as much as possible about different learning styles. It is then possible to adapt teaching styles to learning styles in order to produce a learning process that proceeds as smoothly as possible. We will now describe in broad terms the area of study covered.

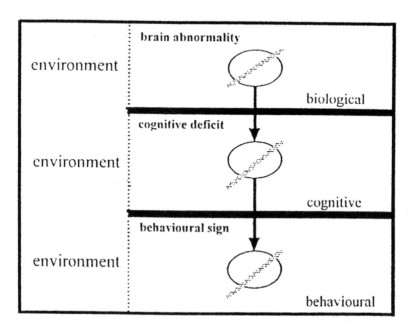

Figure 6.2 How dyslexia might develop from a brain abnormality.

Learning (cognitive) style and metacognition

When a teacher is in the process of teaching a child to read, there are three sets of factors that come into play:

- those relating to the child
- those relating to the teacher
- those relating to the general situation or environment.

No two teachers are the same, nor are any two children. The various classroom situations across the globe in which the teaching takes place will often, but not always, differ widely. The teaching situation has been widely studied for generations, but in recent decades interest has focused on those parts of the teaching situation over which the teacher and the learner have some degree of control. Here we shall concentrate on the child's approach to learning.

There are many characteristics within each child that are capable of influencing how he learns to read (or indeed learns anything else), but two in particular have received much attention. These are:

- learning (or cognitive) style
- metacognition.

Learning style

Learning style relates to a person's individual approach to assimilating and processing the information available. Because different children have different learning styles, it would obviously be to their advantage if teaching styles could be adapted to match, with each child being taught differently from the next, but all in a manner best suited to them individually.

It has been claimed that learning style develops relatively early in life. Measurable differences have been found between boys and girls, and it is possible for some changes to occur over time. There also seems to be a link between learning style and personality, and also with ethnic groups. Learning style can influence academic attainment and appears to be quite independent of basic ability. That is to say, two people of the same intelligence level can apparently have two quite different learning styles. It has even been claimed that learning style is a good predictor of attainment in reading and arithmetic.

Unfortunately, it has not been easy to prove that there are individual differences in the way in which people approach learning and studying, as evidence is elusive. In 1990, Snider concluded that:

The *idea* of *learning styles* is appealing, but a critical examination of this approach should cause educators to be sceptical.

Since then a new, two-dimensional model of learning style has been put forward. These dimensions are:

- the wholist-analytic dimension (i.e. does the learner process information as a whole or in parts?)
- the verbal-imagery dimension (i.e. does the learner represent incoming information in verbal form or as a visual image?).

This model has been placed within a larger and more general model or overview of the individual's learning process.

This general area of learning seems quite promising, but more investigation is required. We need to know the links between learning styles and related areas of brain activity, and also to what extent, if any, a particular learning style is linked to some other particular factor. Are they discrete? Are they linked? Are they shared?

In terms of usefulness in schools, a great deal more information is needed before teachers will be able to help pupils to recognize their personal learning styles and utilize them more effectively.

There are hints that a link is possible between teaching approaches on the one hand, and learning/cognitive styles of learners on the other. Pupils do appear to learn more when using their preferred manner of processing and in their preferred setting. If child A is more 'wholist' than 'analytic' and also more 'verbal' than 'visual imagery', then he will require material to be presented by the teacher in a clearly structured manner by means of verbal descriptions. If child B is at the opposite end of each of these two learning dimensions, he will learn better if the materials are presented generally (so that he can impose his own structure and organization on them) and in visual form (e.g. using pictures, charts, models, graphs, diagrams, maps, etc.) rather than by verbal description.

Metacognition

Metacognition can be briefly defined as 'thinking about how we should think'. It is a person's awareness of just what thinking processes he uses when attempting to learn. We should be able to reflect on our learning and ask ourselves questions such as: Where am I up to at this point? How did I get to this stage? Am I going about this in the most efficient way? What is the best way of proceeding to the next stage? It involves skills such as planning, monitoring, questioning and double-checking. Metacognition can be described as an awareness of the processes of thinking and remembering.

There is evidence to suggest that metacognitive skills are linked to learning difficulties, as children with such difficulties seem to be poor in making spontaneous use of memory control strategies. Pupils should be encouraged to use self-regulation, and they must be active participants in the teaching and learning process, taking part in classroom discussions.

A pupil's metacognitive strategies should be assessed. This will provide the starting point for plans to help the pupil develop skills already mastered or develop new skills. A 'think aloud' framework of questions and answers may be used; planned educational activities along these lines may help the pupil to become a more self-regulated and active learner. One framework that has been suggested as effective for developing metacognitive strategies is reciprocal teaching. It was developed specifically to assist pupils with improving reading comprehension skills, and focuses on the four reading comprehension strategies of:

1. summarising
2. questioning
3. predicting
4. clarifying.

A number of studies have shown that reciprocal teaching is an effective method for improving certain literacy skills, particularly that of reading comprehension.

The cognitive control model

For the past 10 years researchers at Birmingham University, led by Riding, have been building up a body of research investigating the relationship between cognitive style and a variety of other independent variables. They have also proposed a model of 'cognitive control', shown in Figure 6.3, which functions at three distinct levels.

In learning, experiences of the outside world are first perceived and processed, using memory and intelligence. The incoming information is thus analysed and passed to a deeper level (that of cognitive control) where learning style plays a part in processing the messages received. While this is in operation, messages are passed backwards and forwards to an even deeper, primary source in which knowledge and cognitive history (e.g. memory of positive and negative past experiences) also have a part to play in shaping the learning process.

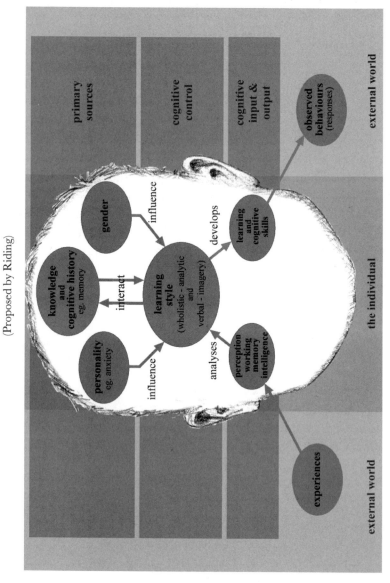

Figure 6.3 The cognitive control model (proposed by Riding).

Other factors will also impinge on this process, related to personality (e.g. anxiety) and gender (as well as possible others).

The outcome of this very complex interaction between two different levels of cognition and at least four separate types of influence, is that a learning strategy results, and this, in turn, produces some response or observed behaviour which the outside world views as a response to the initial learning experience.

As will be appreciated, the crucial part of the entire process is at the cognitive control level, as it is here that the external world and the internal cognitive state of the individual encounter one another. It is this cognitive control which will determine the response made to the external world, imposing on it its own structure and view.

Chapter 7
Dyslexia examined

We need to start by explaining the meaning of the word 'dyslexia'. It comes from the Greek words 'dys', which means difficult, painful or abnormal, and 'lexicos', which means the words of a language. Hence, dyslexia means 'a *difficulty* with *words*', and is understood to refer to written words (reading, writing and spelling) as opposed to spoken words.

It can be appreciated from this that dyslexia is merely a description of a child's difficulties and can in no way be taken as an explanation of what those difficulties are or indeed anything else about them. (This may be stating the obvious, but it is the cause of at least *some* of the misunderstanding and confusion about the subject.) Therefore saying, for instance, 'My child cannot read because he is dyslexic' is no more informative than saying 'My child cannot read because he has difficulty making out words written down'. It does not tell us any more than if we were to say a person is bleeding badly because he has a haemorrhage or that someone has a high temperature because he is feverish. Of course a parent might say, 'My child cannot read properly, because he has dyslexia' and in doing so intends only to convey the message that the poor reading is not due to the child being generally slow or lazy or not having attended school.

The word 'dyslexia' appears in a large number of terms - 'acquired dyslexia' and 'surface dyslexia' are just two taken at random from a long list. It is also associated with other terms that do not contain the words 'dyslexia' or 'dyslexic' but nevertheless are considered by many people to mean the same thing ('specific learning difficulties' and 'specific reading retardation' are two examples).

Table 7.1 lists 51 terms used in the books and articles about dyslexia to which I referred while writing this chapter. All of them are, or have been, used to refer to dyslexia at different times and by different people - doctors, psychologists, researchers, etc.

Such a long list (and there is no guarantee that it is complete) inevitably leads to a great deal of confusion and misunderstanding. As a result, a maze has grown up, through which only a comparatively small number of people can find the correct path - the majority of people become lost when they come across the subject of dyslexia for the first time. For many people, it is by no means clear as to why there are so many terms and whether similar-sounding terms mean the same as one another. Could they refer to different but related conditions? The confusion increases when an interested parent attempts to read up about the subject and discovers that the use and meaning of many of the terms are challenged by some workers in the field of dyslexia. We will now attempt to find some kind of pathway through it all and, it is hoped, clear up some of the confusion.

The large number of terms associated with dyslexia is best explained by relating them to the whole range of learning difficulties that are found within the general school population. We need to start with the total population of schoolchildren and sift through them

Table 7.1 Terms used in relation to dyslexia

Acquired dyslexia	'L'-type dyslexia
Acute dyslexia	Mind blindness
Alexia	Mixed dyslexia
Amnesia visualis vebalis	Morphemic dyslexia
Analfabeta partialis	Phonological dyslexia
Attentional dyslexia	Phonological processor dyslexia
Auditory dyslexia	Primary reading retardation
Bradylexia	'P'-type dyslexia
Classical sequential dyslexia	'R'-type dyslexia
Congenital dyslexia	Secondary dyslexia
Congenital symbol amblyopia	Semantic processor dyslexia
Congenital typholexia	Sequential dyslexia
Congenital word blindness	Specific developmental dyslexia
Constitutional dyslexia	Specific dyslexia
Deep dyslexia	Specific language disability
Developmental aphasia	Specific learning difficulties
Developmental dyslexia	Specific reading difficulties
Direct dyslexia	Specific reading disabilities
Dyseidetic dyslexia	Specific reading retardation
Dyslexia	Strephosymbolia
Dysphonetic dyslexia	Surface dyslexia
Familial dyslexia	Traumatic dyslexia
Graphemic processor dyslexia	Visual dyslexia
Hyperlexia	Visual processor dyslexia
Language learning disorder	Word blindness
Legasthenia	

stage by stage, in a gradual process of elimination, until we end up with those who have dyslexia.

When the total school population is considered, it is agreed by most education workers and researchers that 80% of schoolchildren go through their school careers without any difficulty. Obviously those with dyslexia will not be found within this large, problem-free group and so we must consider the other 20%. This group of 20% will experience learning difficulties of one sort or another at one time or another during their school lives. We should explain here that the term 'learning difficulties', used *in this context*, has a very general meaning and is not to be taken in the literal sense. For example, children with physical handicaps or sensory difficulties are described as having learning difficulties, as are those children in delicate health or with emotional/behavioural difficulties. Any individual child who experiences these difficulties could be quite competent at general learning and be very able at reading, writing, spelling and number work. The official definition of 'learning difficulties' in the way the term is used here was set out in the 1981 Education Act. It refers to *any* difficulty of such a nature that the child requires something *more than*, or *different from* the majority of other children of the same age in order to benefit from the education process.

Although this group of children - the 20% - need extra resources in order to benefit fully from the education process, many of them do not have any difficulty with the actual process of learning itself. In fact, many of them are high achievers at school. This 20% of all children will therefore be composed of a mixture of competent readers and poor readers, but the exact proportions of each are not known. Of this mixture, the competent readers do not concern us and we shall concentrate on the remainder.

Considering the poor readers, a proportion of these will be of below-average intelligence and so their reading difficulties will be explainable by this fact. There may be some within this group who also have dyslexic difficulties but these difficulties could well be masked by their general learning difficulties and might therefore be more difficult to identify. Hence we must consider the others whose difficulties are more easily recognizable.

Many descriptive terms have been given to this remaining group - poor readers of reasonable or good intelligence - in whom we are interested. The system of identification we have just described is summarized in the flow chart in Figure 7.1. Of the 51 terms in Table 7.1, 10 have been mentioned in the flow chart, and it can be seen how they relate to one another. Further explanation is required to show the manner in which many of the remainder are used and how they inter-relate.

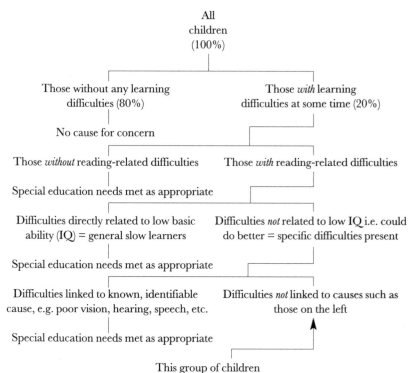

Figure 7.1 Where dyslexic children are found within the range of learning difficulties.

The word 'dyslexia' is, strictly speaking, a general term and refers to two distinct types:

- *acquired dyslexia* - which is sometimes called *alexia*
- *developmental dyslexia* - which is the type we are concerned with in this book, as it applies to children. It is sometimes referred to as congenital dyslexia and at other times as specific developmental dyslexia.

Each type will now be further explained.

Acquired dyslexia

This is sometimes called 'alexia' and also 'traumatic dyslexia' and was first identified more than a century ago. It is a condition found in medical patients (usually adults) and refers to the loss of the ability to read, which had previously been fully developed. This acquired condition results from some form of brain damage and is usually caused by accidents, tumours, strokes, drugs, psychiatric disorders or ageing. The term 'word-blindness' has also been used to describe this same condition.

In all cases of acquired dyslexia there are both 'hard' signs and 'soft' signs of brain damage. 'Hard' signs are the physical injury or wound, and 'soft' signs are such features as co-ordination difficulties, abnormal reflexes or an unusual electroencephalogram (EEG) pattern.

Attempts were made in the mid-1970s to distinguish between different syndromes of acquired dyslexia, with patients classified into groups according to the types of reading or spelling errors that they made or the particular literacy skills they appeared to be lacking.

A survey of just five books published between 1983 and 1991, with a total of 10 editors, writers and researchers, shows that six different names have been used to describe subtypes of acquired dyslexia. Any particular researcher has usually claimed the existence of only two or three types and the question arises as to how close any subtype claimed by one worker is to that claimed by another, even though different names are used.

At the time of publishing their respective books the authors concerned held the posts as given below:

- Colin Tyre was responsible for the Educational Psychology Service of South Glamorgan
- Peter Young was an editor for the Open University Press
- Peter Bryant was Watts Professor of Psychology at the University of Oxford
- Lynnette Bradley was senior research officer in the Department of Psychology at the University of Oxford
- Vera Quin and Alan Macauslan ran the Learning Disabilities Clinic at St Thomas' Hospital, London
- Tim Miles was Professor Emeritus of Psychology at the University College of North Wales in Bangor
- Elaine Miles was course adviser on teacher training at the Dyslexia Unit of the University College of North Wales in Bangor

- Peter Pumfrey was professor of education at the Centre of Educational Guidance and Special Needs, School of Education, Manchester University
- Rea Reason was senior educational psychologist at the Centre of Educational Guidance and Special Needs, School of Education, Manchester University.

The six subtypes of acquired dyslexia mentioned in the five books are:

- surface
- deep
- phonological
- direct
- visual
- attentional.

The subtypes mentioned by each pair of writers are set out in Table 7.2. As can be seen, the subtypes of surface dyslexia and deep dyslexia are mentioned in all five books, with the other four being mentioned less frequently. It is fair to say, then, that among researchers, it is popularly believed that adults with acquired dyslexia do not all present as exactly the same but can be divided into subtypes. There would appear to be at least two subtypes, but there is no agreement on the exact number. However, it is more likely to be a small number (such as two) than a large number (such as ten).

Surface dyslexics

Surface dyslexics are described as reading silently 'by ear', recognizing words by sounds and not by their written appearance. There is

Table 7.2 Six subtypes of acquired dyslexia

		Surface	Deep	Phonological	Direct (hyperlexia)	Visual	Attentional
Young & Tyre	(1983)	✓	✓	•	•	•	•
Bryant & Bradley	(1985)	✓	✓	✓	•	•	•
Quin & Macausland	(1986)	✓	✓	•	•	•	•
Miles & Miles	(1990)	✓	✓	✓	✓	✓	✓
Pumfrey & Reason	(1991)	✓	✓	✓	✓	•	•
Total		5	5	3	2	1	1

nothing wrong with their phonological skills (which will be discussed later) and they are able to read nonsense words. However, they are likely to be caught out by homophones (similar sounding words, e.g. sail/sale; where/wear; hole/whole). Often, they attempt to read these words phonologically and in doing so turn them into nonsense words (e.g. 'broad' read as 'brode'). They have difficulty in remembering what words look like and depend heavily on working out their meaning via the rules about letter-sound relationships. Therefore their greatest difficulty is with words that cannot be read simply by letter-sound correspondence.

Deep dyslexics

Deep dyslexics are described as being unable to use phonics because they are unable to connect what they see on the page with the *sound* of the word. Deep dyslexics look at a word and are likely to read it as an entirely different one, but with a related meaning (e.g. 'city' could be read as 'Liverpool', 'rose' read as 'daffodil', 'pixie' read as 'gnome'). Also, two words of similar 'shape' can be confused (e.g. 'top' can be read as 'hay') as each occupies a shape like:

and 'pond' can be read as 'gash', as each has the following shape:

Words that are concrete in meaning (such as man/house/tree) are more likely to be read correctly than are abstract words (such as hope/love/peace). Deep dyslexics cannot read nonsense words (e.g. nate/toge/borm) and deep dyslexia itself is considered to be the most serious subtype of acquired dyslexia because the symptoms suggest that several components of the reading system are damaged.

Phonological dyslexia

Phonological dyslexia is described as being a similar, but less drastic, form of deep dyslexia, involving difficulties with the analysis of sounds as well as the inability to read irregular or nonsense words. Phonological dyslexics rely heavily on the visual appearance of a word and tend to make derivational errors, e.g. 'weigh' may be read as 'weight', 'wise' as 'wisdom' and 'camp' as 'cape'). A phonological dyslexic cannot analyse a word into its phonological segments and has a tendency to add to, remove from, or change the beginning or end of a word (e.g. 'thinking' may be read as 'think').

Phonological dyslexia has been described as the 'mirror image' of surface dyslexia and is a relatively recent addition to the list of subtypes of acquired dyslexia.

Direct dyslexia

Direct dyslexia is often called hyperlexia. Those adults affected are accurate in terms of the actual oral skills of reading but show poor comprehension of what they have read.

As the acquired form of dyslexia is not the main concern of this book, no information about the other claimed subtypes needs to be given here. Acquired dyslexia has been described solely for the purpose of rounding out the picture so that developmental dyslexia (which is the main object of our interest) can be viewed in its correct perspective, and we move on to consider it now.

Developmental dyslexia

Developmental dyslexia, which is the type found in children, is the main subject of this book. It is referred to by a variety of names (as seen in Figure 7.1), and this tends to produce some confusion. Various researchers have attempted to distinguish subtypes of developmental dyslexia, as it is vital to know whether all children are identical in their dyslexic reading difficulties or display two, three or even more subtypes. If all children display the same difficulties, then the task facing teachers is obviously much easier as one teaching approach (or set of techniques) can be applied to all children equally.

The 10 editors, writers and researchers whose work we referred to earlier describe a number of different attempts to define subtypes of developmental dyslexia. A few brief comments will be made about each of five different classifications. There are others, but these are the ones that are referred to most often:

- The Johnson and Mykelbust classification (made in 1967) is divided into two subtypes: visual dyslexics and auditory dyslexics.
- The Boder classification (made in 1973) is into three subtypes: dysphonetic dyslexics, dyseidetic dyslexics and mixed dyslexics.

- The Seymour classification (made in 1986) is also divided into three subtypes: semantic processor dyslexics, phonological processor dyslexics and visual (graphemic) processor dyslexics.
- The Snowling classification (made in 1987) is divided into two subtypes: phonological dyslexics and surface (or morphemic) dyslexics
- The Bakker classification (proposed in 1990) divides developmental dyslexics into two types, which he calls 'P' and 'L'.

These five attempts to classify developmental dyslexics are not the only attempts that have been made and each one has its critics. You will notice that surface, phonological, and visual are all used to describe both a possible type of acquired dyslexia *and* a possible type of developmental dyslexia also. However, it must not be assumed that these have the same meaning when used in relation to acquired and developmental dyslexia. We can summarize what we have said so far in Figure 7.2.

The subtypes of acquired and developmental dyslexia will be dealt with more fully later in the book. However, it is important for parents to realize that they feature in the research being carried out into the causes and nature of dyslexia, as well as in relation to possible ways of helping dyslexic children. If dyslexic children can indeed be divided into subtypes, then this could be an important signpost as to the cause of their condition. Also, if any subtypes of acquired dyslexia in adults can be found to have similarities with a subtype of developmental dyslexia found in children, this could be a vital step to unravelling the many threads that still surround the causes of dyslexia. A simple set of comparisons might be useful for future reference, and one is set out in Table 7.3.

From what we have covered so far we have learned that:

- 'dyslexia' is a word which only *describes* what a particular difficulty is, IT DOES NOT EXPLAIN ANYTHING
- dyslexia is a general term that covers two main types: acquired and developmental
- developmental dyslexia is the type found in children
- both types have been called by more than one name
- there have been claims that each type exists in a number of different forms.

However, we have not yet attempted to explain much about dyslexia or to answer the simple but all-important question: 'What is

DYSLEXIA

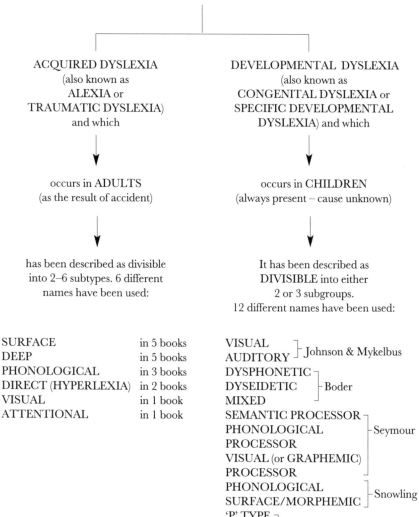

This is a general term and is used to describe TWO different conditions:

ACQUIRED DYSLEXIA
(also known as
ALEXIA or
TRAUMATIC DYSLEXIA)
and which

DEVELOPMENTAL DYSLEXIA
(also known as
CONGENITAL DYSLEXIA or
SPECIFIC DEVELOPMENTAL
DYSLEXIA) and which

occurs in ADULTS
(as the result of accident)

occurs in CHILDREN
(always present – cause unknown)

has been described as divisible
into 2–6 subtypes. 6 different
names have been used:

It has been described as
DIVISIBLE into either
2 or 3 subgroups.
12 different names have been used:

SURFACE   in 5 books
DEEP   in 5 books
PHONOLOGICAL   in 3 books
DIRECT (HYPERLEXIA)   in 2 books
VISUAL   in 1 book
ATTENTIONAL   in 1 book

VISUAL
AUDITORY ⎤ Johnson & Mykelbus

DYSPHONETIC ⎤
DYSEIDETIC ⎬ Boder
MIXED   ⎦

SEMANTIC PROCESSOR ⎤
PHONOLOGICAL   ⎬ Seymour
PROCESSOR
VISUAL (or GRAPHEMIC)
PROCESSOR   ⎦

PHONOLOGICAL   ⎤ Snowling
SURFACE/MORPHEMIC ⎦

'P' TYPE ⎤ Bakker
'L' TYPE ⎦

(3 subtype names are common to both: VISUAL, PHONOLOGICAL and
SURFACE. It must not be assumed that any of these words mean the same in both
adults and children.)

Figure 7.2 Features of acquired and developmental dyslexia.

Table 7.3 Comparison of acquired and developmental dyslexia

Acquired type	Developmental type
• Occurs in adults	• Occurs in children
• The adults have previously learned to read	• The children have not previously learned to read
• Is a difficulty in re-establishing an already learned skill	• Is a difficulty in learning a skill
• Caused by damage to brain	• Cause not known
• 'Hard' signs present in all cases	• No 'hard' signs present (in the majority of cases)
• 'Soft' signs present in all cases	• No 'soft' signs present (in the majority of cases)
• At least 6 different sub-types have been claimed	• At least 12 different sub-types have been claimed

dyslexia?' Unfortunately, there is no simple, quick or exact answer, as we shall see.

Over a 31-year period, from 1968 to 1999, nine different bodies or groups of people have produced definitions of dyslexia or dyslexic-type difficulties. All of these bodies are renowned and highly respected, so we can have confidence in the quality of what they have to say.

The actual definitions are *not* given in this chapter (with the exception of the final one), but they may be found in Appendix I. Instead, each definition has been analysed into its component parts, as shown in Table 7.4, so that an easy comparison may be made.

There are five types of information displayed in the table, arranged in columns numbered 1 to 5. We shall deal with each column in turn, starting with the left-hand column. Column 1 lists the letters A to I, each representing the source of one of the definitions concerned:

- definition A was produced by the World Federation of Neurology in 1968
- definition B was produced by the British Dyslexia Association in 1989
- definition C was produced by the World Federation of Neurology in 1968
- definition D was produced by Rutter, Tizard and Whitmore in 1970
- definition E was produced by Tansley and Panckhurst in 1981
- definition F was produced by the Dyslexia Institute in 1989

Table 7.4 Nine important definitions of dyslexia/dyslexic-type difficulties

Key: ● = definitely; ↗ = possibly

	Name Used (2)	How described (3)	A	B	C	D	E	F	G	H	I	Points of agreement (out of max 9)
5 Conditions applying													
No Organic Damage			●	●	●	●	↗	●	●	●	●	1
No Sensory Defect			●	●	●	●	↗	●	●	●	●	1
Age Factor			●	●	●	↗	●	●	●	●	●	1
Cognitive Disability			●	●	↗	●	●	●	●	●	●	1
Socio-cultural Opportunity			●	●	↗	●	●	●	●	●	●	1
Constitutional in Origin			●	↗	↗	●	●	●	●	●	●	2
Had Been Taught			↗	●	↗	●	↗	●	●	●	↗	4
Below IQ/Ability Level			↗	●	↗	↗	●	●	↗	●	●	4
4 Areas definitely/possibly affected													
Behaviour			●	●	●	●	●	↗	●	●	●	1
Working Memory			●	●	●	●	●	↗	●	●	●	1
Motor Skills			●	↗	●	●	●	↗	●	●	●	2
Oral Work/Speech			●	↗	●	●	●	↗	●	●	●	2
Musical Notation			●	↗	●	●	●	↗	●	●	●	2
General Language/Information Processing			●	↗	●	●	●	↗	●	●	●	2
Number Work/Maths			●	↗	●	●	↗	↗	↗	●	●	4
Spelling			↗	↗	●	●	↗	↗	↗	↗	↗	7
Writing/Essay Work			↗	↗	●	●	↗	↗	↗	●	●	5
Reading			↗	↗	↗	↗	↗	↗	↗	↗	↗	9
Origin of definition			A	B	C	D	E	F	G	H	I	
A	Dyslexia	disorder										
B	Dyslexia	difficulty										
C	Specific developmental dyslexia	disorder										
D	Specific reading retardation	low attainment										
E	Specific learning difficulties	problem										
F	Specific learning difficulties	deficiencies										
G	Specific reading difficulties	problems										
H	Dyslexia	—										
I	Dyslexia	—										

- definition G was produced by the Department of Education and Science in 1972
- definition H was produced by a committee of the Health Council of The Netherlands in 1997
- definition I was produced by a working panel of the Division of Educational and Child Psychology of the British Psychological Society in 1999.

Column 2 tells us the names used in the definitions for the reading problem(s) they are attempting to describe. Four call it 'dyslexia' and two 'specific learning difficulties'; others using 'specific developmental dyslexia', 'specific reading retardation' or 'specific reading difficulties'.

Column 3 lists the one- or two-word descriptions of the reading problem. Five different names are used in column 2, and in column 3, the reading problem is given various descriptions, two calling it a 'disorder', two using the word 'problem(s)' and others 'difficulty', 'low attainment' and 'deficiencies'. The last two make no attempt to produce a description.

Column 4 sets out all the areas that are claimed to be affected (or possibly affected) by these types of reading problem. Ten different areas of the child's functioning are mentioned between the nine definitions. As will be noted, **the only point of agreement between all nine is that there is a difficulty with reading involved**. There is a large measure of agreement (seven out of nine) that spelling is also involved and some agreement also (five out of nine) that writing is related to the problem. Beyond that, there is very little agreement.

Column 5 details the conditions that need to apply before a child can be considered to have the type of reading difficulty with which we are concerned. There is less agreement in this area than in the factors discussed in column 4. Only four of the definitions make a point about the child being found to perform below the expected standard, bearing in mind his IQ or level of basic ability. There are also only four that insist that adequate opportunities to learn must have been available. There is even less in respect of the other conditions.

This is why no easy answer can be given to the question 'What is dyslexia?' All we can say in response is that all experts agree that it is A DIFFICULTY WITH READING and that most also claim that spelling and writing are affected, with performance in these areas being below the child's basic ability level.

Definition I, the most recently produced of the set of nine, deserves further comment. The definition itself is as follows:

> Dyslexia is evident when accurate and fluent word reading and/or spelling develops very incompletely or with great difficulty. This focuses on literacy learning at the 'word level' and implies that the problem is severe and persistent despite appropriate learning opportunities. It provides the basis for a staged process of assessment through teaching.

It should be noted that this definition has no exclusionary criteria; any child is to be considered dyslexic if he fits the above definition. This means there is no distinction possible between:

- the dyslexic child and one with moderate learning difficulties
- the dyslexic child and one with sensory impairment
- the dyslexic child and one with hyperlexia, i.e. the child has the ability to read a piece of text without making any errors, yet is unable to properly comprehend the meaning of what he has just read.

The fact that no exact definition has yet been produced is of little consequence. Children without reading problems learn to read in different ways and have different reading styles. Hence there is no justification for expecting that when difficulties arise they will be uniform in nature between one child and another. None of this can alter the fact that as well as those children who are poor readers because of being slow learners, there is another quite distinct group who have difficulty with reading yet are very able in other ways. These children all require early identification, adequate assessment, a proper description of their special educational needs, and an appropriate level and type of specialist provision to help them. For convenience, we refer to them throughout this book as being 'dyslexic' or having 'dyslexia'. Parents, teachers and others understand these words and use them as an easy form of verbal shorthand to describe the children with whom we are concerned.

Having dealt with dyslexia itself, Chapter 8 goes on to consider the effects dyslexia has on an individual child, and thus give the full picture of the problem.

Chapter 8
The dyslexic child

The previous chapter outlined the attempts made to describe dyslexia, the different forms it may take and the difficulties encountered in trying to define it exactly. Little was said, however, of what a dyslexic child is like. As dyslexia and the dyslexic child are two sides of the same coin, we will now complete the picture by discussing the dyslexic child.

This book concentrates on the difficulties dyslexic children experience in learning to read and ways of dealing with them. It does not attempt to cover all aspects of dyslexia in depth - the others can be dealt with only briefly. We know from Chapter 7 that reading was the *only* area of the 10 mentioned on which all nine bodies agreed. It is also the aspect of children's learning difficulties that causes most concern and on which most research has been undertaken.

However, the very fact that nine *other* areas of functioning were listed in the definitions is an indication of the wide variety of possible difficulties that dyslexic children can present with. As we shall learn in this chapter, there are many other causes for concern besides these nine.

The main point of this chapter can be very well illustrated if we consider as an example the case of just one child with whom I have had professional involvement. Peter was referred to the (then) Schools Psychological Service - since renamed the Educational Psychology Service - by his head teacher for assessment and advice. Figure 8.1 gives the details provided on the standard referral form. Apart from details withheld to prevent Peter, his school and the LEA being identified, the referral form is copied in full.

Peter was just a few days short of his tenth birthday at the time of his referral. The referral details, when analysed, are found to tell an

SCHOOLS PSYCHOLOGICAL SERVICE

Telephone:

FOR OFFICE USE ONLY   ALLOCATION

NO PREVIOUS RECORDS

1   2

Date   Date

REFERRAL TO AN EDUCATIONAL PSYCHOLOGIST
IN ACCORDANCE WITH THE AUTHORITY'S GUIDELINES, PARENTAL
AGREEMENT MUST HAVE BEEN OBTAINED BEFORE MAKING THIS REFERRAL

NAME: PETER _____   DATE OF BIRTH:

NAME OF PARENT(S) OR   SCHOOL:

NAME OF GUARDIAN(S)

ADDRESS: CLASS TEACHER:

TELEPHONE NO:

Please list your concerns about this child: CONCERNS ARE ACADEMIC.
VERY POOR SPELLING/WRITTEN WORK /READING. HE IS NOT MAKING
THE PROGRESS ONE WOULD EXPECT. HE CAN TELL A STORY ORALLY BUT
CANNOT WRITE IT DOWN. HE RESPONDS INTELLIGENTLY IN DISCUSSION.
HIS PARENTS HELP WITH SPELLING EACH NIGHT WITH LITTLE BENEFIT.
HE IS UNABLE TO ORDER NUMBERS. HE CANNOT COUNT IN 3's,
4's, 5's. PETER IS WILLING TO WORK BUT IS OFTEN FRUST—
RATED

When you discussed these concerns with the child and parents what was their
view?

PETER GETS A LOT OF SUPPORT AT HOME AND IS BECOMING FRUST-
RATED THAT HIS YOUNGER BROTHERS ARE DOING BETTER THAN
HE IS. MRS. _____ WOULD LIKE TO KNOW HOW BEST
SHE CAN HELP HIM.

Please record the actions already taken to meet these concerns following your
discussions with the child's parents.

PETER HAS BEEN ASSESSED USING THE ASTON INDEX TO HELP
GAUGE THE EXTENT OF HIS PROBLEMS.

Figure 8.1 A completed referral form.

(contd)

What other source of help/advice have you sought e.g. SBRT., EWO, SCMO, EGO, Speech Therapist etc.? (Please include copies of any relevent reports and in the case of a child who has learning difficulties, please enclose the SBRT report):

No OTHER SOURCE OF HELP HAS YET BEEN SOUGHT

Which of the following areas of development do you feel deserve closer investigation:

Independence & Self Help	☐	Concentration & Attention	☐
Motor & Sensory	☐	Language & Communication	☑
Behaviour	☐	Motivation	☐
Attendance	☐	Emotion	☐

Academic Skills - Please state schemes used and where possible results of standardised tests.

Reading: *STARPOL READING SCHEME.*
2.1 YEARS BEHIND CHRONOLOGICAL AGE USING SCHONNELL LAST
Spelling: *7.1 YEARS. VOCABULARY SCORE = 10. USING \ JULY*
ASTON INDEX. LOW SCORES ON WEEKLY TESTS.
Mathematics: *MAJOR CONCERN*
CANNOT LEARN TABLES. UNABLE TO ORDER NUMBERS

Other relevant information:

PETER IS WELL-BEHAVED AND CARED FOR. HE PARTICIPATES IN ALL CLASSROOM ACTIVITIES AND HAS GOOD HOME SUPPORT. HE HAS EXCELLENT LISTENING SKILLS AND IS A TALENTED ARTIST. HIS PERFORMANCE IS WELL BELOW HIS APPARENT INTELLIGENCE LEVEL.

Signed............................   Date............................

Figure 8.1 contd.

all-too-familiar story as far as dyslexic children are concerned. On the positive side, it is seen that Peter:

- can tell a story well
- responds intelligently in discussion
- is willing to work
- behaves well
- participates in classroom activities
- has excellent communication skills
- is a talented artist
- listens well
- has a high level of vocabulary
- has parents who help him
- gets support at home
- has parents who requested help for him.

Despite all these factors in his favour, however, the head teacher had to report that:

- Peter's achievement is less than his ability would lead one to expect
- his spelling is poor (almost 3 years below his chronological age)
- written work is poor;
- his reading ability is poor (2+ years below his chronological age)
- he is unable to put numbers in their correct sequence
- he is unable to count in 3s, 5s, etc.
- maths generally is a major concern
- Peter is unable to learn his 'times' tables.

In short, Peter has a reasonably high level of intellectual ability as well as many other factors in his favour, such as concerned, support-ive parents, a positive attitude to school and certain talents. Despite this, he is poor academically, having difficulties with reading, spelling, writing and number work, and is unable to accomplish some tasks that most other children of his age achieve successfully. Many would consider Peter to be a 'typical dyslexic'.

The fact that many dyslexic children show a collection of difficul-ties - such as those mentioned in Peter's case - has been known for many years. Many studies have been made and reported on but one of the most detailed and interesting was that described by Professor T Miles of the University of Bangor, who has spent some decades dealing with and writing about dyslexic children.

In 1983, he published the findings of tests carried out on 223 chil-dren, each of whom he considered to be 'clearly dyslexic'. (He had actually studied more than 300, but for his study rejected all those about whom he had even the slightest doubt.) The subjects described in his study were, for the most part, school-age children (i.e. aged 7 to 17) and a few older people (aged 18 to 23). There were 210 of the former and 13 of the latter. As well as being able to describe the difficulties encountered in all 223, he was able to select 132 subjects and match each of them up with another, non-dyslexic child of the same gender, age and intellectual level. Thus Professor Miles was able to form a 'matched control' group which he could use to make certain comparisons between dyslexic and non-dyslexic children. Much of this chapter is concerned with summarizing Professor Miles's findings, but first we shall deal with a couple of matters of general interest: how many children are dyslexic and the connection between gender and dyslexia.

The incidence of dyslexia

Because it is not possible to define a dyslexic child precisely and in a universally accepted manner, different groups of workers who have investigated reading and other related difficulties in children, have studied slightly different populations and so have produced different estimates of how common dyslexia is. Apart from deciding whether a child is definitely dyslexic - and there are no clear-cut guidelines - there is also the matter of degree. A child who is dyslexic may occupy any place on a range from quite slight to very marked.

Research has shown that dyslexia occurs in all groups of children irrespective of gender (which we will discuss in the next section), social groups, intellectual level, geographical area, etc. It does not appear to be concentrated within any particular social group, ability level or part of the country. The average percentage incidence quoted is 4%, which, if accurate, would mean that more than two million people in the British Isles are affected. As dyslexia does not appear to be linked to intelligence, then 4% of bright, average and slow-learning children will all be affected. The difficulty is likely to be more readily identifiable in the bright and average children than in those who are slow. Dyslexic difficulties in slow children are more likely to be overlooked because of the general learning difficulties they experience.

If we draw a graph of the range of children's IQs and include on it a separate curve to represent the 4% of the total population who are also dyslexic, then the categories of difficulties show up clearly. If we divide the whole population into three groups, i.e. low, average and high ability, there are six categories, as each of these three groups subdivides into those 4% of children with dyslexia and the other 96% without.

The graph is shown in Figure 8.2. The lower curve - which relates to the dyslexic children - is shown magnified ten times on the vertical scale for the purpose of clarity, and proper allowance must be made for this deliberate distortion.

The six categories into which the children fall have been marked on the graph. They are:

- LW = **L**ow ability **W**ithout dyslexia (producing single difficulty)
- LD = **L**ow ability with **D**yslexia (producing double difficulty)
- AW = **A**verage ability **W**ithout dyslexia (producing no difficulty)
- AD = **A**verage ability with **D**yslexia (producing single difficulty)
- HW = **H**igh ability **W**ithout dyslexia (producing no difficulty)
- HD = **H**igh ability with **D**yslexia (producing single difficulty).

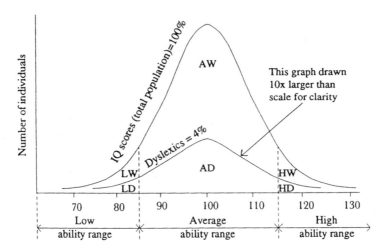

Figure 8.2 How the population divides into six categories.

As we can see, two groups experience no difficulty of any kind (those of average or high intelligence and without dyslexia), three groups experience a single difficulty (dyslexia in two cases and low ability in the other) and one group is unfortunate enough to have a double difficulty. This last group - the children who are of low basic ability and in addition have dyslexia - happen also to be the ones who are most difficult to diagnose because of the 'masking' effect referred to above. Furthermore, the same group of children is also likely to contain those who prove the most difficult to assist once they are identified. This situation is summarized in Table 8.1.

Table 8.1 The range of children's IQs and the categories of difficulties

Group	Number of difficulties	Ease of detection	Ease of remediation
LW	1	–	–
LD	2	Difficult	Difficult
AW	0	–	–
AD	1	Moderate	Moderate
HW	0	–	–
HD	1	Good	Good

As a final word on this topic, it has been suggested by some workers that dyslexia should be considered to be present only in those children of at least average intelligence and that the description 'dyslexia' should not be applied to children in the low ability range.

Dyslexia and gender

Although both boys and girls can have dyslexia, four times more boys than girls are found to be dyslexic. (This is one of the reasons that throughout this book I have referred to the dyslexic child as 'he'.) As with so many other aspects of dyslexia, exact figures are difficult, if not impossible, to arrive at and some estimates have placed the proportions as high as seven to one, but the lower figure would appear to be more likely. (Professor Miles found that in the children he surveyed the ratio of boys to girls was just over four to one.)

Professor Miles's survey results

Reading

In the majority of cases where a dyslexic 'pattern' of difficulties is found, there will be some aspect of reading difficulty present. For most it will be a significant problem but there are occasional cases where reading difficulty does not appear to be the major problem. Of his 223 subjects, 191 (86%) could be described as poor readers and another 24 (11%) as fairly poor (unfortunately Professor Miles does not use exact measurements). He concludes that for many dyslexics, there will be difficulty in learning to read, but they will eventually master the skill. However, they are likely to remain slow readers and reading aloud could present particular problems.

Spelling

There are no figures given that summarize the findings, but a detailed analysis was made of the *types* of spelling error found. Dyslexic children show bizarre spellings - as do non-dyslexic children who are 'out of their depth'. Some errors are plausible in so far as words *could* be spelled that way but in fact are not (e.g. 'asist' for 'assist'), whereas bizarre spellings reveal that the children concerned have little or no knowledge of the relationship that exists between letters and the sounds they represent. Professor Miles gives details of 13 different types of spelling error.

Left-right confusion

In all, 149 of the 223 children (67%) showed uncertainty over left and right. The control sample was used in this when it was found that 87 of the 132 dyslexics (66%) showed confusion compared with only 36% of the control group. Many dyslexic children showed general uncertainty in tasks and were also confused about their body parts (right leg, left ear, right eye, etc.) and the body parts of others. In attempting to give directions to people they made more errors than other children. Even a child who knew the words 'port' and 'starboard' used them incorrectly.

Many right-handed children were helped by remembering the phrase 'I *write* with my *right*'. Many, when young, need to have gloves and shoes specially marked in some way and others make use of body markings such as freckles or scars. It is also common for a dyslexic child to distinguish left from right by means of remembering on which wrist they wear their watch or on which hand they wear their ring, etc. There is good reason to believe that it is only the words 'left' and 'right' that cause the difficulty, not the actual directions themselves as in many circumstances they function normally.

East-west confusion

No statistics were given, but the findings were collected mainly from the older children in the survey. Some dyslexic children are confused about direction and the degree of confusion is related to age, because it is only as children get older that they learn there are four compass points to be used in describing direction and movement around the world.

Confusion over east and west appears to be greater than any other kind of difficulty, but a detailed description of directional errors is not possible.

'b' and 'd' confusion

In all, 146 children, or 65%, showed this type of confusion, and Professor Miles felt there was good reason to think that this was an underestimate, as it was likely that some of the older children had experienced this difficulty when younger. This type of difficulty was particularly persistent, as some children in the higher age range still experienced the confusion. Of course it is not only dyslexic children who confuse 'b' and 'd', but another study (by Bottomley) showed that three times as many errors were made by dyslexics as by non-dyslexics *who had the same spelling age* (as distinct from having the same chronological age).

The letters 'b' and 'd' were not the only letters to be confused. Mistakes over 'p' and 'q' were also reported. These confusions clear up as children get older, but the 'b' and 'd' error persists longer. Professor Miles attributes this to the fact that the *sounds* of this pair of letters are so similar.

Time and date confusion

No statistics were given, but the fact of confusion is noted. Dyslexic children can be late in learning to tell the time and experience difficulty in remembering the days of the week in correct sequence. However, the abstract concept that the passage of time is marked by days of the week, etc., is as well understood by dyslexics as by other children.

Recall of months of the year

In the survey, 55% of the total could not recite the months of the year in correct order. When the matched control group was used, 57% of the dyslexics were unsuccessful compared with 20% of the controls. In addition, some did not know at which month to start the sequence. Many had to resort to memory aids. However, the months of the year are learned, and older children did better than the younger ones.

Subtraction and addition

No statistics are given indicating what percentage of the dyslexic children experience difficulties with these two basic types of calculation, but the observation is made that the difficulties fall into three groups:

- those showing a basic weakness related to calculation in general
- those showing a particular uncertainty in relation to the direction of the number series
- those who needed to use compensatory strategies.

The first group suggests that one cannot assume that a dyslexic child will acquire the basic knowledge of numbers and how they behave in the same way that other children acquire it during the course of everyday experiences at home and school. The second group suggests that there is particular difficulty in getting numbers the correct way round: '7 take away 5' could be confused with '5 take away 7', '62' could be written as '26', and '38' could be read as '83'. (Uncertainty over left and right could well be part of the reason for this.)

Compensatory strategies used were techniques such as counting on fingers or making marks on paper or even drawings, depending on the type of problem they were asked to solve. Despite needing these strategies, the overall picture was one of basically capable children who were quite severely restricted in their ability to carry out some simple mental arithmetical calculations.

Reciting tables

The statistics showed that difficulties over tables are found not only in dyslexic children - 89% of the total of 223 showed difficulties and on the 'matched controls' comparison 90% of dyslexics had problems, compared with 54% of the non-dyslexics. Children tended to lose their place when reciting, made errors of various kinds and often needed to use their fingers to assist them.

It normally takes dyslexic children longer than non-dyslexic children to master a set of tables. Professor Miles found that at age 13 years, some of his subjects could still not recite the 3x and 4x tables. In fact, 16 years was the earliest age at which these two tables no longer presented problems.

Recall of digits

The survey contained the results of testing all 223 subjects on digits presented to them auditorily, but the results of visually presented digits were available for only 42 subjects, as this type of test was not introduced until some time after the survey had got under way.

The 42 children for whom both sets of results were available provided the opportunity for a comparison to be made of these two sensory channels. In the case of auditorily presented digits (i.e. strings of numbers read out to the child by Professor Miles), dyslexic children could not, for the most part, remember as many numbers as others of the same age. (This was true whether they had to recite back the numbers in the order given or in reverse.)

In the case of visually presented digits, the numbers were flashed up on a screen in front of the children for a precise length of time. It was possible to vary the number of digits shown at any one time and also to vary the exposure time. Dyslexic children took longer than non-dyslexics to perceive the numbers correctly.

When the 42 subjects who had been tested both auditorily and visually were subjected to auditory ability-visual ability comparison it was found that they did not fall into the two groups. Therefore it was not possible to describe some of them as 'auditory dyslexic' (having an auditory weakness but no visual weakness) and others as 'visual dyslexic' (the converse). Children who scored high on the visual condition did not necessarily score low on the auditory condition, and vice versa. It appears from this that most dyslexic people find it difficult to process symbolic verbal material irrespective of which channel is used.

Memory for sentences

When given a sentence and asked to repeat it back, many dyslexic children could not do so word for word. In most cases, the *sense* of what was said to them was accurately perceived and repeated back but there was difficulty in getting the actual wording correct.

Other memory problems

Some dyslexic children are reported to have difficulty learning nursery rhymes, and also the alphabet.

Copying from the blackboard

This was also mentioned as a difficulty on many occasions.

Learning a foreign language

Difficulty with a foreign language was often reported; often a dyslexic child can be good at the oral part but have difficulty with writing the language concerned.

Finding rhymes

Professor Miles reports that a small number of the dyslexic children had difficulty in finding a word to rhyme with another word given, e.g. 'a colour that rhymes with head', 'a number that rhymes with tree', etc. He felt they had somehow 'missed out' - were at a loss to know what was required. (The existence of a difficulty on the part of poor readers in recognizing whether words rhyme has also been reported by two other researchers, Bradley and Bryant.)

Bell ringing

Although this may seem rather curious, two of the subjects in the survey had attempted to learn bell ringing but had had to give it up because they could not keep count!

Driving a car

Concerns are often expressed about dyslexics driving cars, usually because of confusion over 'left' and 'right', but it would appear that the confusion relates only to the words and not to the actual directions. There is no reason to think that dyslexic car drivers cannot be good drivers or that they are involved in more traffic accidents than others.

Chess

Dyslexia should not cause any difficulties in chess playing and many dyslexic children are successful at chess. No memory overload is involved as the different moves can be considered separately and do not need to be held in the mind all at once.

Music

Some of the subjects in the survey were gifted musically. Any drawback from dyslexia is related to reading musical notation, not the basic appreciation of the music itself. However, the correct reading of written music can be learned eventually, as can learning to read a book.

Art and craft

Those talents least affected by dyslexia will be the ones most likely to flourish in dyslexic children. Art is one subject in which there are few, if any, dyslexic-type difficulties to overcome. Woodwork, pottery and other craftwork can also be produced to the highest standards.

Creative writing

As Professor Miles puts it, 'Many of my subjects showed remarkable powers of literary appreciation and expression'. Many of the schoolbooks he saw contained good imaginative writing and poetry, albeit often badly spelled and with crossings-out. As he summed it up: 'A weak lexical system appears to be no barrier to creative writing.'

The overall picture presented is that a dyslexic child, apart from having difficulty in learning to read, is likely to have difficulty in a number of other areas of learning and school progress. It is not possible to say which areas of the child's functioning are likely to be affected as no two children will be exactly alike, and even in two with the same areas affected there are quite likely to be differences of degree between one and the other.

As far as schoolwork is concerned, reading, writing and number work (the three Rs), together with spelling, are the ones on which progress is most firmly based and so will cause the most concern if deficient. Other factors, such as confusion over left and right or an inability to put the months of the year in correct order, are likely be viewed as irritations rather than major difficulties and so will cause less concern. Knowing about them certainly helps to round out the overall picture presented by the child and can be an indication of how much he will need to overcome.

Up to this point in the chapter we have described the picture likely to be presented by the young child when first referred for a psychological assessment of his learning difficulties. We shall now look forward and consider what lies ahead.

Professor Miles was unable to carry out a longitudinal study, much as he would have liked to do so. He saw most of his subjects only once and was unable to follow them up in the years after he had seen them. Hence he was unable to report on the progress they made. However, because his subjects embraced a wide age range (most were between 7 and 17 years old), he was able to do the next best thing and compare one age group with another. His results are given below.

Reading progress

The older subjects were much more successful at reading than the younger ones, the average scores on the reading test he used increasing from 18 at age 7 to 92 at age 18. This bears out the results of many other investigations, which show that dyslexic children do improve over time. The rate of progress is likely to depend on the teaching conditions and how favourable these are.

Spelling progress

This also improved over time. At age 7, the average spelling score was 13, but it was 64 in the 17-year-olds. There was a steady improvement, year on year.

Four other tests were studied: digits forward (i.e. the ability to remember a string of digits), digits reversed, months forward and months reversed. In these four tasks, the older subjects were only slightly more competent than the younger ones.

Professor Miles was, in fact, able to do a full reassessment of 21 of his subjects at intervals that varied from as little as 7 months to as long as 7 years 7 months. Gains in reading age were recorded from 1 year 4 months to 6 years 0 months. On average, each child had increased his or her reading age by one year for each year that had elapsed. In other words, since being assessed for the first time, their reading had 'kept up with the clock'. In the same way, spelling was found to have improved by 9 months for each year that had elapsed. Assessment would appear to have made a difference!

The general evidence from this shows that dyslexic children can improve their performance in all kinds of ways as they grow older and that there can even be appreciable gains in reading and spelling, if the conditions are right. Even so, it is clear that traces of the handicap remain.

Now that we have a clear picture of the dyslexic child, our next task is to discuss his assessment. An adequate assessment is essential for a child to be given the help he needs. However, this is not always straightforward, and can give rise to controversy. The next chapter gives a full description of the process and clarifies some of the confusions that can arise from time to time.

Chapter 9
Assessment of the dyslexic child

Each year many children with reading difficulties thought to be caused by dyslexia reach the stage where an educational psychologist is called in to carry out an assessment. The assessment should observe the same basic rules that apply to any assessment of any type of difficulty in any child by any educational psychologist. The assessment of a learning difficulty (or difficulties) in a child is an attempt to answer a question by means of investigative techniques. The question in this case is usually, 'Is my child dyslexic?' or 'Does my child have (a) specific learning difficulty(ies)?'

The assessment should always be a sufficiently full one to produce an answer to the problem posed. More than that, it should also be full enough to justify the answer given. The question could well be asked as to what is a 'full' assessment and, when assessing a child, there can be misunderstandings about whether a full assessment is necessary, or has been requested or has been carried out. A full assessment has never been defined and is probably unlikely ever to be so. There are currently hundreds, if not thousands, of tests, scales, screening devices, profiles and questionnaires designed to gather information about children's skills, abilities, aptitudes, strengths, weaknesses, deficiencies, intelligence, perception, etc. So no matter how many are applied to a child, there will always be some that have not been used. Obviously, a common-sense approach is required. Provided that the assessment of the child is full enough to answer the basic question and so address the difficulty giving rise to concern, then the assessment should be regarded as a full one. In fact, it could be argued that once sufficient assessment has been carried out to provide a diagnosis of the difficulty and the educational psychologist is able to explain the diagnosis she has arrived at, then further assessment is not justified and could be considered a waste of scarce and costly resources (professional's time, pro formas, etc.).

The educational psychologist, in her assessment, has the general aim of investigating the child referred to her and carrying out an assessment of sufficient depth to diagnose why the child has the difficulties described. There are many other aims, such as to be able to explain the reasons for the conclusions reached, to make recommendations as to how the child might best be assisted with his difficulties, to provide a report setting out a description of the child so that all those concerned with his education and development can be properly informed about his functioning, etc.

Different local education authorities (LEAs) have different procedures to be followed when a schoolchild is referred for assessment by an educational psychologist and every educational psychologist has her (or his) own way of working. Because of this, some of what follows will vary in detail between LEAs and even within any one particular LEA. However, the general outcome should be similar.

Educational psychologist's interview/assessment

In order to assess a child, an educational psychologist must gather information. This comes from a number of sources, usually the school, the parents and the child himself. The information is often in written form (e.g. school records and reports) or is gained from interview(s). There is also what the psychologist learns from the child by observing, interviewing and carrying out standardized tests.

All sources of information are important and sometimes a vital piece of information comes from a very unexpected source - often in the form of a chance remark or afterthought. During the assessment process the psychologist must gather as much information as she can.

Background information

Basic details are all-important and should not be overlooked. The spelling of the child's name needs to be checked as well as his date of birth. Sometimes these are inaccurate in the initial set of details provided, which could have serious implications. It is also necessary to know whether the child has ever been known by another name, as hospitals and other agencies could well have records under the previous identity.

The child's educational history can say so much. Has the child attended just one school, has he been to two or have there been frequent changes? What has been the pattern of attendance - quite full, a few lengthy absences or long runs of broken weeks?

Developmental and medical history requires thorough investigation and needs to cover subjects such as eyesight, hearing, speech development, accidents, illnesses, period(s) as a hospital inpatient. If anything of significance arises, it will need to be investigated in more detail and this could, in turn, lead to further lines of investigation.

Some knowledge of family background is vital - the size and structure of the family, and who presently lives in the child's home. An only child with both parents at home is living under very different conditions from another who is one of five with a single parent. For example, the first child might be able to call on more support at home than might the second when it comes to bringing a reading book home from school and hoping to have an adult listen to him. All other aspects of family life will affect a child's development - financial circumstances, material state of the home, the general environment, interpersonal relationships, etc., but the extent of the influence of each is a matter of judgement, taking all other factors into account. When investigating a child suspected of being dyslexic, it is important to find out if there is any history of reading difficulties in the family - particularly in respect of brothers, sisters, parents, grandparents, aunts and uncles.

One line of enquiry that should never be overlooked is to establish whether any close family members have ever undergone an assessment for possible dyslexia. If so, how many are involved and what was the outcome in each case?

Up to this point, the information has related only to the child's background and is of a very general nature. It could be argued that much, if not all of it, should be gathered in the case of every child referred to an educational psychologist, not just those suspected of being dyslexic. After the gathering of as much basic information as circumstances permit, the child himself needs to be interviewed and tested.

No two children are identical and so no two cases referred to an educational psychologist can be identical either. Therefore, there is no strictly laid-down pattern of activity which an educational psychologist must carry out in her work; it would be impossible to produce one that would apply in all cases. Most educational psychologists proceed in their work by drawing up a mental list of possible explanations (normally called hypotheses) as to why the child has the difficulty displayed. This list is arranged in descending order from the most likely down to the least likely explanation. The educational psychologist then goes on to test out the most likely one.

If it is confirmed by the test results, then well and good. If it is not confirmed, then that particular hypothesis is abandoned and the next one on the list is similarly tested. This process continues until one is - or appears to be - confirmed and matters proceed from there. (Sometimes the testing takes place over a period of time, as the psychologist recommends that a particular teaching technique is used and time must then be allowed for it to be properly put to the test.)

Testing

When an educational psychologist starts to assess a child referred to her as possibly dyslexic, she will need to establish two basic facts as a starting point (as we have described in earlier chapters). These are:

1. How well should the child be *expected* to read?
2. How well (or badly) is the child *actually* reading?

Intelligence

As described in Chapter 3, the answer to the first question depends principally on two factors - the child's age and level of intelligence. All other things being equal, a child's reading age should be equal to his chronological age. However, in many cases, all other things are *not* equal, and one of the greatest influences on a child's ability to read will be his intelligence level. A child of high intelligence should have a higher reading age than a child of the same age who is of average intelligence. Similarly the child of average intelligence should read better than a child of the same age who is of low intelligence. In other words, a child's reading age should match his mental age, as we have explained fully earlier.

The answer to the first question is thus provided by the administration of a suitable intelligence scale (or test, to use the popular name for it). The WISC is described in detail in Chapter 3, and I also refer to it here for the sake of continuity. The educational psychologist will be interested in much more than the final IQ figure. She will need to administer 11 subtests (six verbal and five performance) and from them will gain such information as:

- the overall, full-scale IQ
- the verbal and performance IQ's. These will need to be compared to see how closely they correlate
- the individual verbal subtest scaled scores (six of them), to see the range displayed and the pattern exhibited

- the individual performance subtest scores (five of them) for the same reasons as above.

She will then be able to arrive at a conclusion as to the level at which the child should be reading.

Reading

The second question above - At what level is the child *actually* reading? - is answered by the administration of a reading test or a number of reading tests. There are several aspects to reading, any or all of which might repay investigation, depending on the circumstances of an individual child's case.

It can be useful to know how well a child can read single words where there is no chance of his picking up clues from what else is written when he is not quite sure of the word. It is also useful to know how well he reads individual sentences, as well as continuous prose. When a child has read a piece of text and has read out each word correctly, it is useful to know how much he has actually *understood* of what he has just read. A measure of the child's comprehension of text is valuable in diagnosing difficulties. Speed of reading is yet another factor, as a child can read something quickly, at average speed or extremely slowly, and it might be considered necessary to have a measure of this particular reading skill.

The remainder of the assessment procedure will very much depend on whether other difficulties are present, and if so, in what concentration and to what degree.

Spelling

Spelling difficulties invariably accompany reading difficulties and indeed it would be unusual if this were not so. A spelling test will establish a spelling age, and examination of the types of errors the child makes when attempting to spell words too difficult for him can yield useful clues to his difficulties.

Writing

Writing may also be a problem for a child with learning difficulties and can be examined from a number of viewpoints.

Ability to copy is one aspect that may need to be tested. Irrespective of how accurately the child is able to reproduce what is before him, the speed at which he does this could well be a major difficulty.

Ability to take dictation could also repay investigation and be examined for spelling errors, punctuation difficulties and speed.

Free writing will produce further information about spelling, punctuation, grammar, syntax, sentence structure and ability to express ideas, as well as speed of execution.

While assessing a child's writing skills - or lack of them - the type of pen grip he uses will need to be considered, and also whether the child is right- or left-handed. Other factors may also need to be examined, some of which do not usually receive much attention. These include the manner in which the child sits on his chair, how he positions himself at his desk or table and has his book or sheet of paper in front of him, how he holds it steady when writing, etc.

Other test results

Although circumstances will differ from one particular case to another, it can be said as a generalisation that any further testing/assessment carried out will tend to provide information about accompanying problems, or further insight into what type of dyslexic difficulties are involved.

It is argued by some that any assessment should look at such aspects of the child's functioning as laterality, left-right awareness, eye dominance and fine motor control, as well as commenting on matters such as short-term memory, long-term memory, visual skills (such as sequencing and perception) and auditory skills. Others take the view that while such items of information are useful to have, they are not necessary, as they are not likely to be of overriding significance. From the pragmatic point of view, a limit needs to be drawn somewhere and, providing sufficient assessment has been carried out to address the difficulties described, further assessment is desirable but probably not essential. Further assessment after the basic data have been gathered is likely to produce a situation of diminishing returns, such that it will require ever-increasing amounts of professional man-hours of assessment to obtain progressively smaller (and probably less relevant) amounts of information about the child.

After the assessment

The educational psychologist's assessment might need to be spread over two or more sessions. But however many sessions it takes, the child's assessment will eventually be complete and a discussion of the findings will then take place between the psychologist and the parent(s).

This is obviously a valuable opportunity for the parent to compare his or her own impression of the child's difficulties with the psychologist's, to see how closely they match. If there is a mismatch at any point, it can be talked through until the parent is satisfied. The parent should put any questions in his or her mind to the to the educational psychologist for her to answer, and bring up any points they would like to discuss. Differences should also be discussed, and eventually the parent and psychologist should know what is in the mind of the other regarding the child's difficulties. The parent should ask him or herself a number of questions, such as:

- Does the assessment appear to have been a reasonably full one?
- Does the description of my child's strengths and weaknesses agree with what I know?
- Have I had my questions answered?
- Have I had any areas of doubt on my part cleared up?
- Have I learned anything new?
- If I have been told anything which I was not aware of before, does it appear to fit into the overall picture I have of my child?

This set of questions is not supposed to be exhaustive but rather to indicate the lines along which any parent-psychologist discussion should proceed after the assessment is completed. Eventually a report will be provided and this should be a clear and concise summary of what has been discussed. A suggested layout of a report follows.

Loamshire Educational Authority
Main Road, Newtown

21 June 2001

Educational Psychology Service
Educational Psychologist's report on:
John BROWN (dob = 6 February 1993)
26 Canal Street, NEWTOWN, N16 7BR
Attending: Springfield Primary School

Background

Referral details

John was referred to the Loamshire Educational Psychology Service in April 2001. He had become a cause for concern to his

---

school due to his difficulty in acquiring reading, spelling and hand-writing skills by January 2000, at which point he had been entered on to Stage 1 of the Code of Practice of Special Educational Needs, moving to Stage 2 the following September.

John has been the subject of an Individual Education Plan (IEP), which has been deemed as not producing the hoped-for improvements.

John has been seen by me on two occasions, these following on from an initial session spent with his parents, gathering details of his background and developmental progress. My interviews/assessments were carried out over a four-week period covering mid-May to mid-June 2001. My assessment is based on the information available to me from within the school's documentation; that gained from interviewing John's parents and also my interview with and testing of John.

Household details

John, who is aged 8 years 4 months, is the youngest of a family of two children, there being a 10-year-old sister (Stephanie). He lives with his sister and both parents. Mr Brown is presently in full-time paid employment, working regular hours, and Mrs Brown is in part-time (evening) employment.

General health, development and medical details

Mrs Brown informed me that there were no complications relating to John when she was expecting him and that the actual birth process was straightforward. Furthermore, there were no complications in the first minutes and hours of life.

To date John has been fortunate enough to avoid having incurred any serious accidents or suffered any significant illnesses. Consequently, he has never needed any overnight stays in hospital. He does not produce an allergic reaction to any food, clothing or other substance, and he does not require any regular medication.

Educational history

John has had a regular and consistent pattern of education. During his immediate pre-school year he attended the nursery class at Springfield Primary School, enrolling at the school itself in the year following. He is currently a Key Stage 2 pupil, having commenced Year 3 last September.

Assessment

Physical description

John is of average height, weight and build. He has fair hair, a fair complexion and blue eyes. John was very pleasant and relaxed during the two sessions we spent together. He related well and co-operated fully.

Sensory functioning

- Vision - There would appear to be no concern related to vision. John does not wear spectacles nor have any been prescribed for him in the past.
- Hearing - There would appear to be no difficulties related to hearing either, and at present it would appear to be functionally adequate for everyday situations.

Speech, language and communication

I would describe John's general use of speech as normal or above, and the quality of his speech as quite clear. There was no evidence of any stutter, stammer, lisp or other type of defect.

Speech onset was at the normal stage of development and he has never needed to be referred for a speech and language therapy assessment.

Cognitive ability

John's cognitive ability was assessed by me using the WISC-3/UK. The results obtained are as below.

Verbal scale

Information	= 6	
Similarities	= 17	
Arithmetic	= 6	
Vocabulary	= 14	
Comprehension	= 16	
(Digit span)	= (6)	(Total = 59)

Performance scale

Picture completion	= 12	
Picture arrangement	= 11	
Block design	= 12	
Object assembly	= 14	
Coding	= 7	(Total = 56)

Verbal IQ = 110, Performance IQ = 108, Full-scale IQ = 110.

These results show that John's verbal scores range from 6 to 14, a spread of 8, which is greater than would normally be expected and is found in only a small proportion of the population. His performance scores are relatively tightly banded together with the exception of coding. (For a fuller explanation of the WISC-3/UK scores and their significance, please refer to the enclosed information sheet headed WISC-3/UK: description.)

John is a boy of average intelligence overall and his verbal IQ of 110 lies towards the top of the average range (85-115). This score of 110 masks a pattern of underlying strengths and weaknesses that need to be considered when taking John's overall functioning into account. A pattern of this type will be present in only a small percentage of the population.

Basic literacy skills assessment

John's basic literacy skills were assessed and for some of these the Wechsler Objective Reading Dimensions (WORD) was employed. At a chronological age of 8 years 4 months, it was anticipated from the results derived from John's cognitive ability assessment that he would have attainments at or close to the 9 years 2 months level:

1. Reading - Basic Reading (WORD subtest) = 6 years 4 months level
    Reading Comprehension (WORD subtest) = 7 years 4 months level
2. Spelling (WORD subtest) = 6 years 7 months level
3. Handwriting skills analysis - John's handwriting skills were assessed under three different conditions:
    (a) Features related to the task of handwriting - John writes with his right hand and employs the normal type of tripoidal (i.e. three-fingered) grip used by the vast majority of people. He positions the paper on which he writes slightly inefficiently

(approximately two inches too far to the left) and applies a normal degree of pressure on the pen point.

(b) Features relating to the writing produced

    (i) Physical appearance - John writes in a style that is a mixture of cursive and print form. His writing is slightly larger than average, but is reasonably neat and quite easily legible. Letter formation is quite correct and his writing is accurately positioned on the printed line and generally well organized. However, the full width of the line is not always used. Individual letters within a word are accurately spread, as are the gaps between words. When producing dictation and free writing, John made some errors of punctuation as well as some spelling errors. A general deterioration in appearance was apparent as John progressed through the three tasks, mainly due to an increase in the rate of both punctuation and spelling errors.

    (ii) Speed of writing - The most significant feature, however, was the extremely slow speed at which John wrote and it was this aspect which gave cause for most concern. He proved to be able to copy a piece of text at the rate of only six words per minute, to take dictation at only seven words per minute, and to produce a piece of free writing at a rate of between five and six words per minute.

    (iii) Quality of contents - John has good ideas, which are expressed clearly and sequenced in a logical and coherent manner. Any errors in John's handwriting relate entirely to its physical appearance and not to the quality of its contents. When producing free writing he displays a variety of difficulties:

- errors of punctuation, e.g. full stops omitted, capital letters used inappropriately
- errors of omission, i.e. some words omitted, but these are apparently not noticed by him
- substitutions, i.e. one word (a) was substituted for another (I)
- spelling errors. A variety of types of spelling error were demonstrated but the majority consisted of phonetic attempts to spell irregular words.

Self-help and adaptive skills

This area of development gives no major cause for concern. John is capable of looking after himself to the same extent as most

8-year-olds in relation to matters such as dressing/undressing, use of cutlery at mealtimes, being independent in the toilet, etc. Confusion over 'left' and 'right' causes some minor problems at times and he also has some difficulties related to general organization.

Personal and social skills

This area of development is also of no cause for concern. John relates well to immediate family members, his other relatives and to people generally. He is socially aware and competent and also well behaved.

Outside of school hours he likes to play football with his friends, to go swimming and to go fishing with his father. When indoors, he enjoys playing computer games. He has friends among his peer group and these are his preferred choice of company.

Emotional development

Most areas of emotional development have proceeded normally. John sleeps well and is quite easy to feed, showing no marked dislikes of any regular foodstuffs. He is self-conscious about his poor reading and other literacy skills, however, and this causes him some anxiety.

Motor skills development

John has some difficulties with his fine motor skills, but his gross motor skills seem to be quite unimpaired.

Involvement of other professionals

Apart from the family's general medical practitioner, there are presently no other professional personnel involved with John.

Parental views of problem

Mr and Mrs Brown both share the concerns of the school in relation to the difficulties John is encountering in attempting to acquire basic literacy skills.

Young person's view of problem

John is well aware of his difficulties, is becoming more self-conscious about them and would very much like to be able to read, spell and write more competently.

Conclusions

Special educational needs

John has learning difficulties as described below:

1. Despite being of average range intellectual ability and having had adequate teaching, John is significantly underachieving in basic literacy skills. His difficulties are of a dyslexic/specific learning difficulties nature.
2. His reading ability is 2 years 10 months below what would be anticipated and his spelling ability is 2 years 7 months below. Reading comprehension, in contrast, is at a higher level than his basic reading and spelling, but still below (by 1 year 10 months) what would be anticipated.
3. In addition, he also has handwriting difficulties such that he cannot easily express his thoughts on paper at a reasonable rate and in a manner which is free from error.

Objectives of provision

John's future educational provision would enable him to:

- achieve his potential in basic reading skills
- achieve his potential in reading comprehension
- achieve his potential in spelling
- be able to express his thoughts on paper easily and at a reasonable rate and in a manner which is free from error
- be suitably encouraged and supported throughout.

Educational interventions

In my opinion, John would benefit from the educational interventions set out below:

1. An IEP to be drawn up which incorporates as part of its basis the findings set out in this report.
2. A daily period of teaching of at least 30 minutes in either a small-group situation or on a one-to-one basis, aimed at improving John's basic literacy skills.
3. John to pursue reading and spelling programmes shown to have been effective with children who have dyslexia/specific learning difficulties.

4. John to be taught by a teacher experienced in teaching children who have dyslexia/specific learning difficulties.
5. Support and advice to be available from a suitably qualified specialist support/advisory teacher.
6. John to embark on a handwriting skills programme designed to help him with all aspects of writing skills, but principally to increase his rate of output.

Monitoring

This will need to be carried out on a termly basis and the IEP adjusted accordingly. It could assist John's IEP for the opinion of an occupational therapist to be sought and the recommendations made to be incorporated.

At some time in the future it might be considered appropriate for John to be assessed by a specialist teacher, to determine whether it would be appropriate for John to be provided with some form of writing aid.

Signed ....
Educational Psychologist

The separate information sheet referred to in the report follows.

WISC-3/UK - description

The WISC (which stands for the Wechsler Intelligence Scale for Children) is the most widely used test of general intelligence designed for children and allows assessment of a child's problem-solving abilities.

The full-scale IQ summarizes overall performance and provides a broad assessment of general intelligence and the ability to do well in school.

The assessment takes place along two dimensions, the *verbal* (using words) and the non-verbal (or *performance*) (by using hand and eye skills).

The verbal IQ is generally based on performance in the first five of the six verbal subtests and the performance IQ is similarly based on the first five of the six performance subtests. The verbal IQ provides an indication of verbal comprehension, including the ability to use verbal skills in reasoning and solving problems as well as the capacity to learn verbal material.

The performance IQ reflects the efficiency and integrity of the child's perceptual organization, including non-verbal reasoning skills, the ability to employ visual images in thinking and the ability to process visual material.

The subtest scaled scores all range from 1 to 19, with the average score for all children being 10, and most scores grouped within a range of 8 to 12.

The IQs of both verbal and performance scales range from 65 to 135, with the average scores for all children being 100. The verbal and performance IQs of most children match one another quite closely, a discrepancy of a few points being quite common, but larger discrepancies (e.g. 12 or more) being found in only about 5% of the population.

The full-scale, verbal and performance IQs may be influenced by a variety of factors.

This report is only a suggested format and is not being put forward as beyond criticism. However, I do believe it covers all the essentials in the case of the fictitious child concerned, and also provides useful guidelines to the teacher who will undertake work with John. Of course, other aspects of John's functioning could have been investigated and reported on, but whether any highly relevant information would result is a matter for conjecture.

The report produced describes the difficulties John is experiencing, details the assessment carried out, the results obtained and the conclusions drawn. It goes on to specify in *general* terms how John would best be helped, the finer details of the teaching programme being left for John's special needs teacher. She will be able to decide on the approach to adopt, the design of the individual programme to be used, the pattern of work in each session, and the type and amount of home practice required by John each evening, etc.

It needs to be explained that there is an advantage in using a combination of the WISC-3/UK (to assess cognitive ability) and the WORD (to assess reading and spelling skills) over any alternative assessment instruments. This is because the WORD manual includes tables that give *predicted* scores for basic reading, spelling and reading comprehension based on the WISC-3/UK full-scale IQ. Other tables then give the statistical probabilities of the *actual scores obtained* occurring by chance alone.

In the case of John Brown, his WISC-3/UK full-scale IQ was 110, from which could be predicted subtest standard scores of 106 (basic reading), 105 (spelling) and 107 (reading comprehension). The actual scores obtained were 73, 77 and 92 respectively. The discrepancy in each case was, therefore:

- 33 (from 106 - 73) for basic reading
- 28 (from 105 - 77) for spelling
- 15 (from 107 - 92) for reading comprehension.

In the case of basic reading, the tables show that for a child of John's age a discrepancy of 33 standard score points is so large that it occurs by chance alone far less than one occasion in a hundred. In other words, there is far less than one chance in a hundred for John to have produced such a low score naturally. Correspondingly, there are far more than 99 chances in a hundred that some factor (or combination of factors) is causing the discrepancy to occur. In the same way, the low spelling score had less than one chance in a hundred of occurring naturally, and the reading comprehension score had a greater than a one in a hundred chance, but less than five in a hundred - a result that was still quite significant. Obviously these statistical tools are very powerful and useful for psychologists when attempting to diagnose possible dyslexia.

Two aspects of assessment that are becoming more popular deserve a mention. Children's phonological skills are now being assessed more widely, since suitable assessment instruments have been designed and become available in recent years. Phonological skills are explained much more fully in Chapter XI; phonological processing can be broadly defined as the ability to process the sounds of spoken language. Since 1982, tests designed to measure various cognitive processes associated with dyslexia have become available, but over time, the importance of phonological awareness and the different types of phonological skill have assumed greater and greater prominence.

In the Aston Index (1982), one of the nine subtests is 'grapheme-phonemic correspondence'. In both the Dyslexia Screening Test (DST) and Dyslexia Early Screening Test (DEST) (1996), one of the subtests is that of 'phonological skills'. In the Lucid Cognitive Profiling System (CoPS) (1996), one of the nine subtests is 'phonological awareness', but the two tests which are designed to investigate phonological skills most intently are the Phonological Abilities Test (PAT) (1997) and the Phonological Assessment Battery (PhAB)

(1997). The PAT has seven subtests, four of which are devoted to phonological awareness (rhyme detection, rhyme production, word completion and phoneme deletion). The PhAB also has seven subtests, all of which assess phonological skills. These are: alliteration, naming speed, rhyme, spoonerism, rhyme fluency, alliteration fluency and nonword reading.

The second aspect of assessment is that referred to as optometric intervention. This investigates whether a child's reading is improved when using a coloured overlay. The Wilkins Rate of Reading Test, which became available in 1996, investigates the possible beneficial effect of such overlays.

The investigation of phonological skills and possible visual discomfort is far from a routine procedure when assessing a child who is suspected of being dyslexic. For that reason I have not included such investigations in the report on John Brown. However, the trend is sure to grow and it must now be only a matter of time before such investigations are considered part of the general routine.

Psychologists' reports on dyslexic children and adults

Partly for my own professional development, but mainly for the purposes of this chapter, I carried out a survey of psychologists' reports in order to analyse their length, format, scope and general contents.

The reports tested and the psychologists

A total of 25 reports were analysed, selected at random from a larger collection. Of the 25, 18 related to children and seven to adults. However, a total of only 22 people were reported on as three had been assessed on two separate occasions. The total number of psychologists involved was 21, as three had assessed the same person twice (as mentioned above) and a fourth psychologist had assessed two different people involved in the survey. Of the 21 psychologists, 15 were educational psychologists and six were clinical psychologists. Of the 15 educational psychologists, only three were employed by a LEA. Six were employed by an organization (such as the Dyslexia Institute) and six had been consulted privately. Of the six clinical psychologists, five were employed by an organization, and only one was a private practitioner. Taking the 21 psychologists as a group, the majority (11) were part of an organization, seven were private practitioners and only three employed by a LEA.

The reports were written across a seven-year time span, the earliest being dated April 1992 and the latest March 1999. The age range of the people when assessed was more than 30 years, the youngest reported on was 8 years 6 months and the oldest 38 years 10 months.

Length of reports

The contents of the reports will be described in some detail shortly, but first some information about the length of the reports. (The length given refers to sheets of A4 paper with single-spaced type.) The reports fell into two general categories: those intended as full reports (and sometimes to be used as an 'Advice' to a LEA or Appendix 'F' to a Statement of Special Educational Needs); and those intended purely to advise about examination concessions (the person involved having had a 'full' assessment on a previous occasion). The seven 'examination concessions' reports ranged from 2 to 6.5 pages in length, the average being less than 3.25 pages. The 'full' reports ranged from 1.5 to 16 pages in length, the average being just over 8.5 pages. It should be noted, however, that the longer reports contained explanatory information in some depth, e.g. a lengthy explanation of what dyslexia/specific learning difficulties consisted of, as well as detailed descriptions of some of the assessment materials employed and how the results obtained needed to be interpreted, etc.

Contents of reports

When surveyed collectively, the reports showed a certain uniformity in the general areas covered, although there was a wide variation in the contents of a particular area from one report to another.

After a (usually brief) introduction describing how the psychologist and the subject came into contact with one another, the reports then proceeded to cover intellectual ability, literacy skills (reading, spelling, handwriting), other diagnostic information (e.g. phonological skills, miscellaneous information, light sensitivity testing, etc.) and dyslexia screening information. Having covered the information obtained by testing, interview, etc., the diagnosis of dyslexia/specific learning difficulties was arrived at and described in different degrees of detail. Recommendations were then made and often specific books, materials, videos or computer programs were recommended also.

We shall now consider the contents of the 25 reports in greater detail, following the same order as above.

Intellectual abilities

An assessment of the person's intelligence (or general cognitive ability) level was carried out in each case. The scales used were the WISC, the BAS (II) or the WAIS.

IQ OR EQUIVALENT

- Full-scale (or general) IQ or GCA was provided on 24 cases (96%)
- Verbal IQ (or verbal cluster score) was provided on 25 cases (100%)
- Performance IQ (or other similar) was provided on 25 cases (100%).

(Note: in the one report where a full-scale IQ was *not* provided, the report was one written for 'examination concessions'.)

INTELLECTUAL SUBAREAS

(i) Wechsler Scales - related

- scores for information were provided in 12 cases (48%)
- scores for similarities were provided in 12 cases (48%)
- scores for arithmetic were provided in 12 cases (48%)
- scores for vocabulary were provided in 12 cases (48%)
- scores for comprehension were provided in 14 cases (56%)
- scores for digit span were provided in 17 cases (68%)
- scores for picture completion were provided in 14 cases (56%)
- scores for coding/digit symbols were provided in 16 cases (64%)
- scores for picture arrangement were provided in 12 cases (48%)
- scores for block design were provided in 15 cases (60%)
- scores for object assembly were provided in 13 cases (52%)
- scores for symbol search were provided in 4 cases (16%)
- scores for verbal comprehension were provided in 5 cases (20%)
- scores for perceptual organization were provided in 5 cases (20%)
- scores for freedom from distraction were provided in 4 cases (16%)
- scores for processing speed were provided in 4 cases (16%).

(ii) BAS - related

- basic number skills = 20%
- recall of designs = 12%
- recall of digits (forward) = 12%
- word definitions = 12%

- word reading = 12%
- speed of information processing = 8%
- matrixes = 8%
- similarities = 8%
- block design (level) = 8%
- block design (power) = 8%
- immediate visual recall = 8%
- spelling = 8%
- visual recall (delayed) = 4%
- pattern construction = 4%
- quantitative reasoning = 4%
- recall digits (backward) = 4%

OTHER INTELLECTUAL ABILITIES REPORTED ON

- auditory short-term memory = 60%
- speed of information (processing) = 16%
- verbal (conceptual) reasoning = 12%
- visual sequencing = 8%
- immediate visual recall = 8%
- delayed visual recall = 8%
- verbal reasoning skills = 8%
- mental arithmetic = 8%
- visual thinking competence= 8%
- visual conceptual skills = 8%
- visual memory processing speed = 8%
- visuo-motor co-ordination = 8%
- auditory long-term memory = 8%.

In addition to these, there were no less then 45 other intellectual abilities that featured in just one report, i.e. 4%. There are too many to be listed here, but the interested reader can find them in Appendix II.

Literacy skills

READING

The skill of reading was referred to in 14 reports, i.e. 56% of the total. Thirteen of the 14 reports used more than one reading test to assess the skill.

(i) Tests used

The tests employed, given in descending order of popularity were: WORD (subtest) = 44%, Neale (Accuracy) = 36%, WRAT = 32%,

Neale (Comprehension) = 32%, BAS (subtest) = 28%, Schonell = 12%, with 4% for each of: National Adult Reading Test, Vernon, Vernon-Ward, McMullen, Salford, Kirklees, Aarons, Monroe-Sherman and the One-Minute Reading Test.

(ii) Subskills mentioned

Nine different terms were used to describe certain subskills of the learning process, but it was quite possible that more than one term was used to describe the same subskill. These terms, given in descending order of popularity were:

- single-word recognition = 24%
- comprehension (of continuous prose) = 20%
- word attack skills, mechanical reading skills and decoding skills (each) = 16%
- accuracy and speed (each in relation to continuous prose) = 12%
- basic reading = 8%
- reading age (ability) = 4%.

SPELLING

The skill of spelling was referred to in 11 reports (44%). Seven different spelling tests were used, with two of the reports featuring more than one test.

(i) Tests used

In order of popularity we have:

- WORD (subtest) = 28%
- Vernon GST = 20%
- WRAT = 12%
- BAS Spelling Scale and Wide Range ST (each) = 8%
- Diagnostic Spelling Dictation and Schonell GWST (each) = 4%.

(Also, see Handwriting: (i) Tests used.)

(ii) Subskills mentioned

Only one of the 25 reports (4%) attempted to analyse spelling into subskills. Those mentioned in that one report were: sequencing, digraphs and vowel sounds. Two other reports described certain types of spelling error, e.g. letter omissions, applying a phonic approach, sequencing errors, poor knowledge of phonemes.

HANDWRITING

Twelve reports (48% of the total) referred to handwriting and the component skills.

(i) Tests used

Only one handwriting test was referred to and that in only one report (4%). This was the Monroe-Sherman (subtest). (Note: In one report the Two-Minute Spelling Test - which is part of the battery of tests constituting Dyslexia Adult Screening Test (DAST) - was referred to, but only in connection with the *handwriting* skills of the adult being assessed. Whatever spelling score was obtained was not divulged and hence the DAST is not listed above under Spelling, (i) Tests used.)

(ii) Subskills featured or mentioned

I have organized the many subskills related to handwriting under certain headings. I feel there is justification for separating the skills related to the physical activity of handwriting from those related to the actual writing produced. Furthermore, there is justification also in separating this second group into the physical appearance of the handwriting and the quality of the contents.

RELATED TO THE ACTIVITY OF HANDWRITING

- speed = 48%
- pengrip = 28%
- handedness = 12%.

RELATED TO THE WRITING PRODUCED

Physical appearance

- style/form (i.e. print, cursive, block capitals or some combination, etc) = 36%
- punctuation = 32%
- neatness/legibility/letter formation = 20%
- spelling = 16%
- size, positioning on line/organization and sequencing (each 4%).

Quality of contents (in relation to free writing)

- clarity of expression = 36%
- sentence structure/grammar/ grammatical structure = 32%
- syntax/logic = 4%.

Other diagnostic information

PHONOLOGICAL SKILLS

These were referred to in only 10 reports (40%).

(i) Tests used

- Non-word Repetition Test = 12%
- Wepman Test = 8%.

(ii) Skills/features mentioned

These were: alliteration, naming speed (digits), naming speed (pictures), nonword repetition, phoneme deletion, phoneme segmentation, phonological awareness, phonological fluency, rhyme, spoonerisms and syllable counting.

MISCELLANEOUS SKILLS

(i) Tests used

The Aston Index was used in 8% of the cases with four other tests used in 4%. These were: the Benton Test (visual memory), the Bender (Motor Grestalt) Test, the Wide Range Activity Test and the Lincoln-Oseretsky Hand Function Test. (Note: Two other tests were also used, each on one occasion only, but the results obtained were not quoted. These tests were: the Bristol Social Adjustment Guide and the School Situation Questionnaire.)

(ii) Skills featured

Thirteen separate miscellaneous skills were referred to. By far the most popular was that of laterality/directionality, which occurred in 40% of the reports. The other 12 were each featured only once. These were: copying a looping pattern, fixation (time spent on), light sensitivity, map reading, months reversed (ability to recite), motor gestalt, motor skills (fine), motor skills (gross), motor speed, posture, proofreading and visual retention.

ASSESSMENT WITH COLOURED OVERLAYS

This was referred to in only one report = 4%. Light sensitivity syndrome was mentioned in the same report.

ARITHMETIC/NUMBER SKILLS

Arithmetic or number skills were assessed and reported on in 11 (44%) of the reports. Eight tests were used, the order of popularity being:

- BAS/BAS II = 20%
- WORD = 8%
- WIAT = 8%
- WISC (subtest) = 8% and the others 4% (these being One-Minute Test/Addition, One-Minute Test/Subtraction, WRAT (Arithmetic) and the Bangor Dyslexia Test).

DYSLEXIA SCREENING TESTS

Five reports (20%) included the fact that a dyslexia-screening test had been carried out (usually prior to fuller, more detailed assessment). The Bangor Dyslexia Screening was used most frequently (12%), and the other two (Dyslexia Institute Adult Questionnaire, Dyslexia Adult Screening Test) 4% each.

Recommendations

Strictly speaking, the recommendations made in the 25 reports fell into two groups: those related to direct intervention of some kind, and those that recommended the purchase of a particular book, etc., so that the advice/training it contained could be used to advantage. Here I shall deal with only the first group, leaving the other until later.

A total of 64 different recommendations were produced and these could easily be separated into two groups: those related to the learning/studying process (57) and those related to the examination process (7).

The 57 learning/study recommendations divided into general recommendations (24) and specific (33), 18 specific to reading, five specific to spelling and 10 specific to handwriting. The actual recommendations made were as below:

WHEN LEARNING/STUDYING (58 IN TOTAL)

General (24)

- teachers to be made aware of the students' dyslexia (8%)
- techniques for examinations to be studied and practised (8%)
- study skills to be developed (8%).

Each of the other 21 general studying recommendations was made only once each (4%). These were:

- complementation skills (development of)
- computer (portable) (use of)
- Dyslexia Institute Skills Development Programme (use of)
- dyslexia study groups (contact with)
- efficient reading strategies
- examination concessions (to be sought)
- expressive language (opportunities to develop)
- ideas (discussion of with other people)
- metacognition, i.e. self-questioning
- mnemonics (use of, as an aid to recall)
- organisational skills (development of)
- personal organizer (electronic)
- photocopying (extra)
- revision sessions to be on a regular basis
- revision strategies
- specialist provision (via the Code of Practice)
- structured multisensory teaching
- study skills course
- texts (purchase of, essential)
- visual images (use of as an aid to recall)
- word processor (use of).

Specific (33)

Related to reading (18)

Of these 18 recommendations only one - scanning techniques (development of) - was made more than once. In fact, it was made in only two of the reports (8%). The other 17 were:

- breaking down sequences into manageable chunks
- Cloze procedure
- coloured papers/filters/spectacles (use of)
- magnification facilities
- paired reading
- pause-prompt-praise
- reading alone
- reading together
- reciprocal teaching
- specialist eye test

- specialist teaching
- specialist teacher (to be taught by)
- speed reading techniques (development of)
- structured reading programme
- taped reading
- tape recording of some materials to be made
- Toe-by-Toe programme.

RELATED TO SPELLING (5)

Two recommendations were each made in 8% of the reports and these were:

- use of an electronic spellchecker
- simultaneous oral spelling (often referred to as S-O-S).

The other three were:

- cued spelling
- rules of spelling (to study)
- a structure programme for spelling.

RELATED TO HANDWRITING (10)

Each recommendation featured only once. They were:

- answers in note form
- essays (planning of)
- keyboard skills (tuition in)
- outlines (use of simple)
- preparatory cards (use of)
- recording equipment (use of)
- scanning facilities (use of)
- software (use of)
- typing skills (development of)
- word processing (use of).

WHEN SITTING EXAMINATIONS (7)

The recommendations, in order of popularity, were:

- additional time allowance (28%)
- allowance to be made for writing errors (4%)
- to read script to typist (4%)

- to read script into tape-recorder (4%)
- the use of an amanuensis (4%)
- questions to be read to the candidate (4%)
- viva voce (4%).

OTHER RECOMMENDATIONS

Other recommendations, not listed above, were also made. These fell into two groups: books and other related materials, and computer programs. There were 25 different books recommended, all but three of them only once. The most popular were *Easy Type* (Kinlock) (12%), *Spelling Made Easy* (Brand) (8%) and *The Mind Map Book* (Buzan) (8%). The complete list is given in Appendix III. There were six related materials also included in Appendix III.

There were 20 computer programmes recommended. However, 19 of them were all given by the same psychologist. The complete list is given in Appendix IV.

Observations

What does the survey tell us?

We first must acknowledge that it was only a small-scale survey. However, it was a completely random one and represented a fair cross-section both of children (and adults) being assessed for possible dyslexia and of the psychologists who carry out the assessments. Had a much larger survey been undertaken then it would undoubtedly have yielded a much greater body of information, but whether there would have been better *quality* data, i.e. differing statistics in the findings, is open to doubt. There would certainly have been some variation, but I doubt if it would have been significant.

What is almost certain, I believe, is that if a survey were made across time of the nature of such reports, then changes would be noted. Reports written in the seven years prior to our survey period of 1992-99 will, on average, be somewhat different. Similarly the reports written since 1999 will tend to be different yet again. The design of new test materials, the impact of research findings, changes in the law - relating to assessment and the provision for special educational needs - are all bound to wield an influence.

How much common agreement exists?

In the survey there was common agreement on a relatively small number of points. All assessments involved obtaining the intelligence level of the person involved, with all reports but one quoting a full-scale IQ or GCA. All assessments without exception involved the obtaining of both a verbal and a non-verbal IQ so that comparisons of basic verbal and non-verbal ability could be made.

When subtest scores were quoted, a majority had assessed digit span (80%), block design (68%), coding/digit symbols (64%), comprehension (56%), picture completion (56%) and object assembly (52%). All other subtests featured in a minority of the reports.

With respect to other abilities, there was the strong popularity of auditory short-term memory (60%), linked to the assessment of digit span.

Reading was referred to in only 56% of the cases and I was surprised that this was not significantly greater. Spelling and handwriting featured in fewer than half of the cases surveyed. With regard to the latter, many individual handwriting skills were referred to. An observation about/comment on/measurement of speed appeared 48% of the time, but all other handwriting skills were referred to in much fewer than half the cases.

Phonological skills featured in fewer than half the cases, but this is almost certain to increase over time. No particular phonological skills dominated in importance, the one most frequently quoted being nonword reading.

The majority of the reports did not feature any miscellaneous skills. The most popular miscellaneous skill that did feature was laterality/directionality.

Assessment with coloured overlays featured in only one report, and although more suspected dyslexic pupils are bound to be given this type of assessment, it could well be that the work will devolve to opticians rather than psychologists.

Arithmetic/number skills was another area which did not feature prominently. Nor did dyslexia-screening tests. Only 20% of the people reported on had been so screened, but then there was no particular reason why this should be so. Although screening would appear to be more widespread presently than years ago, it seems that the majority of people undergoing a full assessment for dyslexia have not been previously screened. The increased numbers of requests for dyslexia assessment could be in proportion to the increase in the number of people being screened. Also most screenings tend to be carried out on a private basis.

Finally, the recommendations made in the reports were very wide-ranging, but not particularly deep, i.e. very few of the suggested measures were recommended by more than a few psychologists.

In conclusion

A psychologist's assessment of a child's possible dyslexia/specific learning difficulties is quite likely to contain a measure of the child's full-scale IQ as well as his verbal and non-verbal IQs. Close attention is likely to be paid to the child's digit span, block design, coding, picture completion and comprehension subskills. The child's auditory short-term memory will also be noted.

Reading is likely to be assessed and perhaps spelling and/or handwriting. If handwriting is a feature of the child's difficulties, then close attention will be paid to his writing speed. If phonological skills are touched on, then the child's ability to read nonwords is likely to be assessed. Some comment might be made about his ability to distinguish 'left' from 'right'.

Depending on the nature of the child's dyslexia and which specific learning difficulty(ies) is/are of concern, it will be recommended that each of the child's teachers ought to be informed of his dyslexia, that study and other techniques be practised and that examination techniques be practised. The encouragement of scanning techniques will be included, as will the use of an electronic spellchecker and the simultaneous oral spelling technique.

In relation to the examination situation, additional time is likely to be recommended and also that spelling errors should not be penalized.

Books or other materials could be recommended, as might one or more computer program.

In addition to the above likely skeleton of a report, there is the possibility that some of many other skills are reported on and some of many other recommendations made. However, there is as yet no agreement among psychologists or other concerned professionals as to what precisely constitutes a psychological assessment of dyslexia, nor on what ought to be contained in the attendant report.

Parental satisfaction

Throughout the assessment procedure there should be parental agreement with the suggestions made, the steps taken, the contents of the report and the help offered. If there is any disagreement or dispute then it is hoped that matters can be resolved to the parents' satisfaction.

Before referral there should be agreement between the parents and school that the child does have a difficulty and that referral to the educational psychologist is necessary. In most cases this agreement exists, but if the school is not in favour of referral then the parents are entitled to make their own referral to the Educational Psychology Service.

When the child is seen by the educational psychologist there should be an opportunity for the parents to discuss the findings, to ask any questions and to have clarified anything they are not sure about. Obviously if the parents suspect the child is dyslexic and the educational psychologist is of the same opinion, all is well, but if she is not of this opinion then clarification is required.

There are a number of possible areas of disagreement. The parents may feel that insufficient assessment has been carried out to warrant any conclusions being drawn. If they are happy about the assessment procedure itself, then it is possible for there to be disagreement about the conclusions arrived at. Also, it is possible that even if there is agreement on the assessment and conclusions, the recommendations made are a cause for concern.

Any disagreement should be settled as far as is possible by reference to the facts of the case, rather than the feelings or opinions. Any parent could have a justifiable grievance if an inadequate assessment has been carried out, as it could be shown that certain areas of concern were not investigated - or at least not investigated fully.

However, if a full assessment has been carried out (one full enough to investigate all those areas of functioning giving cause for concern) then matters of disagreement rest on much narrower grounds. If, for example, the educational psychologist concludes that a child is not dyslexic but the parents think that the child is, then little progress is likely to be made by the parents simply stating their disagreement; they need to be able to show why they disagree. In these circumstances, a firmly held belief *on its own* is insufficient to produce any changes; it needs to be backed up by hard facts. A solution usually found to be acceptable to all sides when these rare cases occur is for the parents to be given a second opinion, and arrangements for this can often be made by the first psychologist or the principal psychologist of the Service.

It is possible for there to be dissatisfaction with the educational psychologist's recommendations but this is not very likely if there has been agreement reached about the quality of the assessment and the conclusions drawn. It is possible for the parents to feel that insufficient help is being recommended initially and it is always possible that this can be amended to meet parental concern after discussion with the psychologist. Even when parents and the psychologist agree, there is still room for parental dissatisfaction at the next stage of the proceedings - that is, with the amount and type of special help offered by the LEA to the child concerned. Inadequate resources in all areas of education mean that those allocated to dyslexic children are constantly criticized along with the rest as being insufficient. Parents have every right to appeal to their LEA if they feel that their dyslexic child is not receiving adequate help, and should always do so.

The options parents have in the event of a grievance with any part of the assessment process is set out in more detail later (Chapter 13).

The next two chapters look at possible causes of dyslexia. The types of difficulty fall into two groups: one connected with the brain and visual system (which I have entitled 'Biological bases') the other related to how a child acquires phonological awareness (knowledge of the individual sounds that go to make up the words of the language).

Chapter 10
Possible causes (I)
Biological bases

Naturally, any parent of a dyslexic child wants to know *why* their child is dyslexic - exactly what it is that has caused him to have the difficulty he does. Parents are not alone. Countless teachers, psychologists and researchers are also interested in knowing the answer.

Unfortunately, the answer is not known. This is not for want of trying. Over the years since the condition was first recognized - more than a century ago - there have been countless suggestions put forward. Some have been discounted but many remain in a limbo-type of existence, neither proved nor disproved. However, there are a number of lines of enquiry that appear to be quite fruitful. Research continues year in, year out in various university departments and laboratories, and consequently as each decade passes, the basic stock of knowledge relating to the general nature of dyslexia and the factors that affect it grows considerably.

Technological innovations have also played their part, with major contributions having come from magnetic resonance imaging (MRI scans), computerized axial tomography (CAT or CT scans) and positron emission tomography (PET scans), especially in relation to brain functioning.

This chapter is concerned with one group of descriptions and explanations. It covers the parts of the brain and how the brain functions in relation to language, vision and hearing. It also involves the eyes and the visual system generally. It is best described as the biological bases of reading and reading difficulties, hence the chapter title.

The brain: its parts

The human brain is one of the least understood parts of the body, and although much more is known about it today compared with a century and a half or two centuries ago, our knowledge still answers only a very small fraction of the many questions that can be asked. In many ways it is as remote from us as the moon.

The brain controls virtually all the activities of the body - the movement of toes, feet, legs, fingers, hands, arms, eyes, head, jaw and tongue. It also controls those activities that take place without any thought or intention, such as breathing and the beating of the heart. In addition to all this, the brain interprets information about the outside world, which is constantly being delivered to it through the eyes, ears, taste buds, and senses of smell and touch. Information also comes to our brains through other, less well-known senses, e.g. balance, body movement and general body awareness. A third type of work undertaken by the brain is to produce the thoughts, feelings and emotions, together with the many other aspects of a person's detailed and complex personality. Strongly linked to the thought processes are those of communication. Language, of course, is part of this and reading, in turn, is a part of language.

To look at an actual human brain, or even a photograph of one, tells us very little about it. It looks rather like a large mushroom or a lump of drab, grey porridge without any distinctive shape, colour or other features. The brain's surface is arranged in a series of folds and its surface is covered in ridges and clefts. The medical term for a ridge is a gyrus (plural = gyri) and that for a cleft is a fissure (in the case of a deep one) or sulcus (plural = sulci) (for a shallow one). Figure 10.1 shows the brain in position seen from a viewpoint to the left, above and towards the back.

The main feature of the brain is that is divided into two equal-looking halves by a fissure (the longitudinal fissure) running from

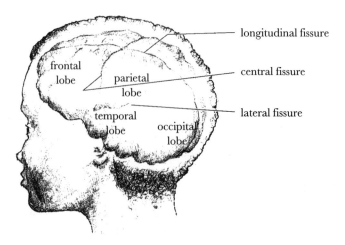

Figure 10.1 The brain, showing the main surface areas of the left cerebral hemisphere.

front to back. The two halves are known as cerebral hemispheres and Figure 10.1 shows all of the left cerebral hemisphere and part of the right. One hemisphere appears as the mirror image of the other. Each hemisphere is divided into four lobes. The central fissure separates the frontal lobe from the remainder and the lateral fissure separates off the temporal lobe (which is close to the ear and temple). At the rear top is the parietal lobe and at the extreme back is the occipital lobe.

We can learn more about how the brain is constructed by studying its appearance when it is cut through in various places. From the outside it looks as if the longitudinal fissure divides the brain completely into two separate hemispheres, but in fact this is not so. The fissure descends so far and then ceases; underneath it, the two halves of the brain are joined together. The means by which they are joined is a massive bridge of brain fibres known as the corpus callosum. This is shown in Figure 10.2. The corpus callosum does much more than merely join the two hemispheres of the brain together. The brain can function normally only if the two halves can communicate, i.e. can pass 'messages' from one half to the other. It is through the corpus callosum that the countless sensations that occur every minute are communicated from left side to right and vice versa. The size and form of the corpus callosum varies between individuals, giving rise to different abilities. People differ in their mental abilities because their brains grow in different forms. Males tend to

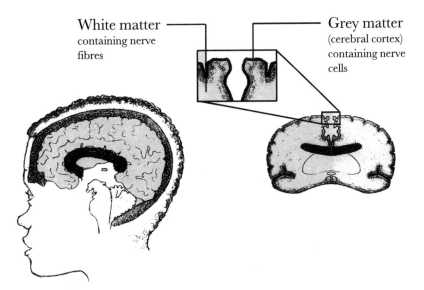

White matter containing nerve fibres

Grey matter (cerebral cortex) containing nerve cells

Figure 10.2 The corpus callosum (shown in black) viewed from the left side and the front.

differ from females, left-handers from right-handers and engineers from musicians.

Cutting through the brain also demonstrates that the grey colour seen on the outside is not continued throughout, but exists only as a thin (3 mm) outer layer or covering. This is the cerebral cortex. Beneath this grey matter is the white matter. It can also be seen that the brain is not solid, but has a number of cavities (known as ventricles) within it.

If you take a very thin section of the brain's cortex and examine it under a microscope you can see that it is composed of large numbers of nerve cells - more than one million million of them (1 000 000 000 000). Each one of these cells can be connected to as many of 25 000 others (the average is 10 000) and so the total number of connections in the entire brain is about 10 to the power of 15. This number is written in mathematical shorthand as 10^{15} and is so enormous that it represents two hundred thousand times the human population of the earth. The numerous foldings of the surface of the brain serve to increase its surface area and hence the number of nerve cells that can be accommodated there. This is shown in Figure 10.2.

How the brain functions

The brain controls the body by means of 'messages' in the form of nerve impulses being passed from the cerebral cortex to the appropriate part of the body. An impulse reaches its destination by travelling down long nerve fibres. The messages/impulses consist of very small electric currents, which are produced by changes in the body's chemicals. The nerve fibres involved act in much the same way as does an electric cable in the home when it carries an electric current to a light bulb or vacuum cleaner after the appliance is switched on.

The nerve fibres to, say, the foot, descend from the surface of the brain down through the body of the brain and into the top of the spinal cord. They descend down to a particular part of the spine, at which they leave and travel down the leg to the foot. However, before they leave the brain, the fibres *cross over* to enter the spinal cord on the side opposite to the cerebral hemisphere from which they originate. This has now transferred the nerve impulse to the correct side in relation to the foot concerned. The left side of the brain controls the right foot and vice versa. In fact, the working of the brain is such that the right hemisphere controls the right side of the head (affecting the eye and mouth movements) but the left side of the body. Toes, feet, legs, fingers, hands and arms are all controlled by that half of the brain which is on the opposite side of the body from them. For this reason the victim of a stroke located on the right side of the brain will have the right side of the face affected, but the left arm and left leg. This situation is illustrated in Figure 10.3.

Despite this, however, it is not correct to say that the two halves of the brain are equal and identical in all respects, each doing exactly the same work as the other but on opposite sides of the body. Some of the functions carried out by one hemisphere are quite different from those of the other.

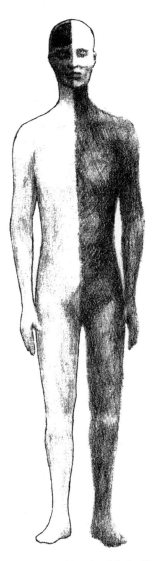

Figure 10.3 Parts of the body controlled by the right half of the brain.

It is thought by some that there is probably an inborn tendency for the two hemispheres to develop differently and for the differences to increase over time through a person's experiences and the general learning processes. The two hemispheres are not equal partners in the organization of movement - the left is the dominant one, for the vast majority of people at least.

The same is true for speech. The left hemisphere keeps the store of learned skills, programmes most movements and also directs the right hemisphere to control the left side of the body while it (the left hemisphere) keeps control of the right side. If the great mass of nerve fibres passing through the corpus callosum is divided, the movements of the right limbs (controlled by the left hemisphere) remain normal but movements of the left limbs become abnormal in a strange way. The person affected cannot comb his hair properly, point the way accurately or trace a circle on the ground with his foot. More automatic movements such as standing and sitting can be carried out quite normally, however. Injury to the right hemisphere will cause some paralysis of the left limbs, but has no effect on the right limbs.

The brain and language

Each activity a person carries out is controlled by one particular area of the brain, and this area will be interacting constantly with other areas as appropriate. The two halves of the brain perform different tasks from one another but also communicate with one another.

In many activities the two halves do *not* have equal control. Instead, one half will take on most of the responsibility for the activity, forcing the other half to have a very much reduced part to play. The most powerful hemisphere is known as the dominant one for the particular activity concerned.

Language is one activity of human beings that is controlled, for the most part, by one side of the brain. In the case of *most* people, their language is processed mainly on the left side with a lesser amount of processing being carried out on the right. However, the situation is not a straightforward one, and while this applies to most people, it does not apply to all. There are some people - a minority - who are different.

Language figures strongly in our interest in relation to dyslexia, because reading concerns the ability to interpret those symbols that represent language. In learning to read, a child must be able to master many skills, such as hearing and understanding speech, seeing and perceiving both handwriting and print, speaking (for reading aloud) and writing. Figure 10.4 shows those particular areas of the left hemisphere that are concerned with the many skills involved in reading and related activities, as well as the manner in which two or more relate in the more complex activities.

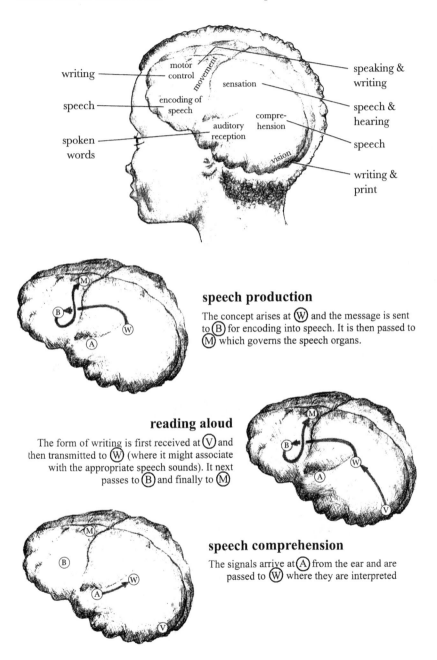

speech production

The concept arises at (W) and the message is sent to (B) for encoding into speech. It is then passed to (M) which governs the speech organs.

reading aloud

The form of writing is first received at (V) and then transmitted to (W) (where it might associate with the appropriate speech sounds). It next passes to (B) and finally to (M)

speech comprehension

The signals arrive at (A) from the ear and are passed to (W) where they are interpreted

Figure 10.4 The language areas of the brain.

A number of researchers believe that dyslexia can be explained, at least in part, by dominance. In most people, while they are engaged in any activity related to language, the left side of the brain plays a leading - or dominant - role. It is felt that dyslexia could result if the language areas are more or less equal in size, as in this case there is evidence to suggest that a greater number of messages need to be passed from left to right across the brain through the corpus callosum. This results in the dyslexic person needing more time to understand what is being said to them or what they are reading. Similarly, they will also need more time to express themselves when replying.

Now that we have covered the basics of brain structure and functioning, it is appropriate to describe one of the most recent and interesting explanations of dyslexia.

The cerebellar deficit hypothesis

This hypothesis proposes that the cause of dyslexia is one part of the brain not being able to function properly. The idea comes from Professor Nicholson and his team of co-workers at Sheffield University; the part of the brain involved is the cerebellum, which lies in the lower rear area, as shown in Figure 10.5.

The explanation is a very attractive and potentially quite powerful one, as it ties together a number of different features of dyslexia into a coherent whole and provides a convincing reason for them.

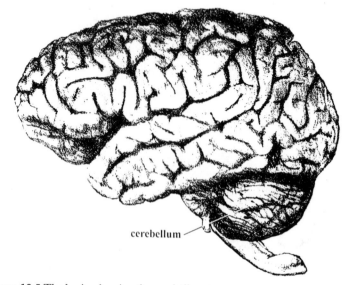

cerebellum

Figure 10.5 The brain, showing the cerebellum.

The longstanding puzzle related to dyslexia is why dyslexic children have difficulty understanding the meaning of print, etc., but can learn about and comprehend so many other things in life without difficulty.

Another puzzle relates to the difficulties dyslexics have in addition to that related to reading. With most dyslexic children, their difficulties with reading, spelling and handwriting have been assessed and investigated quite thoroughly, but other aspects of their development - apparently totally unconnected, or certainly not very closely connected to literacy skills - have been ignored. When large numbers of dyslexic children have been surveyed, however, it has been found that they were also slower to crawl and walk, tended to have slower reaction times, were often slower at talking and later displayed some minor speech difficulties. (This is only a hasty summary of the areas of development affected.)

The underlying difficulty in the two main areas of language and movement is one of automaticity. Dyslexic children tend to be unable to perform both cognitive and motor skills in as smooth, uninterrupted, free-flowing and automatic a manner as their non-dyslexic counterparts.

In the past ten years or so, it has been realized that the cerebellum could hold the answer. The cerebellum has long been known to control independent limb movement, particularly those movements that need to be carried out rapidly and require some degree of skill. Recent research carried out in the US, however, showed that the language areas of the brain had involvement with the cerebellum and that the function of making movements automatic could well be closely connected to making language skills automatic - producing language dexterity also.

A few facts about the cerebellum are appropriate at this point. It is densely packed and deeply folded. It accounts for between 10 and 15% of the total weight of the brain, 40% of its total surface area and 50% of its neurones (nerve cells). It is now realized that the cerebellum is a far more complex part of the brain than was first supposed and that it has connections that reach further forward, including to Broca's language area, than was originally thought.

When dyslexic children were tested by Professor Nicholson's team, they were found to perform significantly worse than non-dyslexic children of the same age and also worse - though not quite to the same degree - as younger children who were at the same reading level as them. The tests related to all skills controlled by the cerebellum.

This is clear behavioural evidence that dyslexic children do show abnormalities associated with the cerebellum (or its closely related pathways). This evidence was confirmed by studies of dyslexic brains, in which differences were found, and also from a 'brain-imaging' study using PET scans in which the dyslexics' brains acted differently from those of non-dyslexics.

The work described here is generally referred to as the cerebellar deficit hypothesis. It is shown in diagrammatic (flow chart) form in Figure 10.6 to explain the different stages and interactions and is also described stage by stage in Table 10.1.

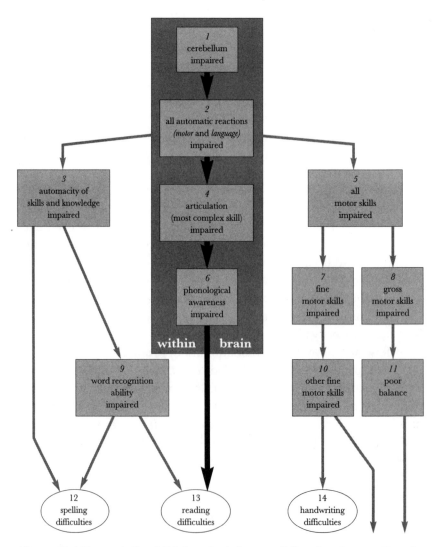

Figure 10.6 The cerebellar deficit hypothesis: how cerebellum impairment affects the acquisition of literacy and other skills.

Table 10.1 Cerebellar impairment: the stages described

1 The child's cerebellum functions imperfectly, the difficulty probably located in the errorfeedback loop.
2 Consequently the child's ability to react automatically in relation to both movement and language skills/dexterity is impaired.
3 He will be slower to sit up, to crawl and to walk, etc. Timing and speed will be impaired.
4 Babbling and the talking stage which follows will each be impaired. He will be forced to concentrate more on articulation and hence less on other skills.
5 The acquisition of movement skills of all types will be slower and less efficient.
6 The processing of the sounds of spoken words – the phonology of language – will be less complete. There will be less awareness of ONSETS and RIMES (described in Chapter 11).
7 Fine motor skills such as hand control and finger movements will be adversely affected.
8 Gross motor skills such as crawling, walking, running and kicking a ball will be affected, as also will balance.
9 The ability to recognize words is impaired as the child has acquired fewer skills, both verbal and non-verbal, and also has less knowledge (3). When the difficulties described in (6) are added to this, the situation becomes much more significant.
10 All fine motor skills, not just those related to handwriting, will be impaired.
11 Poor balance is one of the results of cerebellar impairment and is present in association with the others described.
12 SPELLING DIFFICULTIES result from a combination of impaired skills and knowledge (3) and the impaired ability to recognize words (9). Spelling difficulties tend to be most resistant to remediation.
13 READING DIFFICULTIES result from a combination of impaired phonological awareness (6) and impaired word-recognition ability (9). There is less fluency in reading as well as a slower reading speed. One of the keys to fluent reading is the ability to articulate sub-vocally. The cerebellum is active in this process and consequently its impairment impedes fluent reading.
14 HANDWRITING DIFFICULTIES are a product of the general impairment of the child's motor skills but particularly the fine motor skills. The precise timing and co-ordination of the muscles essential for the task is lacking.

Difficulties or deficits in the way in which the cerebellum functions account very well for how reading, spelling and handwriting skills are acquired more slowly and also for how these skills, once acquired, are slower, much more effortful and less automatic. Dyslexic children have difficulties in making skills automatic despite extensive practice and regardless of whether the skill is a cognitive or a motor one. They also display unusual lapses of concentration and tire more quickly than non-dyslexic children.

It accounts also for how other skills, with no obvious connection to literacy, can be more difficult to acquire and master. It explains why many children with dyslexia are bright in so many ways: it is because the parts of the brain involved in general comprehension and understanding lie towards the front of the brain, some distance from the cerebellum and not influenced by it.

Finally, it needs to be explained in relation to Figure 10.6 that literacy difficulties can arise from several routes, but the central route (which has been highlighted) is considered to be the most important.

The brain and vision

The manner in which our eyes and brain work together to produce the sense of vision is one of the most remarkable features of the human body. We are heavily reliant on vision for survival, as about 95% of our knowledge of the outside world comes to us through our eyes. By means of vision we can detect light and shade, colours, movement and depth. We are also able to interpret what we see about us by converting so many signs into meanings, and this is particularly so in the case of reading, where meaning is derived from the printed or written word.

The process involved in the visual system is extremely complex and although it is not necessary for us to have a detailed knowledge of it, a familiarity with the basic details will help a great deal. Our eyes respond to light rays, which is why we cannot see anything when we are in total darkness. When we are in normal daylight or sufficient artificial light, there are countless rays of light entering our eyes from many directions. The rays themselves are invisible and each one is extremely narrow. Light rays travel in straight lines unless they strike something which causes them to change direction. Usually there are a number of rays found together and when this is so they form a beam of light.

We can learn something about how our visual system operates by considering what happens in just one of our two eyes when we are looking at an object somewhere in the centre of our overall visual field. (What happens in the other eye will be similar.)

The light rays pass from the outside world and strike the front of the eyeball. They pass through two layers (the *conjunctiva* and the *cornea*), a liquid (the *aqueous humour*) the *lens*, then a jelly-like substance (the *vitreous humour*), which fills most of the eyeball, and finally make contact with the *retina*. All five substances through which the rays pass before reaching the retina are colourless and transparent. By the time they reach retina, the light rays have undergone a number of distortions and changes of direction. This results in them placing an image of the object on the retina that is both upside down and back to front in relation to the object itself. When the messages contained in the nerve impulses are passed from the retina to the brain, the brain has to 'interpret' the messages, thereby making sense of the outside world by picturing it as it really is. (Figures 10.7 and 10.8 illustrate what we have said so far.)

The visual pathway

This is the name given to the route taken by the nerve impulses as they travel from the eye through the brain to the right and left visual cortex at the rear.

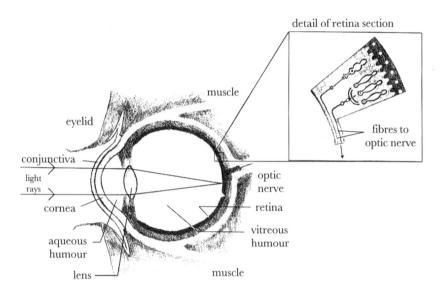

Figure 10.7 The structure of the eye.

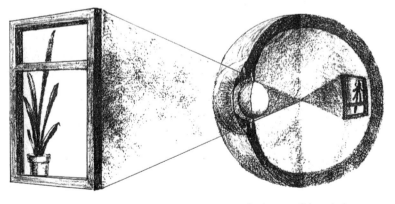

the image of the window
formed on the retina
is upside down and
back to front

Figure 10.8 Image formation in the eye.

The retina at the back of the eyeball is a light-sensitive layer consisting of a mixture of two types of cells (the *rods* and *cones*). The rods respond to differences in light and shade and the cones respond to different colours. The light rays must travel through the seven different layers of the retina in order to reach the light-sensitive part of the rods and cones.

When light falls on the retina it triggers a chemical reaction within the cells and this, in turn, converts into a nerve impulse that is passed out of the back of the eye by means of the two *optic nerves* (there is one from each eye). These run backwards and towards each other, meeting at a particular point (the *optic chiasma*), which plays a very important part in the process of visual perception. The optic chiasma is a crossing point. At this place nerve fibres cross over from one side to the other, but there is not a complete crossing over, only a partial one.

The nerve fibres that leave each retina in a bundle consist of two different groups, those from the left half of each eyeball and those from the right, but it is easier to consider them as belonging to either the outside (temporal) or the inside (nasal) half of each eye. What happens at the optic chiasma is that the fibres from the inside (nasal) half of each eye cross over to the opposite side of the brain and meet up alongside the outside (temporal) fibres of the other eye. (Note: The optic chiasma is not to be confused with the corpus callosum. Although each of these nerve fibres cross over from one half of the brain to the other, the optic chiasma is quite separate from the corpus callosum. It is much smaller in size and located about 0.75 inches (18 mm) below the front of the corpus callosum. Another important difference is that the optic chiasma contains only nerves related to vision whereas the corpus callosum contains a variety of different nerves.)

From the optic chiasma the two sets of optic nerves (now known as *optic tracts*) continue to run back through the brain. The left optic tract consists of nerves from the outside half of the left eye and the inside half of the right eye. The right optic tract, in similar manner, contains the information gathered by the inside of the left eye and the outside of the right eye. The effect of this rather confusing-sounding arrangement has been to collect on the right side of the brain all of the information about the outside world that belongs to the left side of the total visual field, and vice versa. This produces a situation with which we are now quite familiar - that of each side of the brain processing information that relates to the other side of the body (in this case the outside world closest to the other side of the body). Figures 10.9 and 10.10 illustrate the total arrangement.

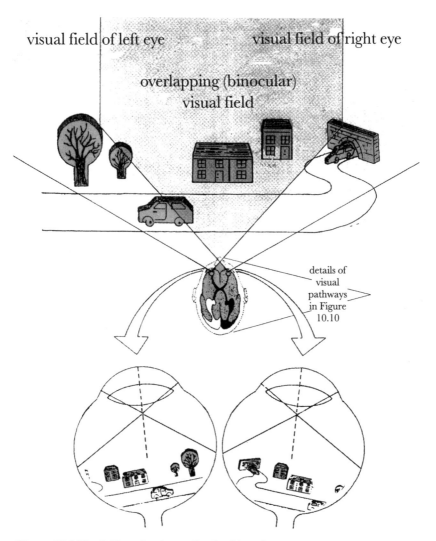

visual field of left eye   visual field of right eye

overlapping (binocular)
visual field

details of
visual
pathways
in Figure
10.10

Figure 10.9 The fields and pathways for visual impulses.

Each optic tract enters another specialized area in the brain (a *lateral geniculate nucleus*). From here nerve impulses are passed to different nerves (*optic radiations*), which continue to pass back through the brain, eventually reaching the visual areas of the brain located in the occipital lobes.

This should give us a very rough idea of just how complex our visual system is. Not only are the total mechanisms highly complicated, but they are still not yet properly understood. The more complex a system is, the more likely it is to have delicate parts and hence the greater the likelihood of something going wrong. Efficient vision relies on the efficiency of two eyes, each of which allows light

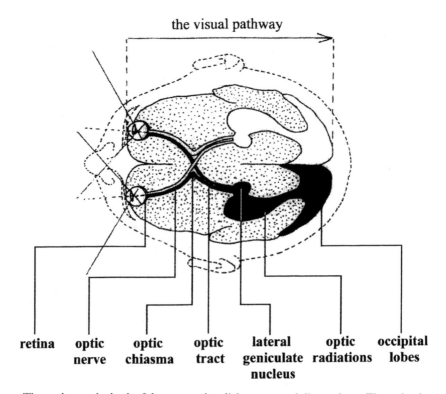

the visual pathway

| retina | optic nerve | optic chiasma | optic tract | lateral geniculate nucleus | optic radiations | occipital lobes |

The **retina** at the back of the eye receives light waves and directs them. The retina is divided into two parts, the inside and outside halves, each of which has a separate bundle of fibres which combine to make the **optic nerve**, which passes out of the back of the eye to the **optic chiasma**. Here the two bundles of fibres cross over sides, each leaving the outside bundle on its own. Each new combination (outside fibres with inside fibres from the opposite eye) is known as an **optic tract** and each optic tract passes into its own **lateral geniculate nucleus**, out of which nerves proceed in a distinct pattern called **optic radiations**. The fibres radiate backwards and outwards to connect up with the visual areas of the brain which are located in the **occipital lobes**.

While proceeding through the visual pathway, the nerve impulses conveying information about what the outside world looks like have been organized in such a manner that the information about the left half of the visual field is gathered on the right side of the brain and vice versa.

Figure 10.10 The visual pathway.

rays to pass through and become distorted in the process, after which sense needs to be made of the distorted image.

Light energy at the retina is converted to chemical energy, which in turn is converted into electrical energy. It is this that forms the basis of the nerve impulse passed from the retina through a series of nerve fibres to the visual cortex at the rear of the brain. The brain must then 'interpret' what the eyes have 'seen' in the outside world, whether it is a house, a tree, a car or a book.

The fact that each retina contains 6 million cones and 120 million rods illustrates the extreme delicacy of the whole system. Something else to take into account is the manner in which the eyeball can change shape in order to focus images, as well as move about within the eye socket and scan the field of view. When what is being scanned is a printed image from which meaning must be derived by also involving the language centres of the brain, a very complex situation becomes many times more so.

This is an appropriate point at which to describe more interesting and up-to-date research findings involving the brain, vision and hearing in relation to becoming literate and the problems of dyslexics.

The neural/sensorimotor basis of dyslexia

This describes the research findings of Professor Stein and his team, who are based at Oxford University's Laboratory of Physiology. In summary, they believe they have identified two different sets of nerve cells, one affecting vision and one affecting hearing, each of which has been found to malfunction in significant numbers of dyslexic people.

In relation to vision, a set of large neurones have been identified in the brain. These specialized cells - known as magnocells - are responsible for the timing of both sensory (mainly visual and auditory) and also motor (movement) events. The proper development of these cells is essential for reading skills to develop appropriately. Specialized cells (magnocells) in the retina of the eye are capable of signalling information quickly to the magnocells which lie behind them and which, in turn, signal on to the visual cortex of the brain and also to the cerebellum. Hence the magnocellular system is essential for controlling eye movements during reading, and prevents the visual gaze from slipping away from any word on which it needs to remain fixated.

It is now felt that in dyslexics, the visual magnocellular system develops less well than in others. It appears to be approximately 30% smaller in dyslexics, and also slightly slower and weaker in its functioning. Difficulties could lead to unsteady eye fixation, which could, in turn, cause letter and word images to move around on the retina of the eye. This results in impaired memory for the visual form of a word and hence for its correct spelling.

Not all dyslexics have visual difficulties; some have auditory/ phonological problems and so are unable to distinguish clearly between two similar but distinct speech sounds. A proportion of dyslexics demonstrate both types of difficulty.

Dyslexics, along with poor readers generally, are significantly worse than good or average readers at detecting sound frequency changes, and it is this ability that a child relies on heavily when, for instance, he needs to distinguish between the sound of a 'b' and that of a 'd'. It is for this reason that dyslexics are worse than others at phonological analyses, as is evidenced by their poor performance in attempting to read nonwords (which was demonstrated by Professor Snowling in 1987).

There is no absolutely clear-cut set of magnocells in the brain's auditory system that compares with those in the visual system. Nevertheless, some large neurones do seem to be specialized to do the work with which we are concerned here - the detection of change in the frequency, amplitude and phase of sounds, particularly those involved in speech. Dyslexics tend to have reduced sensitivity in detecting such changes in sounds, and so it appears quite likely that they may have, in addition to impaired development of the visual magnocellular system, an impaired development of magnocells in the auditory system.

The sensitivity of the visual magnocells may help to determine just how well children develop the orthographic skills they need for reading. If impaired, the magnocells can produce unsteady fixation when reading and hence visual confusion of letter order. This, in turn, will produce poor memory of the visual form of words and so the acquisition of orthographic skills is impeded.

The sensitivity of the auditory magnocells may help to determine a child's phonological skills. Impaired development will lead to auditory confusion of letter sounds and will result in poor phonological development.

Magnocellular systems project to the cerebellum, which plays an important role in the reading process by contributing both to the control of steady eye fixations during reading and also to 'inner speech'.

Professor Stein's research accords very well with what is known about the processes involved during the early stages of normal reading. This is set out in Figure 10.11, and shows that when a learner reader encounters a particular word, one of two alternate processes come into play. If the word has a familiar appearance to the child (i.e. he has met with it in its printed form a few times before), then he will recognize it visually and be able to link this familiar-looking pattern of letters to the meaning associated with them and pronounce the sound of the words that the printed form represents. The means used is the lexical (or visual) route.

If the word is a visually unfamiliar one, then the pattern of letters needs to be tackled one at a time in the correct order for them to be broken down (segmented) and sounded out individually. Having mapped the printed pattern of letters on to a certain sequence of

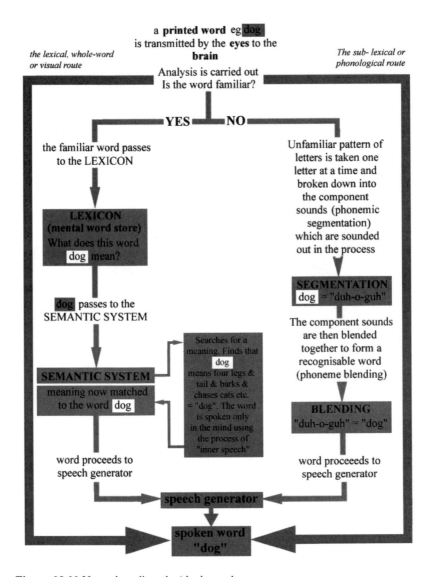

Figure 10.11 Normal reading: the 'dual route' process.

speech sounds, the child must then attempt to blend this particular and unique pattern of speech sounds into a whole, which forms a recognizable word. The word can then be read aloud. This method is the sublexical or phonological route.

For dyslexic children, the most common difficulty encountered is with phoneme segmentation. The child is unable to decode or 'map' graphemes (written words) into their corresponding phonemes (individual speech sounds), and hence cannot easily progress beyond the phonological stage to become an automatic, fluent reader. (Other dyslexics have more difficulties related to the process of visual perception.)

PET scans of the brain, referred to earlier in the chapter, have recently produced some interesting results in relation to dyslexics. Part of the left temporal lobe of the brain was investigated at the Institute of Cognitive Neuroscience in London, and dyslexic readers were found to have less activation than non-dyslexics in that part of their brains when attempting to read and name pictures.

PET scans also produced interesting results when adult dyslexics and non-dyslexics took part in a rhyming task. As can be seen from Figure 10.12, the dyslexics used far less processing power during the task.

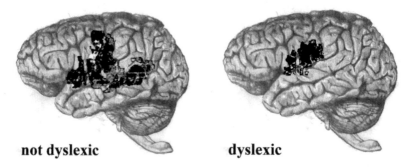

not dyslexic   **dyslexic**

Figure 10.12 Brain activity during a rhyming task.

Results showing a similar trend were produced when the same group of adults were given a task that involved the use of short-term memory (Figure 10.13). (These results were produced by the work of Paulesu, Snowling, Frith, Eden and others.)

We will conclude the chapter with some further information relating to the visual system and some information about hearing.

Eye dominance

Most people prefer one eye to the other, such that they will always (or almost always) use the same eye to look through a telescope. The eye

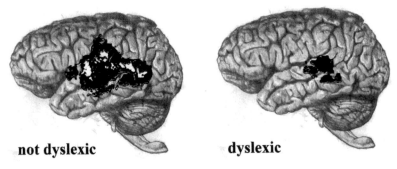

not dyslexic **dyslexic**

Figure 10.13 Brain activity during a short-term memory task.

that is preferred on these occasions is known as the dominant eye and in the case of most people their dominant eye is on the same side as their preferred hand (the one they write with). Most people are right-handed and right-eyed. A child found to have his dominant hand and dominant eye on opposite sides of his body is described as 'cross-lateral', and some tests of dyslexia set out to investigate whether a child is cross-lateral or not.

Several investigators believe that eye dominance is important. When a child is looking at a distant object, the line of sight of each eye is parallel and dominance has no part to play. But when looking at something close, such as a reading book, the sight lines converge and under these circumstances one eye becomes dominant.

Some people believe that dyslexia is associated with a failure to develop consistent eye dominance, and so confusion results as to exactly where letters and words are on the printed page. It has been argued that more than half of the dyslexic population has an unfixed reference eye, but the findings on which this claim was based have been criticized.

Others are concerned that the muscles controlling fine eye movements are more important, because during reading the eyes need to track across the page.

Eye tracking

When we read something printed in English, or many other written languages, we must follow the line of print from left to right across the page. There have been reports that a high proportion of dyslexic people tend to scan a line of print in the opposite direction.

If a dyslexic child follows a line of print from right to left when he is being taught by a teacher who is unaware of this, and who assumes that he is tracking normally, then it is quite possible for that child to develop a learning block associated with the printed word. Reversals and some misreadings of words would also be explained by this difference.

Competent readers are reported not to have a symmetrical visual scan. That is to say they do not 'take in' an equal number of letters to the right and left of any point on the page they are looking at. Rather, they take in 14 letters to the right and only seven letters to the left. Dyslexic children who do not have this particular range and pattern of scan are obviously at a disadvantage.

There is little dispute that the eye movements of dyslexics when reading differ from those of normal readers, but it is extremely doubtful whether this fact holds the answer to the problem of dyslexia.

Lenses and filters

Some children report that they are able to read better if they wear spectacles fitted with specially tinted lenses or read the text through a coloured filter placed over it. The use of lenses and filters is closely associated with Helen Irlen of the Irlen Institute in the USA, and reports of the successful use of lenses and filters have appeared in newspaper and television reports since late 1985. Helen Irlen claims that some people suffer from what she calls 'scotopic sensitivity syndrome' (or SSS for short), which refers to the ability to see when low levels of light only are available. However, there has been confusion, because a coloured filter will remove certain *wavelengths* of light, which is a different matter altogether from altering the *level* of light available.

Psychologists have attempted to test the claims made for lenses and filters, but this has proved to be difficult, as many of the studies carried out (and on which the claims were made) contained serious flaws, such as poor experimental design, lack of control groups, gains in reading being found to be quite low, reading tests being printed on coloured paper, etc. Other investigations have shown that the lenses (of which there are more than 140 possible varieties) acted mainly to absorb light rather than to cut out any particular wavelengths.

Researchers have found that the degree of improvement in reading levels when using coloured overlays during reading is no greater in dyslexic children than in other children. The evidence indicates that visual problems do *not* appear to be a major cause of dyslexia, and also that dyslexic individuals have only minor problems with visual perception, but that they do have a difficulty in recalling names and with 'naming' language. Difficulties of this type will be discussed in Chapter 11.

The brain and hearing

The manner in which sounds heard reach and are interpreted by the brain is very complex, but there are certain similarities to vision. Sounds coming into either ear set up nerve impulses to the brain, but the nerve fibres that carry the impulses divide up so that some go to the half of the brain on the same side as the ear, but others go to the opposite half. However, each set of nerve fibres that crosses over is stronger than the set that stays on the same side. Hence, sounds heard in the right ear are interpreted for the most part on the left side of the brain, and vice versa.

In most people, language is interpreted by both halves of the brain, but the left half has a larger language area than the right, and so is much 'stronger'. The right ear, for most people, is stronger when interpreting speech because it is more closely associated with the large language area in the left half of the brain. The left ear/right side of the brain is better at interpreting non-speech sounds.

It is thought that many severe dyslexics do not have their language areas sited mainly in the left hemisphere. If the brain, owing to incomplete dominance, must attempt to analyse language in both halves simultaneously, the connection between the two halves through the corpus callosum could become overloaded and create confusion as to what needs to be interpreted. Figure 10.14 summarizes the situation.

The next chapter considers an entirely different type of possible cause(s) of dyslexia.

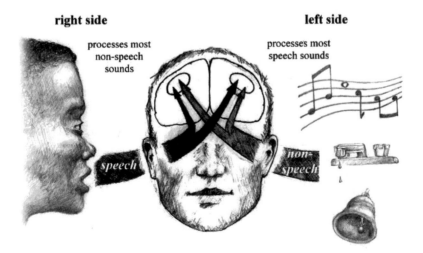

Figure 10.14 The brain and hearing.

Chapter 11
Possible causes (II)
Phonological awareness

The word 'phonology' means the study of the speech sounds of a language, but in relation to dyslexia, it is usually used somewhat more loosely and refers to just the speech sounds themselves. It is how we will be using the word in this chapter.

Phonological awareness is knowledge of these sounds and is something which grows gradually in a child over time. Spoken words have many characteristics and young children are initially aware of a word in its entirety as a solid 'block' of sound, so to speak, and concentrate on the meaning of the word and nothing else. Later on, in the course of development, they become aware of other properties of words and are able to distinguish long words from short words, easy-to-say words from more difficult ones, ordinary-sounding words from 'funny'-sounding ones, 'nice' words from rude words, etc.

The sounds within words

It is only much later that a child is able to concentrate on the sound composition of a word, and to realize that most words do not consist of a solid 'block' of sound, but are in fact, made up of a string of smaller sounds arranged in a set order.

This stage marks the start of the development of phonological awareness. When a child has fully mastered the phonology of his language, and therefore possesses full phonological awareness, he has acquired certain knowledge and a number of skills relating to the smaller speech sounds of language that go together to make up words.

Onsets and Rimes

Two important skills relate to the sounds at the beginning and ends of words. Most words can be broken down into two parts, the begin-

164

ning and the remainder. The beginning is known in phonology as the *onset*. The spoken word 'cat' divides into 'c-' and 'at', with 'c-' being the onset. Similarly the onset of 'dog' is 'd-' and of 'play' is 'pl-'. The onset is, in fact, the part of the word up to the first vowel, and can consist of a number of sounds. 'Cat' and 'dog' each have an onset of just one sound, but 'play' has an onset of two sounds, and the word 'string' has three different sounds in its onset, each one being represented by a different letter of the alphabet - s, t and r - when it is written down. When a child is aware that 'cat' and 'cup' have the same onset, but 'cat' and 'pup' have different onsets, he has achieved some degree of phonological awareness.

A group of words with similar onsets that are placed together in speech is referred to by students of English grammar as 'alliteration' and such groups of words are very popular with young children. Children's authors are well aware of this fact and have named their characters in order to capitalize on it. Earlier generations of children have enjoyed stories about Desperate Dan, Billy Bunter and Milly Molly Mandy. Later there was The Famous Five, Thomas the Tank Engine and Muffin the Mule. Nowadays we have Postman Pat, Bob the Builder and the Teletubbies.

Before moving on, it needs to be pointed out that some words do not have an onset, these being those that begin with a vowel, such as 'am', 'egg', 'ink', 'odd', 'us' (these are just a few short examples).

The second phonological skill relates to the second part of words, the part that follows the onset. This part of a word is known as the *rime*, and is, of course, closely connected to the word rhyme, because when two words have the same rime they will be found to rhyme. A child who knows that the words 'dog' and 'log' have an ending sound in common - '-og' - and therefore rhyme, but that the words 'dog' and 'duck' do not have the same ending sound, has acquired an important phonological skill. Children are fond of rhymes - hence the popularity of nursery rhymes, and also characters with rhyming names, e.g. Andy Pandy, Dennis the Menace, etc.

Segmentation and blending

In achieving awareness of onsets and rimes, a child has started to acquire a third very important phonological skill, which is that of *segmentation*. To be able to consider two words such as 'cat' and 'cup', and to know that they start with the same sound, means that the child has been able to divide (or segment) each word into at least two parts ('c-' and 'at' and 'c-' and 'up') and to recognize that the same sound (represented by the letter 'c' when the word is written down) is present at the start of each. The same applies when he considers 'dog' and 'log' and is sure that they rhyme, i.e. have a rime in common ('-og').

A fourth skill is the reverse process of segmentation and is *blending*. To be able to take the separated sounds of 'm-' and 'an' and blend them together to produce the spoken word 'man' or to take 'fr-' and 'og' to produce 'frog' means the child can successfully blend speech sounds. It is a level of even greater sophistication to realize that the spoken word 'man' is made up of three speech sounds and not just two, and to realize that 'frog' is likewise actually composed of four speech sounds. (It so happens that in each of these words each separate speech sound is represented by a single letter of the alphabet when the spoken word is represented in writing (or print), but more of that later.)

Deletions and additions

A fifth skill which a phonologically competent child possesses is that of speech sound *deletion*. When this is carried out one part of a given word can be dropped out and the remainder pronounced accurately. Sometimes it is possible to alter a word in such a way that another word results, but most of the time it will be a nonword. The spoken word 'stick' without the sound represented by 's' will produce 'tick' and without the 't' sound will produce 'sick'. Similarly, 'switch' without the initial sound produces 'witch', and with both of the first two sounds deleted will produce 'itch'.

Closely linked to sound deletion is sound addition. A child who is phonologically aware will realize that if the word 'sing' is considered, it is possible to insert a 'w' sound after the initial 's' to produce another word: 'swing'.

Spoonerisms

Another closely linked skill relates to sound transpositions between pairs of words which usually occur together. These occurrences are usually known as spoonerisms, and are named after a university lecturer in Victorian times. He became famous for his many 'slips of the tongue', which were of a particular type. When speaking, he would occasionally swap over the beginnings of two words so that when he meant to say 'the down train' it came out as 'the town drain', and 'the dear old queen' became 'the queer old dean'. A student who had missed all of Spooner's history lectures was accused of having 'hissed all my mystery lectures'. Obviously, spoonerisms will not always make sense, as nonwords will often be produced. For example, 'King John' will become 'Jing Kohn' and 'crowded ship' will become 'shrowded crip'. Whether or not, they almost always produce a humorous reaction, and there is at least one British comedian who builds his act on spoonerisms, reciting the 'Tairy Fale' of 'Rindercella', her 'Gairy Fodmother', the 'sugly isters' and the 'prandsome hince' with the 'sass glipper'. A child who can produce spoonerisms is able to segment a word into its component parts, manipulate each from the donating to the receiving word, and then blend them together to form the new words (or nonwords, as the case may be). He has mastered three different phonological skills.

The significance of phonological awareness

It is generally acknowledged among researchers into dyslexia that during the past 20 years or so the major achievement has been in identifying that poor phonological skills are very closely linked with dyslexia difficulties. Many, probably most, believe that inadequate phonological skills are the main, and perhaps the only, cause of children's reading problems. Some feel that this is perhaps too extreme a stance to adopt, but none deny that phonological skills are of great importance, as is evidenced by the work of researchers such as Bradley, Bryant, Snowling, Stanovich and Vellutino.

Phonemes

Phonological awareness, as we have said, relates to a general awareness of the speech sounds of our language. So far we have spoken only in quite general terms and have named only two types of speech sounds: onsets and rimes. We now need to go into more detail about the smaller sounds that go together to make up the words we speak. In particular, we must go into some detail about phonemes.

Spoken language and written language have only two things in common: sentences and words. We speak in sentences and these are composed of distinct words. We also write down words arranged into sentences. Writing, if there is enough of it, is organized so that the sentences are grouped into paragraphs. And the paragraphs, if there are enough of them, will be grouped into chapters, which can in turn be compiled into books, which can in turn be ordered into separate volumes, depending on the nature of what is written.

Sentences, whether spoken or written, are strings of words that make sense. A sentence may be long or short, simple or complex; it is immaterial, providing that it makes sense.

Sentences can be broken down into phrases, phrases into words, words into syllables, onset and rime, or phonemes. An example should help in clarification. Take, for example, the sentence: John is a bricklayer in London.

This can be broken down into two phrases:

- John is
- a bricklayer in London.

A phrase is part of a sentence and therefore does not make complete sense when considered alone, but at the same time is capable of conveying some meaning. Other examples of phrases are: the black dog, a heavy cargo, in the box, along the road, etc.

The sentence can also be broken down into words. There are six of them. We shall select just one - 'bricklayer' - and analyse it.

- Onset and rime = br - icklayer (a rime can be subdivided into nucleus and coda, but we do not need to go into such detail here).
- Syllables = brick - lay - er. There are three syllables. A syllable in a word is similar to a beat in music. A syllable occurs wherever a vowel (a, e, i, o, u, and occasionally y) is present. Sometimes there are two vowels together (ee, oo, ou). Sometimes the single (or double) vowel has one or more letters before it and/or one or more letters after it. The three syllables of 'bricklayer' are based on the three vowels that occur in the word: 'i', 'a' and 'e'. The 'i' has 'br' in front of it and 'ck' after. The 'a' is sandwiched between 'l' and 'y' and the 'e' has just the letter 'r' immediately following. The process of splitting a word into its component syllables is known as syllabification.
- Phonemes = b-r-i-ck-l-ay-er. The ten letters in the printed word are clustered together in such a way as to represent the seven different sounds that go to make up the sound of the spoken word 'bricklayer'. The letters 'b', 'r', 'i' and 'l' each represent a speech sound. The letters 'ck', although being two different letters represent just one sound. The same applies to 'ay' and 'er'.

Phonemes, then, are the basic speech sounds of our language. In fact, a phoneme is the smallest unit of sound present in a spoken word. Phonemes are vitally important because they are, so to speak, the building blocks of our spoken language, and it is vital in speaking and listening that every phoneme is pronounced clearly by the speaker and heard accurately by the listener. If this does not happen, then either one word could be changed into a different one or, more likely, nonsense will result.

Once again, a simple example should illustrate the importance of what we are discussing. The word 'pen' consists of three separate and distinct speech sounds (phonemes) and it so happens that each phoneme, when the word is written down, is represented by a single letter of the alphabet. If the initial sound were to be substituted by a different one, we could end up with entirely different words (such as 'den', 'fen', 'hen', 'men', 'then', etc) or with nonsense words (such as 'nen', 'ren', 'sen', 'chen', 'shen', etc.). Similarly, changing the middle sound will produce 'pan', 'pin' and 'pun'. A change to the final sound would produce 'peg', 'pep' and 'pet'.

The ability to read successfully relies heavily on the learner reader knowing about the phonemes within a word - that is, on having *phonemic awareness*, which is a sub-branch, so to speak, of phonological awareness, but probably the most vital of them all.

The phonemes of the English language

Each one of the hundreds of thousands of words that go to make up the English language is made up of one or more phonemes. However, when the many thousands of words are analysed they are found to consist of various combinations of a much smaller number of basic sounds or phonemes - between 40 and 50, in fact.

The human vocal system is capable of producing many speech sounds but no one particular language ever makes use of all of them. There are speech sounds made by Chinese, Russians, Arabs and South American Indians that are never heard in English, and the converse is also true. (The scientific study of human speech sounds generally is known as *phonetics* and the study of how the sounds of a particular language are arranged in patterns so as to convey meaning is known as *phonology*.)

In the case of English, it is not possible for anyone to say precisely how many speech sounds are used by the many millions of English-speaking people in the world when they are conversing together. An American, a Scotsman, a New Zealander, a Yorkshireman and a Cockney will all use slightly different speech sounds. In fact, it is possible to claim that there is no such thing as *the* English language, but rather that there are a number of English languages, each of which has a large area of overlap with the others.

Because of this, agreement was reached long ago as to what was to be regarded as correct and proper. This is usually called the received pronunciation (RP) of a language. Since the late 19th century there has been in existence an International Phonetic Alphabet (IPA), which was developed to produce suitable symbols for the sounds of any language. It has been revised from time to time, most recently in 1989. It is sufficiently rich to label the phonemes of any language and to handle the contrasts between them.

In the case of English there is a total of 44 phonemes in RP, 20 of them vowel sounds and the others consonants. These are given in Table 11.1.

Table 11.1 The phonemes of the English language

THE PHONEMES OF THE ENGLISH LANGUAGE

Vowels (20)		Consonants (24)	
Symbol	Sound (or value)	Symbol	Sound (or value)
aɪ	try – write	b	back – rubber
aʊ	noun – now	d	day – rudder
ɑ	father	dʒ	judge – George – raj
ɒ	wash – odd	ð	this – other
æ	cat – trap	f	few – puff
eɪ	day – steak – face	g	got – bigger
əʊ	go – goat	h	hot
ɛ	get	j	yet
ɛə	fair – square	k	car – key – clock – trekked – quay
ɜ	her – stir – word – nurse	l	lip
i	he – see	m	much – hammer
ɪ	ship	n	now – runner
ɪə	hear – here	ŋ	sing
o	force	p	pen – pepper
ɔ	north – war	r	round – sorry
ɔɪ	noise – toy	s	see – missed
u	lunar – pool	ʃ	ship – mission
ʊ	foot – put	t	ten
ʊə	pure	tʃ	church – latch
ʌ	bud – blood – love	θ	three – heath
		v	very
		w	will
		z	zeal
		ʒ	decision – treasure

(Total = 44)

One of the things an English-speaking child needs to learn is the manner in which the everyday speech he both listens to and uses comprises simpler sounds than words - the 44 phonemes. As we have stated above, the child needs to know that a word is not just one 'block' of sound, but is made up of a number of shorter sounds blended smoothly together to make the one longer sound that is the word. The child must eventually learn that a word such as 'happy' consists of two 'beats' or syllables - ha and ppy - which in turn consists of a total of four phonemes - h - a - pp - y (pronounced 'huh-ah-puh-ee') - which, if written in the International Phonetic Alphabet, would be: h/ae/p/i.

A further complication for the reading process is that the 44 different speech sounds are represented in print or writing by only 26 letters of the alphabet. Because there are insufficient letters to provide a one-to-one relationship with sounds, the letters are used singly or in pairs to represent different sounds. Conversely, any one sound can be represented by different letters from one word to the next. For example:

- the *oo* sound in 'shoot' is also
- *ou* (in soup)
- *u-e* (in chute)
- *ough* (in through), etc.

Similarly:

- the *er* sound in 'her' is
- 'ir' (in sir)
- 'ur' (in fur), etc.

These are only a few of the countless examples that exist. All in all, our alphabet of only 26 letters is thoroughly unsuited to the job it must do, and the task of learning to read is not made any easier.

We need to explain again that at first, children are not aware of the individual phonemes that go together to make up a word. At a young age, children are aware of only the *meaning* of a word or a sentence, and it is only when they start learning to read that they begin to think about the sounds within words.

The question arises as to whether young children who are insensitive to, and uninterested in, rhyme are likely to be dyslexic readers later in life when they are in school and attempting to master the skill of reading.

The child's development of phonology

Our phonology or speech-sound system is concerned purely with the sounds of words, and particularly those smallest units (phonemes) that go to build up words. The system is not concerned with the meaning of words, nor with the rules of grammar, which govern how words are arranged in order in a sentence. A person's individual phonology obviously needs to match exactly the general phonology of the social group in which he lives, otherwise misunderstanding and confusion could result. A person who is fluent in his own language and then moves to an area where a different language is spoken will need to be fully competent in the second language in order to fully comprehend situations and function easily. Obviously a child born into an English-speaking family that lives in an English-speaking environment will need to develop the phonology of English.

At birth a child has no knowledge of phonology, as he can neither understand what is said in the world about him, nor reply using language. However, he has the potential to develop a perfectly adequate phonology by means of the phonological system with which he is born, and requires only adequate stimulation over a certain period of time to be brought to full competence.

Initially, a very young baby will simply be aware of the different levels of sound and will react appropriately to noise (particularly loud noises), gentle soothing sounds or silence. Eventually, he learns to distinguish the human voice from other sounds, and later still the voices of individuals - particularly those of his mother/carer and others in close daily contact. Voice tones (e.g. warning tones, etc.) will come to develop meaning at a later stage, and after that the significance of certain words (e.g. no, yes, good, bad, mummy, daddy, etc.).

When these important stages of development are under way, the child's phonological system is starting to develop his individual phonology in line with that of the people about him. The phonological system manifests itself in a number of phonological skills that are distinct from one another but, at the same time, closely interlinked. The skill of phonological awareness can be identified, as without it no further development could possibly take place. The skill of phonological processing can also be identified, as without such a skill the child would not be able to 'filter out' speech sounds from the ocean of sounds that will often surround him; nor would he be able to respond to them appropriately. At a later stage, although presumably while other skills are still developing, the skill of phonological production comes into play. The child makes many sounds with his voice in the early weeks and months of life, but gradually speech sounds related to his own culture's language start to increase while correspondingly, those with no 'language value' in his particular culture decrease and become more or less extinguished. The child of an English-speaking family living in an English language environment will start to produce a range of English language phonemes and other speech sounds, modelling his vocal output on what he is hearing on a regular basis, and eventually going on to produce recognizable words.

The phonological system cannot be defined precisely and its exact structure is not known, nor is the dynamic and complex manner of the development of the various skills that go to make up its final form and means of operating. An attempt to illustrate what is known is given in Figure 11.1, but not all workers in the field would agree on its details.

Full competence in phonology is usually developed by the age of 8 years. At this stage, a child will be able to segment, analyse, compare and contrast, identify differences and similarities, produce alliteration and rhymes, delete phonemes from any part of a word, add phonemes, transpose them, produce spoonerisms, read nonsense words, etc.

Phonology and learning to read

When children start learning to read they need to be able to deal with phonology more proficiently than when they learned to speak. They need to understand the *alphabetic principle* - that is, to realize that the phonemes within a word are represented by individual letters (or combinations of letters) of the alphabet. They also need to know that the differences they detect between two spoken words will be represented by differences in how the words appear in print form. Different phonological structures are represented by different orthographic patterns.

Spoken language is both fast and complex. Normal speech is produced at a rate of between 10 and 20 phonemes per second. In normal speech, one phoneme is only half sounded out before the next in the sequence is embarked upon, and occasionally a phoneme is dropped altogether. What is said must be only half heard by the listener. Nevertheless, the speaking/listening situation for the majority of the population is a highly developed, speedy and automatic

The **PHONOLOGY** of an individual

develops through the mechanism of his
PHONOLOGICAL SYSTEM which:
- cannot be defined accurately
- developes over some years, and
- is composed of a number of

PHONOLOGICAL SKILLS or **ABILITIES**, the
principal ones of which are:

PHONOLOGICAL AWARENESS which:
- can be implicit or explicit
- can be analysed at different levels
- is demonstrated by knowledge of
  rhymes and alliteration
- eventually reciprocates with literacy skills
- developes **PHONEMIC AWARENESS** and
- underlies the development of

PHONOLOGICAL PROCESSING which:
- takes in
- analyses
- categorizes
- selects and
- orders speech sounds in order to prepare for

PHONOLOGICAL PRODUCTION i.e. speech
and its various dimensions e.g. fluency,
naming speed, spoonerisms, etc.

PHONOLOGICAL PROCESSING and PHONOLOGICAL PRODUCTION are
each mediated and strongly influenced by **PHONOLOGICAL MEMORY**

NOTE: 1 Each phonological skill can demonstrate a deficit/impairment but these
          can be improved by phonological skills training
       2 Many researchers believe that dyslexia/specific learning difficulties is
          characterized by a marked deficit or impairment in phonological skills
          (which are quite independent of intelligence)

Figure 11.1 The development of phonology.

one, which hangs together quite solidly and proceeds quite efficiently. Much of speech will be only half spoken by one person and
only half heard by the other, but nevertheless, will be perceived accurately. A person who has just been introduced to someone is quite
unlikely to speak to them in a slow, precise manner, fully sounding
out every individual phoneme. Their natural speech will be quite
rapid and imprecise; it could probably be represented quite accurately as:

- 'Pleeztermeechya'

but will be perfectly well understood to mean:

- '(I-am)-pleased-to-meet-you'.

The speaker will have composed, blended and spoken the component phonemes at great speed. The listener will have heard, segmented and comprehended them equally quickly, and quite automatically, without conscious effort being involved.

As explained earlier, for a child to be able to learn to talk, all that is required is that he is in contact with people who talk. To be able to read, the child needs to undergo the process of being formally taught. Countless generations of brain evolution has produced speech naturally, but literacy is an artificial, man-invented phenomenon, and hence cannot be acquired automatically or without the intervention of somebody already so skilled. It is no more natural than playing a game of chess or programming a computer. Phonology needs to be dealt with more consciously when learning to read than when learning to speak.

However, once the alphabetic principle has been grasped, then there is at least some basis for the reading skill to develop, grow, become refined, and also become automated and fluent.

Research into reading difficulties

It is easy for anyone to make guesses as to why some children are poor at reading, but this is not good enough. What is needed is hard evidence. The question 'Why are some children dyslexic?' has been asked countless times and reasons have been suggested, but generally speaking most of the time people in the past have not got it right. Generally, they have put forward reasons based on inadequate evidence. One investigator (Hinshelwood) claimed that dyslexia was caused by 'a difficulty in acquiring and storing up in the brain the visual memories of words and letters'.

If some particular difficulty within children were responsible for those children's reading difficulties, then dyslexic children should, in one specific way at least, be quite different from other children. Most researchers in the past have taken a group of dyslexic readers, given them a test in a particular skill (such as memory for words), compared the results with those from a matched group of non-dyslexic children and found that the dyslexics perform badly in comparison. The researchers have then assumed that the reading difficulties are caused by the poor skill involved.

On the face of it, of course, this appears to be a perfectly reasonable assumption to make, but unfortunately, there is a big snag involved. The snag is that in many cases the researchers have confused *cause* with *effect*. That is to say, the poor skill (such as poor memory for words) might be the *result* of not being able to read properly, rather than the *cause* of it! In fact, there are at least four situations that might exist in relation to the poor skill and the dyslexia:

- The poor skill might be present in the child from early on, well before he goes to school, and so might cause the dyslexia later.
- The skill might develop poorly over time due to the dyslexia, and so be a result of dyslexia.
- The poor skill and the dyslexia might exist quite separately, but happen to be present together in the same child (or children) by sheer coincidence.
- The poor skill and the dyslexia might each be brought about by some third factor, as yet unknown to us.

As we said above, the majority of studies carried out have used control groups, which are essential to the design of the study. Unfortunately, the control groups have been used incorrectly as they have controlled inappropriate parts of the study. In comparing dyslexic with non-dyslexic children, what has usually been controlled has been the size of the groups, the gender balance, the intelligence levels, the social factors, etc. In other words, all factors likely to affect the outcome have been matched between the groups, *except* the ability to read.

The criticism of these studies is that it can be quite misleading to compare such groups of children by means of age, as the results will not tell the researchers what it is they are hoping to discover. If two groups, each of the same age and intelligence range are matched, then this is a mental age match. But the groups need to be matched by reading age, not mental age, for meaningful results to emerge. That is to say, there is nothing to be learned from comparing 10-year-old dyslexics who have a reading age of 7 with 10-year-old non-dyslexics who read normally (i.e. have a reading age of 10 years). What *should* happen is that the 10-year-old dyslexics should be compared with 7-year-olds who read normally (i.e. have a reading age of 7 years also). This would place both groups, the dyslexics and the controls, at the same level of reading ability and would thereby produce a reading-age match instead of a mental-age match. If this is done and some differences are found, we know that it could not possibly be caused by a difference in reading levels, as both groups are the same. Therefore, the finding would be a significant one.

Having said that, the ideal type of research is difficult to carry out. Ideally, the research would need to be carried out in three distinct stages in relation to dyslexic children:

1   A 'reading-age match' type of study would need to be carried out, as described above. This would show that there actually was some genuine difference (such as a weakness in a particular skill) between dyslexic and other children.
2   A large-scale study carried out over a period of time (likely to be some years in an investigation of this type) would be necessary to determine whether this particular skill weakness could predict future difficulty with learning to read.
3   If the link between this particular skill weakness and future reading progress was found to be strong, the weak skill would need to be improved by teaching, to demonstrate that when this occurs, reading ability also improves.

If something (that we shall call x) causes dyslexia, then it must be present in a child *before* the child starts to make attempts at reading. It is hoped that it would be possible to detect x before the child embarks on the reading process, as described in point 2 above. This kind of study, because of the length of time involved, is described as longitudinal, and would involve children being tested in the years before they start school and being followed up for some years after they have been enrolled. A comparison of the test results obtained at the beginning of the study with success or difficulty in reading later on would show whether there is any relationship between x and dyslexia.

As a word of caution, it should be mentioned that any results obtained might not be as straightforward as they appear, because it is possible that both x and dyslexia are caused by a third unknown factor. Researchers must be constantly on the alert for this type of situation.

Stage 3 above describes the technique that should be used to get around this potential difficulty. Children need to be trained over a period of time in relation to x, the factor being studied. Naturally, a control group of children who are not given any training would be required. If the investigator is correct in her suspicions that x causes dyslexia, then the 'trained group' should show an improvement in reading skills, which the 'non-trained' group will not show.

By using experimental techniques such as those described above, researchers have been able to produce two valuable types of result. First, they have been able to show that a number of long-held beliefs relating to dyslexia do not hold water. Second, they have been able to show that there *is* convincing evidence in relation to phonemic awareness for at least some of the difficulties faced by dyslexic children. Taking the first-mentioned, strong doubts have been cast on the beliefs that dyslexics:

- produce mirror-image reversals when writing
- are particularly poor at perceiving or remembering shapes
- have greater difficulty with cross-modal perception (cannot relate the spoken with the printed word)
- have greater difficulty in producing the correct word when they want to say something
- have poor memory for words.

Research into phonological awareness

With regard to phonological awareness (the main subject of this chapter), more and more attention has been paid over the past 20 or 30 years to children's awareness of the sounds that go to make up the words they hear and use every day.

One study (carried out in 1974) explored the difficulties children experience when attempting to divide up speech into phonemes. The young children, when given some examples of what was expected of them, showed that they could divide words up into syllables quite easily, but found much greater difficulty in separating out the individual phonemes. None of the children aged 5 was able to do the phoneme task; fewer than 20% of those aged 6 were successful; and only 70% of the 7-year-olds were able to do what was required.

Since then, further research has shown a link between this ability to divide up words into phonemes (phonemic segmentation) on the one hand and reading progress on the other. For instance, children have been tested on their ability to find 'the odd one out' in a group of three or four words spoken to them. Sometimes the different phoneme was at the beginning of the 'odd' word:

- bud - bun - rug - bus

sometimes in the middle:

* m<u>u</u>g - pig - dig - wig

and sometimes at the end:

* run - bu<u>t</u> - gun - sun.

The children tested were aged 4 and 5 and had not yet begun to read. When retested three or four years later, there was a close relationship between the scores at 4 and 5 years and their reading ability when aged 8 and 9. The same also applied to their spelling ability and this difference held true even when allowances were made for differences in intelligence.

Children who had made no progress in reading by the age of 6, but who were then given practice in sounds over a two-year period, were found to make more progress in reading than similar children not given such practice.

In another study, two large groups of children, one dyslexic and the other not dyslexic, were compared. The dyslexics did not do well at tasks that required both groups to detect and produce rhyme. This poor performance by the dyslexics resulted despite the fact that both groups were matched by reading age, i.e. the dyslexics were older. Also, the task involved only spoken and not written words. The dyslexics were found to be between three and six times worse than the controls. This is evidence of a definite and specific defect among dyslexic children. Although the dyslexics could actually read as well as the control group, they were far behind in their ability to know whether groups of words rhymed or not.

Studies carried out in Sweden, the US and England have shown that children who have a poor awareness of, and sensitivity to, rhyme during the years before they start learning to read will not be able to read or spell as well as other children some years later. This finding holds true even when children of equal intelligence are compared. Furthermore, the finding holds good only for reading and reading-related skills such as spelling. It has no effect on success in mathematics, for example. In addition, the connection has been found to remain strong for as long as three years. It must be an important factor and other work has confirmed that this is so.

Much research into phonological awareness has been carried out, and continues to be carried out, in many parts of the world. Even a summary could fill at least one book of this size, and probably several. The foregoing is meant to give just a flavour of the type of work that is ongoing and producing some insights.

To people not constantly working with children who are learning to read and sometimes experiencing difficulties, much of what has been said might be rather puzzling. It is difficult for many adults, particularly those who have never had reading problems themselves, to understand why a child should not be able to realize immediately that a word such as 'cat', when spoken, is made up of three smaller sounds (which we will represent as kerr-urr-tuh). At first this seems to be a very easy demand to make on a child, but it is not. Even when a young child is able to distinguish between 'cat' and 'cap' or 'cat' and 'mat' it is still possible for that same child to be completely unaware of the three segments/phonemes in each word and that there is only one segment (or phoneme) difference between each pair. Those who believe that phonemic awareness (or, rather, lack of it) lies at the root of dyslexic children's difficulties claim that it is only when children begin to learn to read that they actually start to think about the small sounds within words. They claim that it is reading that produces an awareness of phonemes and not the other way round. To the dyslexic child, words remain just words - indivisible and impenetrable. What is more, a dyslexic child may be unaware that written letters correspond to sounds, and even after being taught the fact, will not find it easy to connect a particular letter (or pair of letters) with the related sound.

A brief mention should be made of *syntax*, as many people feel that dyslexic children have difficulty with this also. Syntax is the grammatical (that is, correct) arrangement of words in speech or writing so as to make a sentence. For example, it is bad syntax to say or write 'John was running along the road not looking where she was going', as the word 'she' should actually be 'he'. In the same way, it is incorrect to say 'I am going to telephone Mary and speak to them'; 'them' should be 'her'. For the syntax of a sentence to be correct, there must always be consistency with regard to gender, number and tense.

It is interesting to note that semantics (the meaning of words) plays no part in the difficulties shown by dyslexic children. Semantics is closely linked to intelligence, but phonological awareness is very much less so.

Irrespective of the exact cause(s) of dyslexia, a dyslexic child needs help. A variety of approaches can be used to help a child overcome his dyslexic difficulties, and a general picture of these is given in Chapter 12.

Chapter 12
Help for the dyslexic

During the last century and more since dyslexia was first described, and particularly in the past 20 years or so, a considerable body of knowledge has been building up about ways of helping the dyslexic child to read competently. Knowledge about how to help with spelling, handwriting and other skills has also grown, and continues to do so. Older methods have undergone revision and updating. And in recent years there has been a significant growth in reading programmes designed for use with a computer/word processor.

This chapter is intended to summarize the types of help available. It is not possible in a work of this nature to go into great detail, and the aim is to give an overview only.

There are a few general principles on which the overall work is based and these need to be mentioned at the outset. It is acknowledged that those children who are most severely dyslexic tend to make little progress with ordinary teaching methods. However, it is absurd to suggest that they are incapable of ever learning because they have failed to respond to these methods. (You will recall that in Chapter 8 the point was made that dyslexics do make progress over time, given the appropriate help.) However, dyslexic children do not all exhibit the same signs and symptoms, nor is any one symptom present in all dyslexic children to the same degree, so what will be an appropriate teaching method for one child will not necessarily be appropriate for another. The characteristics of the dyslexic are that the dyslexia can be severe, it is often very resistant to normal methods of remediation and it may be accompanied by other difficulties, e.g. visual, auditory or motor. The typical dyslexic child needs to be taught literacy skills for at least part of each day on an individual or small-group basis, and there are arguments to be put forward that certain children will respond best to one approach whereas others - those with different symptoms - will require something different.

There are so many forms of help available for the dyslexic child in school that there is a danger of someone such as a parent, who is attempting to find out about the subject for the first time, becoming confused. Clear-cut information on the subject is often difficult to find.

Any help available is part of the overall situation in which remedial provision is laid on for children, and that help is, in turn, part of the very wide field relating to the normal teaching of reading throughout the country. Because of this, a large number of terms are used, often with no common agreement as to what is meant by any particular one. Different terms used by different writers can mean the same thing. Any parent attempting to find out what help is available is likely to be overwhelmed by such terms as: reading scheme, programme, approach, technique, method, strategy, resource, procedure, system, etc.

An example will make this clear. One recent book describes ARROW, which stands for *A*ural - *R*ead - *R*espond - *O*ral - *W*ritten. The book says:

> This *approach* has been further developed by Lane (1990) under the aegis of the University of Exeter, School of Education in his ARROW *technique*. The *method* has its origins in infant teaching/learning approaches and was originally developed as a *technique* to help in the education of learning impaired pupils with marked difficulties in language skills attending a unit attached to a mainstream school. Children using the *system* will use at least one, and probably all, of the five components of ARROW.

The emphasis in italics is mine, and is there to point out that even in these few lines ARROW has been described as four different things - an approach, a technique, a method and a system. In the normal course of events, one would expect that the teaching approach would be something quite fundamental, indicating the particular direction, so to speak, in which the teaching would be aimed. The approach having been decided, a programme would be planned out, starting at 'Stage 1' and moving through a number of other stages in a set order until the goal of full literacy was reached. Throughout the programme a number of techniques or methods would be employed, particularly if sticking points or places of difficulty were encountered, and to assist in the overall task various aids and items of equipment would be used.

If this is an acceptable description, then by broadening our viewpoint and looking at the overall situation relating to the dyslexic child we can see that there are five main factors involved:

- the *teacher* herself
- the *conditions* under which the child and teacher meet
- the general *approach* followed
- the particular *techniques* or *methods* used from time to time (within a more general *programme*)
- the *equipment* available to the teacher in her task.

The teacher

All teachers must have basic teaching qualifications, which for most newly trained teachers today means a university degree and a Certificate in Education, these two qualifications representing four years of full-time study. Those teachers employed to work with children with special educational needs, tend to have at least one other qualification, usually a Diploma in Special Education, which is awarded after a further full year of study.

The average remedial teacher (who might be called a specialist reading teacher or support teacher, as titles vary from one LEA to another) will usually have a number of years of teaching experience, as the study for the Diploma in Special Education is usually undertaken only after some years of general classroom teaching. In LEA schools throughout the UK, the teachers who provide specialist teaching for children with reading difficulties will vary when it comes to the number and type of qualifications they possess. They will also vary with regard to the number of years of teaching experience they have had, and the type of pupils with whom they have gained their experience.

It will be a proportion of these specialist teachers who will be assigned or appointed to teach dyslexic children. Some, throughout the course of a working week, will be teaching only dyslexics, others will be teaching some dyslexics and some others with reading difficulties due to other causes. Some specialist teachers have had additional training in various approaches/techniques/methods designed specifically to assist dyslexic children. There are many of these, and 30 of them are listed in Table 12.1. They represent most of the major approaches/techniques/methods presently in use in those institutions that specialize in identifying and helping dyslexic children.

As will be apparent, these 30 approaches were published over a period of 58 years (from 1943 to 2001), during which time six of the earlier ones were revised, the latest in 1999. We have described them as approaches/techniques/methods because of the confusion about names that was explained earlier. As we can see, 12 of the 30 are not

Table 12.1 Samples of specialized teaching approaches

1	Fernald Multi-sensory Approach	1943	
2	Gillingham–Stillman Alphabetic Method	1956	
3	Edith Norrie Letter Case	1960	Revised 1970
4	Slingerland Approach	1960	
5	Orton–Gillingham Method	1967	Revised 1987
6	Bannatyne's Colour Phonics	1969	
7	Alpha to Omega	1975	Revised 1990
8	Hickey Method	1977	Revised 1991
9	Peabody Rebus Reading Programme	1979	
10	Bangor Teaching Programme	1982	
11	Aston Index (Revised)	1982	
12	Aston Portfolio Checklist	1982	
13	Spelling Made Easy	1984	
14	Academic and Developmental Learning Disabilities	1984	
15	Children's Written Language Difficulties	1985	
16	Alphabetic Phonics	1985	
17	Tactics for Teaching Dyslexic Students	1986	
18	Dealing with Dyslexia	1986	
19	Bangor Dyslexia Teaching System	1989	Revised 1992
20	Icon Approach	1990	
21	Dyslexia: A Teaching Handbook	1990	
22	Jolly Phonics	1992	
23	Phonological Approach To Teaching	1993	Revised 1999
24	Toe By Toe	1993	
25	Multi-Sensory Learning	1994	
26	Beat Dyslexia	1994	
27	Activity Literacy Kit	1998	
28	Phono-Graphix	1999	
29	Multi-Sensory Teaching System for Reading (MTSR)	1999	
30	Checking Individual Progress in Phonics (ChIPPs)	2001	

given any description, four are called approaches, four phonics, three methods, two programmes, two systems and one each checklist, index and tactics.

The rate at which these approaches/techniques/methods grew in number shows an interesting trend:

- in the decade 1940-49 there was one
- in the decade 1950-59 there was one
- in the decade 1960-69 there were four
- in the decade 1970-79 there were three (plus one revision)
- in the decade 1980-89 there were 10 (plus one revision)
- in the decade 1990-99 there were 10 (plus four revisions)
- in the two years 2000 and 2001 there was one.

Figure 12.1 shows the rapid growth rate, and it could well be that the decade 2000 to 2009 will outstrip those of the 1980s and 1990s.

There are a number of points to be made about these approaches in relation to the teacher. First, there are many available on the market and any specialist teacher is likely to be familiar with at least one and probably more. Second, the approaches themselves vary a great deal in form and content. With some, all is explained in a manual, but with others the teacher is required to attend a training course to become familiar with what is expected.

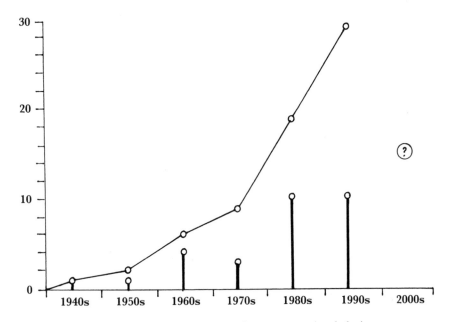

Figure 12.1 The growth in specialized approaches to overcoming dyslexia.

The conditions

The conditions under which a dyslexic child receives specialist teaching can vary tremendously, and will be influenced by a large number of factors, such as:

- the LEA area in which the child lives
- the particular school he attends
- the general facilities available
- the policy of the LEA on such matters
- the wishes of the parents
- the results revealed by the child's assessment

- whether the child has been provided with a Statement of Special Educational Needs (SEN), etc.

The two major factors, which underlie everything, are the amount of specialist teaching provided to the child each week and the setting in which this takes place. A child might be taught for a comparatively short or lengthy total amount of time each week, and the pattern of provision might be twice daily, once daily, twice weekly or some other. The child might be taught by one teacher, or more than one, and each teacher might be a staff member of the institution the child attends, or a visiting specialist.

The child could be taught individually or in a small group (the size of which can vary). He might be withdrawn from his class or be given support within it. It is also possible for the teaching to take place in the child's local school, in a special unit or in a special school. If the special school happens to be the site where the teaching is provided, then this could be either a day school or a residential-type school. At the time of writing, in-class support would appear to be experiencing the highest rate of growth. This fact is influenced strongly by the DfES's policy on inclusion, the aim of which is to have as many of the nation's children as possible educated within a mainstream setting. Running concurrent with this, and to some degree related to it, is the aim of reducing the number of Statements of SEN issued, while at the same time maintaining the type and level of provision the Statement would have described had it been issued.

Many LEAs are of the opinion that dyslexic children do not require segregated provision, and the current move to produce as many 'dyslexia-friendly' schools as possible will go some way towards justifying their stance. Many parents of dyslexic children do not share this philosophy, however, and are determined to have the LEA produce a Statement for their child and, in some cases, to place them in a specialist school or unit.

Other variations are also possible. The direct teaching of reading and other literacy skills is supplemented with various types of support. This may be provided at the systems level of the school, so that teaching groups can be organized, the curriculum planned and teaching materials adapted. It could be that arrangements are made for there always to be two teachers in the classroom (one of whom is always available to assist a special needs pupil), or for parents to be available in a supportive role, or even for other school pupils to help. Paired reading is often used. This could take the form of relaxed reading, shared reading, 'pause, prompt and praise' peer tutoring, etc.

The approach

We shall consider two types of approach that a teacher might make - general and special.

General approaches apply to most children in the course of learning to read, and also to those with difficulties other than dyslexia. Fortunately, there are many approaches to reading that can be taken, and it is part of the teacher's work to ascertain which is most suited to the child. This is bound to depend on matters such as the child's age, his reading attainments, his general intelligence, whether there are literacy difficulties apart from reading, what methods have so far proved to be unsuccessful and whether there are other factors involved, e.g. poor speech. Also, it is possible for a child to be taught by two or more approaches at the same time.

Paired reading has been used with much success in many cases. In recent years, computer-assisted learning (CAL) has developed greatly and opened up a range of opportunities for children with many types of learning difficulty, including dyslexia. The range and quality of the software available to help not only with reading, but also spelling (via the text processing) and handwriting (via the print-out facility) increases almost daily. For well over two decades there has been a growth in the number of publications linking the results of individual assessments with the type of instruction advised for children with literacy difficulties. These have not been designed specifically for children with dyslexia, but nevertheless many dyslexic children have benefited. (Some indication of these is given in Table 12.2.)

Some approaches to teaching dyslexics are much more specialized, and we have already listed 30 of these in Table 12.1. Most of the specialized approaches concentrate on improving the child's ability to develop and use the phonological (particularly the phonemic) skills, which are poorly developed in many dyslexics. Pupils with dyslexia need to be taught many basic skills that most children acquire quite easily. While some believe in building up the weaker skills, others concentrate on a child's strengths, and still more attempt both at once. In many cases, dyslexic children are taught in exactly the same way as non-dyslexics, but there is greater emphasis on matters of structure, detail, assessment, systematic teaching, over-learning and record keeping. Ultimately, much time must be invested, and there is no magic wand that can be waved, nor any kind of instant cure.

Table 12.2 Materials linking assessment and teaching

Early Detection of Reading Difficulties	Clay	1979
Preventing Classroom Failure	Ainscow and Tweddle	1979
Educational Applications of the WISC-R	Nicholson and Alcom	1980
Development of Reading and Related Skills with Pupils of Secondary Age (DORRS)	ILEA	1981
Barking Reading Project	Barking and Dagenham LEA	1982
Classroom Observation Procedure	ILEA	1982
Aston Index (Revised)	Newton and Thompson	1982
Aston Portfolio	Aubrey et al.	1982
Cloze Procedures and the Teaching of Reading	Rye	1982
DATAPAC	Akerman	1982
Linguistic Awareness in Reading Readiness	Downing et al.	1983
QUEST Screening, Diagnosis and Remediation Kit	Robertson et al.	1983
Special Needs Action Programme (SNAP)	Ainscow and Muncey	1984
Making Sense of It (Miscue Analysis)	Arnold	1984
Direct Instruction	Science Research Assoc	1985
Teaching with Precision	Raybuild and Solity	1985
Special Needs in the Primary School: Identification and Intervention	Pearson and Lindsay	1986
Learning Difficulties in Reading and Writing: A Teacher's Manual	Reason and Boote	1986
The Primary Language Record	Barrs et al.	1988
Early Identification of Special Needs	Wiltshire CC Ed Dept	1988
Bromley Screening Pack	Bromley LEA	1989
Touchstones	NFER	1989
Computer-assisted Learning Programmes with Speech Enhancement	Davidson	1990
Sound Linkage Programme	Hatcher	1994
Cognitive profiling System (CoPS)	Lucid	1996
LASS (Secondary)	Lucid	1999
LASS (Junior)	Lucid	2001

Programmes, techniques and methods

Often a teacher will design an individual programme for a child. This is excellent in principle and something to be aimed at for any child with learning difficulties. There are also many commercially produced programmes available today which teachers tend to draw on, either an entire programme or part(s) of one, which fit in well with what they feel the child requires.

The commercial programmes have a lot in common. Most help the child to decipher print by using a phonic approach. To a greater or lesser extent they also employ multisensory methods. Programmes tend to be comprehensive and detailed and they often recommend a particular teaching order. The work is cumulative in so far as a typical programme will start with single letters and build up to words. Also, rote learning is considered necessary, as is over-learning.

Such programmes meet the characteristics recommended by the British Dyslexia Association that teaching should be:

- structured
- sequential
- cumulative
- thorough.

Some commercially produced programmes are:

- Reading Recovery (1988), developed in Ohio, USA
- The English Colour Code Programmed Reading Course (1976)
- Patterns of Sound (1968)
- Pictogram System (1973)
- Signposts to Spelling (1978)
- ARROW (Aural - Read - Respond - Oral - Written) (1990)
- Attack-a-Track.

Some of the many teaching techniques and methods used in the UK are:

- SOS (Simultaneous Oral Spelling)
- self-esteem enhancement
- psychomotor programmes
- embedded pictures
- mnemonic drawings
- the use of tape recorders (often of special design)
- the use of plastic letters
- finger spelling
- syllabification
- cursive script.

As will be apparent, techniques and methods are designed for one specific part of a programme - some to assist with just writing, others designed for spelling, etc. There is a large measure of support for the view that no single approach, method or technique is appropriate for all dyslexic children at all stages in the development of their reading skills. It is unlikely that any two dyslexic children will experience identical approaches, programmes and techniques throughout the years of their school lives.

In 1990, a survey was carried out to find out the opinions of certain important organizations on a number of matters relating to dyslexia. Those contacted were:

- the Department of Education and Science (DES) - since retitled the Department for Education (DFE), and afterwards the Department for Education and Skills (DfES)
- the British Dyslexia Association
- the Dyslexia Institute
- the Dyslexia Unit at the University of Bangor
- the National Association for Remedial Education
- the Assistant Masters and Mistresses Association
- the United Kingdom Reading Association
- National Association of School Masters and Union of Women Teachers (NAS/UWT).

One of the aims of the survey was to discover which teaching approaches, programmes, techniques, methods or types of teaching assistance were recommended by each. The results are given in Table 12.3.

Table 12.3 Types of approach and recommendations

Type of teaching approach/programme, etc.	Recommendations (out of total of 8)
Multisensory	7
Phonics	4
Perceptual training	4
Memory training	3
Contextual clues	3
Curriculum support	3
Study skills	3
Objectives	3

Others that received a mention were:

- support from specialist teacher
- sequencing training
- motor skills training
- spelling rules
- language skills

- automaticity
- number
- enjoyment of reading and writing
- word processing
- use of tapes
- letter-formation training
- word recognition
- reading strategies
- writing strategies
- metacognition
- essay practice
- paired/peer reading
- behavioural skills
- counselling.

(A number of other recommendations were made by the eight organizations and these were of a wide-ranging nature covering matters such as the training of teachers, the design of school buildings and the equipment that should be made available.)

Equipment

The basic equipment available to the teacher will be exactly the same as for any teacher, in as far as the dyslexic child can be taught by means of everyday classroom equipment. Greater importance is attached to the manner in which the teaching is done. The teacher and child should, therefore, have such items as a blackboard, access to a photocopier, and books (including dictionaries), work books and work sheets.

There should also be relevant wall charts, letters of the alphabet available on cards (for example, as in the Edith Norrie Letter Case), letters in plastic mould form, letters cut from sponge, rubber and either 'fuzzy felt' or magnetic ones (preferably both). A sentence maker and flash cards are also likely to be required.

Games that involve letters and words are very valuable to children with reading difficulties, and Scrabble, Snakes and Ladders, Lexicon, etc, should be available. Much can be learned even in a play situation. Advances in information technology have recently brought what was formerly very expensive equipment well within the budget of schools and units. Nowadays it is quite commonplace for a school to have a tape-recorder, audio-cassettes, portable typewriters, small electronic spelling machines and computers capable of word processing. In the past few years - since the mid-1990s - word-processing facilities have 'mushroomed' in schools, and all schools now have a 'computer suite' (and sometimes more than one). Peripherals such as printers are also quite common. All of these can be used to advantage by a dyslexic child.

More specialized equipment also exists, some of it at reasonable cost. Triangular-sectioned rubber pencil grips benefit those with writing difficulties and are quite cheap. The Edith Norrie Letter Case referred to above has proved invaluable over the years since its introduction, as has the SALVA machine (*See-And-Learn-Visual-Aid*).

Support teaching

Having described the overall scene in relation to helping the dyslexic child, it should be said that most children are helped by remaining within their class and being given support teaching. This is a growing trend. There are many reasons for this, but generally the trend is for greater inclusion of children with special educational needs. A survey carried out in 1987 found 14 different forms of support for learning available in mainstream secondary schools, and another survey in 1988 found a mixture of sets, withdrawal, support teaching and special classes. (Withdrawal and support teaching were the two most widely used.) The general philosophy underlying the present approach to children with learning difficulties, is that:

- all members of staff should be aware of, and attempt to help, these children with difficulties
- the children should be given access to the whole of the curriculum
- their learning should be supported
- if possible, the curriculum should be differentiated for them, i.e. delivered at a level and pace appropriate to the learning difficulties they are experiencing.

Earlier in this chapter we gave a brief description of the manner in which support teaching could be organized for a dyslexic child within the ordinary classroom, and there is no need to repeat it here. However, to give some details of the types of outcome of such support, we can list the following:

- specially prepared worksheets
- teaching any specialized vocabulary prior to a lesson
- providing a tape recording of literature being studied

- providing photocopied notes (to save note taking)
- arrangements to tape record notes, etc.
- arrangements for transcribing work from a tape recording
- use of a word processor - including tuition
- tuition related to work organization
- a remedial programme to overcome a specific weakness.

Obviously, many of these will be of assistance to other children with difficulties, not just dyslexics.

We shall complete this chapter by setting down the *principles* on which the teaching of dyslexic children should be based:

1. Teaching to be undertaken only after a full assessment of the child.
2. The diagnosis of the child's difficulties to be made as early as possible.
3. The general approach to be based on utilizing strengths and minimizing weaknesses.
4. Daily tuition to be provided for the severely dyslexic child.
5. All books, etc., used to be stimulating and interesting.
6. Books, etc., not to be those associated with previous classroom failure.
7. The vocabulary used to be controlled.
8. The teaching to be carried out with an individual child or a small group of similar children (although this teaching does *not* need to be on an all-day basis - see point 10).
9. All pressure to be removed from the child.
10. The child to remain with his or her intellectual peers in class and be withdrawn for regular, short spells of individual assistance.
11. Less written work to be expected than from others.
12. Class marks to be awarded on the basis of *oral* responses.
13. Dyslexic child to sit at the front of the class, not in the back row feeling neglected.
14. Dyslexic child to be given access to correct spellings.
15. Teacher to let child have his own alphabetically indexed note-book.
16. Teacher to let the child do homework/classwork with textbooks open.
17. Dyslexic child not to stay on one book too long. After a while a book should be substituted for a different one at the same level.
18. Writing done on the blackboard always to be very clear.
19. Important new words to be written up clearly.

20. Teacher to avoid giving *long* lists of spellings to be learned, as small successes are better than total failures.
21. Like-sounding words (homophones) not to be put together.
22. Mistakes in written work should never be read out in front of the whole class.
23. Emphasis should be placed on the child competing with himself, not others.
24. Withdrawal timetable to avoid impinging on favourite lessons.
25. A time limit for homework should be set.

The next chapter gives various types of advice. It is hoped parents will find all of it useful when trying to get help for their child. Most parents are not familiar with the law relating to special educational needs, nor are they always aware of their rights and the rights of their child. 'A guide through the maze' is required, and Chapter 13 attempts to provide this service.

Chapter 13
Advice for parents

If our society were better organized, then all dyslexic children would be identified early, assessed adequately shortly afterwards, reported on in an efficient manner with their needs fully described, and provided with assistance of the correct type and quality to meet their needs. Unfortunately, real life is far short of what it could be, and so this does not happen for all children.

The aim of this chapter is to provide advice for parents of dyslexic children, describing the difficulties they might encounter at any stage of the process from when the suspicion of dyslexia first arises to when assistance is eventually provided. Suggested courses of action are given for each possible point of difficulty. There are three main stages in the process, each of which can be spread over an indefinite period of time and also broken down into a number of smaller stages. The main stages are:

- when dyslexia is first suspected
- the assessment
- the provision.

Dyslexic children are children with special educational needs (SENs) and, therefore, must always be dealt with by the same overall framework and general processes laid down in law for all such children. We will describe them briefly here so as to be familiar with the overall context in which all education personnel must operate.

The Revised Code of Practice

The Department for Education and Skills (DfES) suggests that schools should attempt to meet a child's SENs by embarking on a staged process. The process was originally set out in 1994 by the DfE (as it then was) in the 134-page booklet entitled 'Code of Practice on the identification and assessment of special educational needs'. However, a revised Code has been in preparation since 2000, and was produced in draft form in July 2000 for the purposes of consultation with concerned parties. It is linked to Part IV of the 1996 Education Act.

Some serious criticisms of the draft revised Code were made by parents, schools and both Houses of Parliament, and all of these were taken into consideration, but at the cost of delaying the production of the final form of the revised Code of Practice. Its implementation has been delayed until January 2002, having originally been intended for January 2001.

What had previously been a five-stage process will now be reduced to three:

- Early Years Action/School Action - (replacing Stages 1 and 2)
- Early Years Action Plus/School Action Plus (replacing Stage 3)
- referral for statutory assessment (replacing Stages 4 and 5).

At Early Years Action/School Action, the educational setting (Early Years setting or school) carries out assessment and lays on the required provision. At Early Years Action Plus/School Action Plus, the setting/school brings in outside specialists to assist in assessment and/or provision. The next step in the sequence, as under the original Code, is to refer for a statutory assessment.

In the revised Code, a very high priority is given to partnership with parents. Parent partnership services will need to be available and LEAs will need to set up a conciliation process. One important new principle embodied in the revised Code will be that the views of the child are to be sought, and taken into account, and should not be influenced by the parent.

In dealing with specific learning difficulties, the draft of the revised Code deals with the nature and range of special learning difficulties, how progress can be defined and how action ought to be related to levels of SEN. It mentions 'evident difficulties in tasks involving specific abilities, such as sequencing, organisation or phonological or short-term memory abilities'. It also states that 'higher levels of difficulty may be indicated by ... literacy performance in the first or second centile' (i.e. at the level of the lowest-performing two percent of the population) and also by' ... 'inability to overcome these weaknesses...'. A final statement of interest to us is that 'Overcoming specific learning difficulties may call for carefully targeted interventions using particular teaching techniques (such as multi-sensory approaches, a focus on phonological awareness, or motor programmes). More generalised support may not be adequate.'

Many agencies, including those concerned with dyslexia, protested that the proposed revised Code had replaced an LEA's duty to 'specify' the special educational provision it intended to make available to a 'Statemented' child, with a requirement to merely 'set out' such provision. The DfES accepted that such a change might be interpreted as the encouragement of vague, rather than clearly defined specialist provision, and has undertaken to amend the guidance on the quantifying of provision.

Finally, additional guidance on implementing the revised SEN Code of Practice will also be published in the form of an 'SEN Toolkit' made available to schools, LEAs and others.

Documents related to the revised Code

This is probably the most appropriate point at which to mention other relevant Acts, government reports, papers, etc.

It was the 1993 Education Act which required the Secretary of State to issue the Code of Practice to all LEAs and the governing bodies of all maintained schools. Certain amendments were made to this Act by the Education Act 1996, but there were no substantial changes made to the law on special education.

A Green Paper, 'Excellence for all children: meeting special educational needs', was published in October 1997, and concerned raising standards, shifting resources to practical support and increasing inclusion. There was emphasis on early identification of difficulties and appropriate intervention, the right of parents to express a preference for a special school place for their child, and an improvement in the monitoring of school-based SEN provision. Local schemes should develop active links with voluntary bodies; parent partnership schemes ought to be employed in resolving parent-LEA disagreements; and children with SENs should be enrolled in ordinary schools unless there are 'compelling reasons' for doing otherwise. Children with SENs are to be treated no less favourably than others.

A related document, 'Meeting special educational needs: a programme of action', was produced in 1998, and not only summarized by timetable the action taken over the previous three years, but described a 'programme' which builds on the 'Green Paper' of 1997.

Underlying assumptions about SENs

That said, the purpose of the Code is to give practical guidance; it cannot and does not attempt to provide every detail of what ought to be done in each individual case. However, it does set out general principles that apply to all children with SENs as well as going into more detail in relation to more specific types of SEN.

Schools have been expected to have SEN policies since 1 August 1995, and these are, of course, available to parents. There are a number of underlying assumptions contained in the Code of Practice, and these can be summarised as:

- The staff of every primary school will be made aware that any child admitted may have (an) as-yet-undetected SEN(s).
- Each child with difficulties ought to be identified, sooner or later, from the overall picture of the child, which will emerge when information from various sources is combined.
- These sources are:
  - the child's performance - as monitored by the teacher
  - the outcomes of baseline assessment
  - the child's progress in the National Literacy and National Numeracy Strategy Frameworks
- the child's performance when following the National Curriculum
- screening instruments
- assessment tools.
- The concerns of parents, and any information provided by them is highly relevant.
- It can also be assumed that in the initial stages of concern:
  - the National Curriculum will be differentiated and/or adapted
  - learning activities will also be differentiated
  - the school will make full use of all available classroom and school resources before calling in outside resources.

Specific learning difficulty/dyslexia

The revised Code devotes five pages to describing in some detail various aspects of how it is to be applied to dyslexia. It covers the nature and range of dyslexia, how progress can be defined and how action taken is to relate to level of need. It also gives three case studies.

In relation to the nature and range of specific learning difficulties, it mentions:

- fine or gross motor skills (difficulties)
- low attainment in one or more curriculum areas
- the fact that there are indications that the difficulty is not global
- signs of frustration
- difficulties with sequencing, organization, phonological skills or short-term memory
- limited skills in verbal exchanges
- delays in forming concepts related to sensory experiences.

Lower and higher levels of difficulty are differentiated.
   In relation to progress, this can be measured by:

- comparing the dyslexic child with non-dyslexics of the same age
- comparing the dyslexic child's 'weak' areas with his 'strong' areas
- comparing the rate of progress now with that made by the child in the past.

In relation to attempting to match the child's level of need with appropriate action, the revised Code acknowledges that for some children the more generalized support may not be adequate. The interventions mentioned for these children with greater need include:

- careful 'targeting'
- multisensory teaching approach
- an emphasis on phonological awareness
- motor programmes
- adult support
- access to information and computer technology (ICT)
- the teaching of study skills
- additional time for key curriculum areas.

The final three listed are described as possibly more effective and less costly than adult support.
   The thinking behind the document is quite clear. The DfES expects all schools to go through a set procedure for every child suspected of having SENs in the belief that this will ensure a thorough assessment of the needs of each child. (It also goes some way to making the assessment process uniform from one LEA to another.)
   The DfES also works on the basis that all children with SENs, when considered as a group, will show great variation from one to the other. There will be a gradient starting with children who have

quite mild needs at one end, progressing through an ever-increasing continuum to severe, multiple and complex needs at the other. The DfES, therefore, expects each child to be 'matched up' to the correct type and quantity of extra assistance that is appropriate for his (or her) individual case. The three suggested stages are set out in Table 13.1.

The description given relates to the procedures to be followed in the primary phase of education, as it is within this phase that the majority of dyslexic children are identified.

What these stages mean, in practical terms, is that once a school identifies a child as a cause for concern, then the school should do its best to see if it can meet the child's needs from within its own resources. If this is tried for an appropriate period of time and found not to be effective, then a specialist teacher or other relevant person should be called in to advise, and the school should act on that. In the event of this not being successful, referral needs to be made to the Educational Psychology Service so that the school's educational psychologist can assess the child and give appropriate advice.

Should the psychologist feel that the child would benefit from a full multidisciplinary assessment she will inform the LEA of her opinion and the LEA will decide whether to proceed with this. In the event that they do so, they must finally consider all the evidence presented to them and decide whether the child has difficulties that are severe and/or complex, etc.

If the LEA decides that the child does fall into one or other of these two categories, then it must issue a 'Statement of Special Educational Needs', in which not only the child's needs are described, but also the provision that is going to be laid on to help meet those needs. The school or unit where it is intended the needs will be met should also be included. (The Statement is aimed at safe-guarding the child's rights to be provided with something different or extra. Once the Statement is issued, the provision *must* be laid on and the child's right to such provision becomes legally protected.) The Statement cannot be amended or withdrawn without sound educa-tional justification. The child should be monitored and reported on, at least annually. The Statement must then be reviewed in the light of the findings, with provisions amended as appropriate. That is to say, the LEA must increase the provision if the level is found to be insufficient, but it can also decrease or even terminate it, if this is felt to be justified. Any changes must be noted in the Statement, and when it is felt that extra provision is no longer required, then the Statement is withdrawn.

Table 13.1 Stages, action to be followed and agency involved during the primary phase relating to a child with special educational needs

STAGE	ACTION	AGENCY
School Action	• Child's class teacher (CT) consults with parents and together they AGREE that child may need further support, etc. • Assistance of SENCo is sought • CT and SENCo collect all available information about the child and seek additional information from the parents • SENCo takes the lead in further assessment, planning support, monitoring progress and reviewing action • CT remains responsible for working with the child on a daily basis • SENCo and CT decide on the ACTION needed to help the child progress • SENCo draws up an Individual Education Plan (IEP) for the child	School
School Action Plus	• School consults outside specialist • External support services should advise about new IEPs/fresh targets etc., provide more specialist assessment and also support for particular activities • SENCo with CT and co-ordination external specialists consider different teaching approaches/ appropriate equipment/suitable materials/use of IT so that: • A new IEP can be produced	School
Referral for Assessment	• The LEA decides quickly whether a statutory assessment of the child's SENs is necessary by working co-operatively with the parents, school and other agencies • If so, conducts the assessment in co-operation with the parents, etc. • Considers the evidence and decides whether to draw up a 'Statement' or not • If not, produces a 'Note in Lieu' of 'Statement' • If so, produces a proposed (draft) 'Statement' for the parents to consider. Part 4 (placement details) will be left blank • When appropriate, produces a final 'Statement' for the parents • Gives parents written notice of their rights of appeal to the Tribunal for Special Educational Needs (due to be retitled to include Disability) • Gives parents the name of the LEA person to whom they may apply for information and advice	LEA

So much for the theory. As will be appreciated, the Code of Practice is set out in very general terms because it applies to all children with SENs, not just dyslexics. Children with SENs form a very wide-ranging group and display many types of difficulty. Most of these can be present in a child in varying degrees as well as in various combinations. It is generally held that 20% of children will have SENs at some stage during the 11 or more years of their statutory education, but that only 2% will have needs that are sufficiently serious to justify the provision of a Statement.

We must now consider each of the three important stages we mentioned at the beginning of the chapter. (These are not to be confused with the three stages of assessment set out in the Code of Practice.)

When dyslexia is first suspected

A number of problems can arise with dyslexic children, as any parent will appreciate. In the first place, many dyslexic children come to the attention of parents and teachers as having difficulty with reading, and so it can often be difficult, depending on the circumstances, to distinguish a dyslexic child from a child who is generally slow. It could well be some time before the true nature of the child's reading difficulty becomes known. Another possible problem is that it could be the parents, rather than the school, who first suspect dyslexia, and in this case they will need to bring their suspicions to the head teacher's attention. Whoever first suspects dyslexia is not important. What *is* important is that the suspicions must be shared immediately - parents with school or school with parents. At this stage, it is the communication that is vital, in order to speed up getting help to the child, as well as home-school co-operation.

Generally speaking, matters are probably more likely to proceed in a straightforward manner if the school is first to suspect dyslexia and then informs the parents, as in these circumstances parents tend to co-operate fully in what the school suggests. However, if it is the parents who first bring their suspicions to the school, it is more likely that misunderstandings or delays could arise. In most cases, the school will do all it can to allay parents' worries and meet their wishes, but sometimes the school will not be of the same opinion as the parents, or feel that the evidence available is not strong enough to support such suspicions. In some cases, they may even believe that the parents are over-anxious. It could also be the case that the school would like further time to work with the child before reaching a decision as to whether dyslexia is involved.

Ideally, it will require only a discussion between parents and head teacher to produce agreement on both sides about what is to be done, and the timing of such action. If, for whatever reason, it is not possible for parents and school to agree on the nature of the child's difficulties, then the matter can easily be resolved by referring the child to the educational psychologist. Should the school be reluctant to refer the child, it is quite in order for the parents to make the referral themselves, but this is probably best achieved by the parents writing direct to the LEA.

Of course, the school and parents could be in complete agreement that dyslexia is the cause of the child's difficulties, but the school might consider it unnecessary to refer him to the educational psychologist. The school might feel that the severity of the problem is not as great as the parents believe it to be, or that the child can be helped sufficiently from within the school's own resources. Obviously, parents should carefully consider what the school has to say on the matter, but if, in the final analysis, there is disagreement, then the parents are quite entitled to make the referral themselves.

The assessment

When, by whatever means, the educational psychologist is brought into contact with the child, there are some aspects of the process that might cause parental concern, or at least give rise to questions. It is to be hoped that the child will be seen shortly after referral or at least without too long a delay. If the educational psychologist has a lengthy waiting list, there is little that can be done except to request that some priority is given. This might result in an earlier referral, particularly if the parents are willing to accept an appointment at short notice in the event of a cancellation.

Of more importance, is the actual assessment itself (including the results, the psychologist's interpretation and the recommendations). The parents should be satisfied that the assessment was sufficiently thorough to properly investigate the child's difficulties, describes them accurately and leads to some conclusions being drawn. Some impression will be gained from what the psychologist says in interview afterwards, but the parents can only act on what is contained in the written report.

If the parents feels that the assessment was not sufficiently thorough, then they can request that the psychologist does further investigations. If the parents are unhappy about the actual findings because, for instance, they do not conform with what they themselves know about their child, then it is always possible to request a second opinion. The same applies if the parents agree with the findings but not the recommendations. For instance, if the psychologist does not feel that the child should undergo the 'Statementing' procedure, but the parents wish for it to happen, then an appeal is also possible in this situation.

The provision

Dyslexic children vary considerably from one to another, particularly in the degree to which they are affected, so it is not possible to discuss the provision for such children in more than vague terms. What also complicates the overall picture is that the provision available for dyslexic children varies from one LEA to the next, and even between schools within the same LEA.

What is important is that any particular dyslexic child gets the correct type and quantity of assistance to adequately remedy his difficulties *irrespective* of whether a 'Statement' has been issued or not. After the child's needs have been adequately assessed, and the necessary help agreed on, then that help *must* be provided. As part and parcel of the same process, regular reviews of the child's progress need to be carried out so as to ensure that what is being provided is effective. If parents feel that provision is inadequate or inappropriate, then they have the right to ask for their child's situation to be reconsidered.

Figure 13.1 summarizes the stages that a dyslexic child with a significant degree of difficulty is likely to go through before being provided with a 'Statement of Special Educational Needs' by his LEA, and given the necessary help. The flow diagram also includes details relating to a child whose difficulties are less serious.

It would be incorrect to assume that the general situation is a pessimistic one, and that assessment and help will never be provided for a dyslexic child unless the parents embark on a lengthy and bitter battle with their LEA. In fact, the opposite is true. Over time, teachers and their LEAs have become more aware of dyslexia, its prevalence and the need for resources to assist with it. More children are being recognized, assessed, diagnosed and recommended for specialist help. More teachers are undergoing the necessary training to be able to provide the requisite expertise. As time progresses, the situation for dyslexic children is seen more and more to be one of constant improvement. The fact that specific learning difficulties were described in the original Code of Practice is tangible confirmation of this.

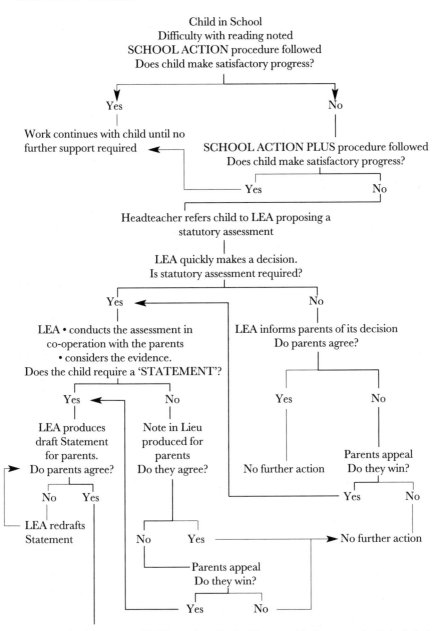

- STATEMENT of SENs produced in final format with placement details included
- Written notice of parental rights to appeal to a TRIBUNAL is given
- The name of the LEA PERSON who will provide advice and information is given

- Extra educational resources assigned to the child
- Progress is kept under regular review
- Statement is maintained/amended/withdrawn as appropriate

Figure 13.1 Stages leading to the production of a Statement of Special Educational Needs.

Of course, the rate of improvement in the situation is not as rapid as parents would wish, and needs are not yet being fully met, but the overall situation at present is definitely an improvement on that of some years ago. The aim of this chapter is to provide guidance to those comparatively few parents who *might* encounter some difficulty at some stage. It is not thought that all or even most parents will face any serious problems. (For those who may find it useful, the whole process has been summarized in Table 13.2.)

Parents' rights

Today's parents have far more rights with respect to their children's education than ever before. When a child has SENs, parental rights become particularly powerful and far-reaching.

It is probably worthwhile setting these out in detail, as not all parents are aware of just what rights they have when problems arise with their child's educational progress, such that assessment is required and SENs are diagnosed. It is also worth knowing that there are many independent agencies that a parent can turn to for advice and support if they encounter difficulties when attempting to gain help for their dyslexic child. Different rights apply to different stages in the assessment procedure, and so have been gathered together accordingly in the box below.

Parents' rights in relation to their child's SENs and the assessment of those needs under the 1996 Education Act

Parents have the right:
When choosing a school...

1. ...to obtain in writing general information about the range of special educational provision available with their LEA. (Each LEA produces a booklet, which is updated annually.)
2. ...to obtain in writing specific information about a particular school or schools. (Each school produces a booklet, which is updated annually.)
3. ...to visit any school to ask questions, etc.

In assessment procedures...

4. ...to request an assessment of their child at any stage.

(contd. p 208)

Table 13.2 The resolution of parental grievances

Area of concern	Possible action
Parents concerned that a child has reading difficulties but concern not shared by school	Seek clarification from the class teacher and the SENCo
School shares parental concern but feels that dyslexia is not the cause	Request the opinion of an LEA (or other) specialist teacher. If still unresolved request the educational psychologist (EP's) opinion.
Parents and school agree dyslexia the likely cause but school feels not severe enough to warrant further action	Contact the LEA's Director of Education and request an EP's assessment
Child assessed by EP but parents unhappy about the nature of the assessment (e.g. not full enough)	Discuss with the EP and request more detailed assessment. If still unresolved contact the principal EP (PEP)
Parents satisfied with the assessment itself but disagree with the finding (e.g. they contradict what parents feel)	Discuss with the EP. If still unresolved a second opinion can be sought via the PEP
Parents satisfied with the assessment but not with the conclusions (e.g. child not thought to be dyslexic)	as above
Parents satisfied with assessment in general but not with the EP's recommendations (e.g. no extra support required)	as above
Parents satisfied with the EP's assessment but not with the LEAs decision (e.g. not to carry out a formal assessment)	Appeal against the LEA decision to a Special Educational Needs Tribunal
Parents agree with all aspects of the formal Assessment but not with the type and/or the amount of provsion proposed	as above

5.   ...to make a complaint if this request is refused and they consider the refusal to be unreasonable.

For children under 5 (not relevant in the case of dyslexic children)...

6.   ...to refuse an LEA request for an assessment if their child is under the age of 2 years.
7.   ...to be informed by the health authority if it considers that their child under 5 has SENs.
8.   ...to obtain from the health authority information about any voluntary agency, which it believes, might be able to help them.
9.   ...to be advised by their LEA, if their child is under 2, of the best way of helping their child (e.g. nursery provision, etc).

If the LEA requests an assessment...

10.   ...to early consultation and full discussion about their child's difficulties.
11.   ...to have their views and feelings taken into account (i.e. be given an opportunity to put them in writing and have them circulated to concerned professionals).

If the LEA decides to go ahead with assessment...

12.   ...to have explained to them the procedure that is to be followed.
13.   ...to be given the name of someone in the LEA who can be contacted for more information.
14.   ...to be given 29 days to make a 'representation' to the LEA (i.e. be given the opportunity to tell the LEA whether or not they agree with the decision and to gather any reports, etc., in support).

When the assessment is being made...

15.   ...to attend any interview their child has.
16.   ...to expect that relevant professionals are supplied with a copy of their representations.
17.   ...to be informed of the purpose of any examination, also where and when it is to take place, how to get more information and how to make their views known.

18. ...to refuse permission for a move to another school for a short period.

After the assessment...

19. ...to be informed, in writing, of the LEA's decision whether to produce a Statement of Special Educational Needs.
20. ...to be given a draft version of the Statement for their comments.
21. ...to be given an accompanying copy of all reports and evidence submitted by the various professional advisers.
22. ...to ask for a meeting with the LEA to clarify anything they are unsure of, etc. (This request is to be made within 15 days.)
23. ...to request a further meeting after this one to question any of the professionals. (This request must be made within 15 days of the first meeting.)
24. ...to put their final comments about, and criticisms of, the draft Statement to the LEA, and also to make their own alternative proposals.

Getting help...

25. ...to consult their own advisers and get a second opinion from, for example, The Panel of Independent Experts on Special Educational Needs.

The Statement of Special Educational Needs...

26. ...to appeal against the LEA decision not to produce a Statement if they believe one should be produced.

Appealing against the Statement...

27. ...to appeal against the Statement or any part of it if they feel there is justification in doing so.
28. ...to be given 14 days' notice of the time and place of the appeal, and for it to be held in an accessible place, at a convenient time.
29. ...to have a friend or representative at the hearing of the appeal.
30. ...to have witnesses at the appeal.

31. ...to submit written statements from experts.

The appeal...

32. ...to be informed in writing of the decision.
33. ...to appeal in writing if still unhappy.
34. ...to complain if they feel that the behaviour of the appeal committee was unfair.

Reviews and reassessments

35. ...to be fully involved in the annual review procedure.
36. ...to complain if this is refused.
37. ...to request reassessment of their child if a change in circumstances occurs.
38. ...for their child to be the subject of a special annual review when in year 9 and for the annual review to involve the Connexions Service which will consult with the head teacher in the drawing up of a transition plan.
39. ...to request reassessment if they move to another area.
40. ...to have their child in receipt of full-time education up to the age of 19 years.

General advice

In all your contacts with your LEA or other organisation keep all letters you receive, make a copy of any letter you send out, note the date of *receipt* of any letter as well as the date *on* the letter) and keep a note of any telephone calls you make or receive. Always note the name of any person to whom you speak, as well as their title, telephone number, extension number, etc., what was said on either side, etc. If anything of importance is ever said to you in interview or over the telephone, request that it be confirmed in writing within the near future.

When writing to the LEA, particularly if protesting about, or appealing against a decision, be as factual as possible and not emotional. State your case as plainly and simply as possible in the first instance, and then add your reasons for thinking what you do. Give as many facts and as much evidence as possible to back up your case.

Try to be positive rather than negative and critical in what you write. State your case from your child's point of view rather than your own, or that of another person. Prepare what you want to put across in rough first and check it in case there are any flaws or contradictions that need to be amended. (Getting a friend to go over what you have prepared can be very useful.) At all times when writing, *concentrate on your child* and not on anyone or anything else.

Parents who might become involved in a Special Educational Needs Tribunal might like to know that between 1995 and 2000 the number of appeals to the Tribunal increased by more than 100%. Parents won 72% of 'Statement' appeals, 64% of 'Assessment' appeals, and 85% of those relating to insufficient provision.

For the sake of completeness, the next chapter covers issues not yet dealt with, but which are often encountered by a parent quite early on in the process of trying to learn about dyslexia.

Chapter 14
Other issues and questions

The subject of dyslexia gives rise to many arguments between individuals and groups. A parent attempting to learn what he or she can about dyslexia is bound to run up against these debates sooner or later, and before long could be in a position where it is necessary to 'take sides'. Parents will disagree with LEAs, LEAs will disagree with bodies such as the British Dyslexia Association (BDA) and Dyslexia Institute (DI), one psychologist will disagree with another, and the medical world is likely to be in dispute with the field of education.

There are many matters that give rise to arguments, but there are three in particular that cause more disagreement than most:

- Does dyslexia exist?
- Is dyslexia more a medical or an educational matter?
- Should difficulties with reading, spelling, writing, etc., be called dyslexia or is specific learning difficulties (SpLDs) more accurate?

The professionals also disagree over other matters, such as whether dyslexia can be diagnosed accurately, whether it is useful to talk about a child's potential in relation to dyslexia, whether differences between children are basically those of kind (qualitative) or merely degree (quantitative), and how accurate it is to claim that there are different types of dyslexia. However, the three singled out above get much more publicity than others, and so we shall lead with them.

Does dyslexia exist?

The existence of dyslexia is not accepted by every worker in the field of literacy difficulties. Many dedicated and highly respected psychologists and educationists, most of whom are based at universities and constantly involved in research, argue against the existence of such a phenomenon as dyslexia.

The attitude generally adopted is that those children referred to as dyslexic are not a separate group from other children who have reading difficulties because they are generally slow. They argue that dyslexic children are part of the whole group of children with reading difficulties and that the children in this group blend into one another in a gradual manner as part of a continuum. In other words, dyslexic children are not different *in kind* from other poor readers, but only *in degree*. They will agree that there are *quantitative* differences, but not *qualitative* ones.

Because of the nature of the difficulties shown by the children we are concerned with, it is easy to understand why some workers should adopt this stance. In 1972, the Advisory Committee on Handicapped Children, which produced the Tizard Report, accepted that some children did experience severe and often long-lasting difficulties in learning to read, but found that there was no evidence to show that a collection of symptoms (i.e. a syndrome) of developmental dyslexia existed. However, the precise pattern of abilities that characterized the children considered to have a specific reading difficulty of any sort remained obscure. The Advisory Committee could not specify any procedure that could be used to identify such children.

About 30 years have passed since then, but the debate continues. In 1979-80, education and medical bodies (the Schools Council, the CSE Board, the GCE Board and the British Medical Association) were unable to formulate a working definition of the term dyslexia. In 1981, the Undersecretary of State referred to dyslexia as a condition 'which is difficult to define', and also said, 'There is much stale argument over what is or is not dyslexia.'

In 1983, a government circular stated, 'Many educational and child psychologists had, and still have, serious reservations concerning the validity of the concept of dyslexia.'

At the present time, some psychologists are willing to use the term dyslexia in a descriptive manner only. Others refuse to use the term at all, as they consider the evidence on which the claim for the existence of dyslexia is based to be insufficient. The concept of dyslexia has come in for some very strong comments from some quarters. The late Professor Meredith, of Leeds University, referred to it as 'the unidentified flying object of psychology', and other critics have described it as a syndrome shown by the children of middle-class parents. However, most workers with objections to the concept of dyslexia express their reservations in a context of soundly based professional reasons.

The term 'dyslexia' is criticized because of the lack of an agreed working definition, as well as there being no universally agreed means of alleviating the condition. The arbitrary nature of the dividing line between children considered to have some specific type of reading difficulty and those outside tends to be a matter of controversy. In our present state of knowledge, which is rather limited, we still do not know:

- the cause(s) of dyslexia
- the exact signs or characteristics by which we can be sure that it is present in a child
- how to identify it in every case
- how to predict the manner in which it will develop within any particular child
- exactly how to counteract its effects.

For a condition to exist in medicine or psychology, one or more of these five characteristics should be present, otherwise we are on rather shaky ground. On the other hand, many conditions in the past were known to exist before they could be described so precisely.

Because the task of accurately defining and identifying dyslexia has been such a difficult one, a working party was set up in 1998 by the Division of Educational and Child Psychology, and this resulted in the definition of dyslexia given in Appendix I (definition I). How widely it will be accepted, however, remains to be seen.

The fact that any child who demonstrates reading and spelling difficulties (after experiencing appropriate learning opportunities) is to be regarded as dyslexic *irrespective of the child's general, overall ability* will not sit easily in some areas of the dyslexic world. This is not to deny the ethical worth of the aim of providing as much assistance as possible to all children with reading and spelling difficulties, irrespective of exact causation. Unfortunately, worthy aims often meet with unsuccessful applications. Parent groups have already voiced their concerns that the definition seems to rule out early identification. The words '...persistent despite appropriate learning opportunities...' imply that dyslexia will be identified only after the child has been taught for some time, whereas they, understandably enough, seek as early identification as possible.

We now turn to the second main bone of contention.

Is dyslexia a medical or an educational matter?

The fact that two different professions have until recently been in dispute as to who was, so to speak, the rightful 'owner' of dyslexia goes back to the very origins of the discovery and description of dyslexia.

Because dyslexia relates to reading and reading-associated skills, it is not surprising that it did not become properly detected or reported on by any professional person until education became more widespread, and it was quite commonplace for ordinary people to be able to read and write.

It was not until 1877 that the loss of an adult's ability to read was professionally reported by a German physician, Kussmaul. However, as a point of interest it should be pointed out that the condition had almost certainly been encountered and remarked upon by others. For instance, the classic reforming novelist Charles Dickens in *Bleak House*, which was published in 1852, describes the character of Mr Krook, a ship's chandler, who is almost certainly dyslexic. He knows all the letters of the alphabet and can copy words from memory, but cannot read them, despite having tried for the previous 25 years. He pastes up alphabets in the back room of his shop and is described as 'grubbing away at teaching himself to read and write, without getting on a bit'. He spells out words from papers that he has, 'chalking them over the table and the shop wall and asking people what this is and what this is...'. Another character says of Krook: 'Read! He'll never read. He can make all the letters separately and he knows most of them separately when he sees them; he has got that much under me; but he can't put them together...'.

It is quite probable that this description, published 25 years before Kussmaul described alexia (which he called 'word blindness'), is not the earliest one available.

The subject of dyslexia was virtually the exclusive property of the medical profession for the next 50 years or so, as Table 14.1 shows. It lists the earliest historic milestones in the development of our knowledge about dyslexia.

A dyslexic-type difficulty was first officially reported in 1877, but was then called 'word blindness'. The German physician Kussmaul was describing the condition he had found in an adult who had originally been able to read but had then lost the ability to do so. The term 'word blindness' is an inaccurate one, but nevertheless, has stuck in the public mind and entered everyday speech, becoming quite firmly linked with the condition and giving it a medical type of

Table 14.1 Milestones in knowledge about dyslexia

Date	Name	Profession	Occupation	Term used	Had studied
1877	Kussmaul	**Medicine**	Physician	Word blindness	Adults
1887	Berlin	**Medicine**	Professor	Dyslexia	Adults
1895	Hinshelwood	**Medicine**	Eye surgeon	Word blindness	Adults
1896	Kerr	**Medicine**	Medical Officer of Health	Congenital word blindness	Children
1896	Pringle-Morgan	**Medicine**	General Practitioner	Congenital word blindness	Children
1925	Orton	**Medicine**	Psychiatrist	Specific reading difficulties	Children

association. The condition Kussmaul described would nowadays be called alexia or acquired dyslexia.

The term 'dyslexia' was not used for a further 10 years, until Professor Berlin used it to describe the acquired condition, again in an adult. The developmental condition, which is found in children, was not reported officially until 1896, and in that year two different people, by sheer coincidence, did so. Both Dr James Kerr (a medical officer of health in Bradford) and Dr Pringle-Morgan (a general practitioner from the south coast) described various children they had encountered with the condition. They each used the term 'congenital word blindness', which was able to convey the point that it was a condition the children had possessed throughout their lives; it had not been acquired as in the cases of adults described by the earlier reports. The term 'congenital word blindness' used by these two doctors is today known as 'developmental dyslexia' (which in this book we call simply 'dyslexia') and Kerr and Pringle-Morgan are acknowledged to be the discoverers of dyslexia in children.

The medical profession was the only one to describe or report on the condition for many decades, as the first educational psychologist in Great Britain was not appointed until 1913. (This was Cyril Burt -

who was later knighted - appointed to the London County Council). Psychologists during this period (the late 19th and early 20th centuries) did a great deal of work designed to help children and their parents overcome difficulties related to literacy. Cyril Burt produced much work of this nature, and the majority of educational psychologists who followed him into the profession have shown similar interest.

When it is appreciated that medical personnel place emphasis on disorder, disease and treatment, but that psychologists place emphasis on learning processes and development, it is easy to understand that contrasting interpretations are inevitable. In 1981, McDonald Critchley (a neurologist) wrote that 'I have always insisted that the diagnosis of specific developmental dyslexia is a *medical* responsibility'. But in the same year, Whittaker (an educational psychologist), wrote: 'We do not have a medical condition called dyslexia, we have an *educational* problem about how to teach more effectively'. These two workers and their viewpoints sum up the issue in the debate very effectively.

As a final comment we need to say that the BMA has advised its members that dyslexia is not basically a medical problem. For the sake of balance it also needs to be said that neurologists disagree with this. We now turn to the third area of contention.

Dyslexia versus specific learning difficulties (SpLDs)

The debate centres on which of these two is the more appropriate term to use when referring to children who have reading or other literacy difficulties. As will be appreciated, the whole study of dyslexia has been disadvantaged from the earliest days by the use of different terms to describe the type of reading difficulties we are concerned with. We know from Table 14.1 that 'word blindness' and 'dyslexia' were used in the case of adults, and 'congenital word blindness' and 'specific reading difficulties' were used to refer to children. With the passage of time the labels have multiplied, each new one being introduced in an attempt to clarify matters and produce general acceptance.

'Congenital word blindness' is unsuitable, as the condition is not any kind of blindness. 'Strephosymbolia', which was used by Orton (who is listed in the table), means the twisting of symbols. It is not a suitable term, as the confusion of letters such as 'b' and 'd', or words such as 'saw' and 'was', is only part of the total picture. 'Developmental dyslexia' has much to recommend it, as the word 'developmental' clearly indicates that children and not adults are involved.

The manner in which dyslexia or dyslexic-type difficulties has been defined by various organizations over the past quarter century or so, gives insight into the confusion and arguments that exist today. We have discussed these at some length in Chapter 7 and analysed the essential elements of them, comparing one with another, although it has not been necessary to give each definition at length. Of the five different names used by the nine different bodies/organizations dealt with in Chapter 7, it has been found that, over the years, three have dropped out of use, with only two - dyslexia and specific learning difficulties - remaining. However, these two survive in an atmosphere of strong dispute. A number of different attitudes have been expressed, each by its own group of supporters. These are:

• dyslexia and SpLDs are different
• dyslexia and SpLDs are the same
• dyslexia is one of a number of SpLDs
• it does not matter whether they are the same or not.

Generally speaking, dyslexia is the term favoured by most workers in the medical field, whereas SpLDs tends to be used by those in education. There is also the general assumption that dyslexia is a part (or subset) of SpLDs. Over the years psychologists have come to accept that there could be a variety of specific developmental dyslexias (which is abbreviated to 'dyslexia') and that these could all be included within SpLDs, as these constitute a wide group of difficulties.

Many parents, teachers and psychologists are in agreement that such matters are irrelevant, and that all energy ought to be invested in identifying the children concerned more effectively by accurate assessment methods, as well as helping them by using more effective teaching techniques.

Other questions

We finish this chapter by answering a number of questions commonly asked by parents, but not covered earlier in the book.

Is dyslexia inherited?

For almost a century it has been known that any child with dyslexia is likely to have one or more close relatives who are dyslexic also; dyslexia runs in families. However, until recently, it was not known for certain whether this situation arises because dyslexia can be inherited or rather because the dyslexic family members shared the same environment which brought the dyslexia about.

Recent studies have concentrated on twins (both identical and non-identical types) or other family members. The results have shown that there is a genetic cause; dyslexia *can* be inherited. In fact, this is a gross over-simplification of the situation. What is inherited is not dyslexia itself, but aspects of phonological processing which, if deficient, can produce difficulties in learning to read. Further work has shown that deficits in phonological skills are themselves the result of an inherited weakness in segmental language skills; the situation can be summarized roughly as in Figure 14.1.

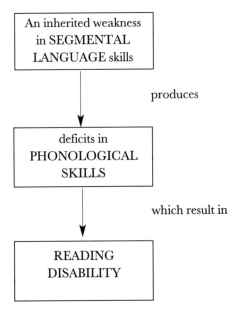

Figure 14.1 Heredity aspects of dyslexia.

The exact means by which the dyslexia is inherited is not yet known, but there are several possible mechanisms. Every human being develops from a single egg, which contains 23 pairs of chromosomes. One of each pair comes from the father and the other from the mother. All of our chromosomes are set by the contents of this first single cell. Each chromosome is made up of a string of small genes and each gene carries the hereditary chemicals which distinguish our characteristics - height, weight, skin pigmentation, eye colour, susceptibility to disease, etc. Each pair of chromosomes is different from all other pairs. They have been numbered for identification purposes and the genes strung out along them are in the process of being mapped out in great detail. Deficits, weaknesses and mutations are passed on from one generation to the next if one gene on one chromosome becomes altered appropriately. One pair of chromosomes determines the sex of the individual, and sometimes defects are passed on by genes on these chromosomes and so become sex-linked characteristics.

It is possible that dyslexia is brought about by the combined influence of a number of genes, but there is also evidence to suggest that it is caused by a single dominant gene. The exact situation is far from clear-cut and work is still ongoing. Some research has produced evidence that chromosome 15 is linked to dyslexia, but other studies have not confirmed this. There is also evidence for a linkage on chromosome 6, and this evidence has been gathered from at least two independent sources and was reported on in late 1994. (Interestingly, the point on chromosome 6 that has been identified is in the same region as the human leukocyte antigen complex, and may explain an often-reported association between dyslexia and autoimmune disease.)

Using a new technique and a far more accurate gene map than has been available before, Professor Stein (of Oxford University) has discovered that the region of interest on chromosome 6 contains many genes, but the relevant one has not yet been identified. This discovery will hopefully go a long way to dispelling the myth that dyslexia is merely a 'middle-class' syndrome.

People working in the field of heredity/genetics have shown that there is as much as a 50% probability of a boy becoming dyslexic if his father is dyslexic. The chances drop to about 40% if it is his mother who is affected. There is a lower probability still of a girl developing dyslexia in similar circumstances. However, to put the situation into its correct perspective, it needs also to be stated that environmental factors play a substantial role in the word-recognition skills of children with dyslexia.

One of the most important environmental factors is reading experience. In other words, reading will improve more in a child the more that child is exposed to the printed word. This applies even to those children who have severe deficits in their phonological skills. Hence genetic influences may constrain the speed or ease of reading development, but environmental factors - such as improved reading instruction and greater reading experience - may compensate for the constraints imposed.

Dyslexics can eventually achieve high levels of word recognition, but still tend to remain deficient in phonological coding skills. Hence, reading experience alone may not be sufficient, and recent work has looked at matters such as the training of particular language skills in children who are at the pre-reading stage. Such training may reduce the likelihood of reading difficulties later on.

Why are more boys than girls dyslexic?

Dyslexic boys outnumber girls by a ratio of 3, 4 or even 5 to 1. One suggested reason is that dyslexia is a sex-linked phenomenon, but it is also suggested that it is because boys develop more slowly than girls.

Are there signs by which we can identify dyslexic children?

There are no 'hard' signs and the question of whether there are 'soft' signs is one surrounded by confusion. Complications at the time of birth can lead to some children having reading difficulties later in life, but this does not apply in all cases. There is no single 'soft' sign associated with dyslexia and so searches have been made for a group of signs. Signs such as difficulty in sequencing, mirror writing, letter reversals, cross laterality and finger agnosia have been suggested. However, there is no general agreement about their significance as they are often present in efficient readers.

Are reading difficulties associated with speech problems or delayed speech?

There is a substantial amount of evidence confirming that some children with speech defects have dyslexia or retardation in reading.

Do hearing problems cause reading difficulties?

Yes, in all children affected, irrespective of whether the difficulties are dyslexic or not.

Are dyslexic children likely to have behaviour problems?

It is quite possible that these will develop. The DfES makes specific mention of them in the Code of Practice. It talks about behavioural difficulties (linked to signs of frustration and/or low self-esteem) that are sometimes associated with SpLDs. It also mentions factors such as avoidance of tasks, disengagement from learning and non-attendance at school.

Do dyslexic children have handwriting problems or do they produce mirror writing?

Some dyslexic children demonstrate handwriting problems, as do some non-dyslexics. The same applies to mirror writing. The cause could be maturational lag or some kind of generalized response in some children when they start learning to write. It could be that these children are paying attention only to a letter's shape and not its orientation, i.e. they could be learning a bad habit very efficiently. It is also possible that poor handwriting and reversals are caused by uncertainty and confusion about how to write down what they want to say.

Is dyslexia the result of a language deficiency?

Research suggests that various deficits in language are at the root of reading problems, but the link is a tenuous one. A more reasonable explanation could be that the language difficulties are the *result* of a child's lack of reading progress. Also, many children who have no language deficits still find reading difficult.

Chapter 15
Useful information

It goes without saying that it is hoped that every parent of a dyslexic child will meet with goodwill and co-operation from all concerned in the education system, and that as a result their child will be identified early, assessed without delay, have their needs fully described and then met; and that the LEA will lay on appropriate resources to an adequate degree, keep the child's progress under regular review and maintain the situation while the needs remain.

Even were this ideal situation actually to be borne out, there is no doubt that the parent concerned would still benefit a great deal from knowledge about their rights, their child's rights, and the existence of voluntary agencies and support groups, etc.

In the case of a parent who encounters hostility, indifference, opposing viewpoints, lack of action and unwarranted delays, support is vital. One of the best forms is to provide the parent with the information they need to be able to muster support for their child so as to present his case as strongly as possible.

That is what this chapter is all about - to let parents know about useful publications, support agencies and organizations that are able to provide information, guidance and general help. They have been grouped under three main readings relating to local education authorities (LEAs); independent organizations, which exist in order to assist in any type of case of special educational needs; and finally those concerned only with dyslexic children. As a preliminary you might find it useful to know the whereabouts of the Department for

Education and Skills (DfES), which is responsible for the education system of England and Wales:

The Department for Education and Skills
Sanctuary Buildings
Great Smith Street
Westminster
London SW1P 3BT
Tel: 020 7925 5000, Fax: Various, depending on department
Email: Various, depending on department, Website: www.dfes.gov.uk

Your local education authority (LEA)

Every LEA must produce a booklet of general information for parents and update it annually. You may have one free of charge on request. It ought to set out the LEA's policy on children with special educational needs, and give a description of what resources it has to meet those needs.

Every LEA school must produce a booklet describing the school's:

• philosophy
• policy on relevant matters and
• details relating to special educational needs.

You should be able to obtain a copy relating to the particular school your child attends (or one at which you are considering enrolling him). If a change of school is suggested as a means of helping with his dyslexia, you will require a copy of the booklet relating to the proposed school. Again, these booklets are to be updated annually.

Independent bodies (special needs in general)

If you have been involved in an Appeal held in connection with the assessment of your child's special educational needs and you feel that the behaviour of the Appeal Committee was unfair, then if you live in England or Wales you can complain to:

Council on Tribunals
22 Kingsway
London WC2B 6LE
Tel: 020 7947 7045, Fax: 020 7947 7044
Email: enquiries@cot.gsi.gov.uk, Website: www.council-on-tribunals.gov.uk/

Residents of Scotland need to get in touch with:

The Scottish Committee
44 Palmerston Place
Edinburgh EH12 5BJ
Tel: 0131 220 1236, Fax: 0131 225 4271
Email: scot@gtnet.gov.uk, Website: enquiries@cot.gsi.gov.uk

who may arrange a hearing for you.

If you are unhappy about the manner in which your LEA has dealt with your child's SENs, you may appeal to the Secretary of State and have your case heard at a Special Educational Needs Tribunal. The details are:

SEN Appeals Tribunal
6th Floor
Windsor House
50 Victoria Street
London SW1H OHW
Tel: 020 7925 6925, Fax: 020 7925 6926
Email: demi.akerewusi@sent.gsi, Website: www.sentribunal.gov.uk

You may find that being a member of a group will be of assistance to you. There may be a local Campaign for the Advancement of State Education (CASE) group in your area. More information can be obtained from:

Campaign for the Advancement of State Education (CASE)
158 Durham Road
London SW20 0DG
Tel: 020 8944 8206, Fax: 020 8944 8206
Email: tulloch-case@mcr1.poptel.org.uk, Website: www.casenet.org.uk

Information and advice about all aspects of the state education service is offered by ACE, whose address is:

Advisory Centre for Education
1c Aberdeen Studios
22-24 Highbury Grove
London N5 2DQ
Tel: 020 7354 8321, Fax: 020 7354 9069
Email: ace-ed@easynet.co.uk, Website: www.ace-ed.org.uk

Free telephone advice is available between 2 pm and 5 pm, Mondays to Fridays.

ACE also publishes the *ACE Special Education Handbook*, which you will probably find very useful and informative.

The Centre for Studies on Inclusive Education (CSIE) aims to ensure that LEAs, individual schools, parents and others, establish effective and stable integration schemes for children with special needs. It produces a wide range of leaflets, reports and surveys. It also arranges conferences, and provides support for families:

Centre for Studies on Inclusive Education (CSIE)
Room 2S-203
S Block
Frenchay Campus
Cold Harbour Lane
Bristol BS16 7OL
Tel: 0117 344 4007, Fax: 0117 344 4005
Website: inclusion.org.uk

Free information and an advice service (on all aspects of law and policy affecting children and young people in England and Wales) is offered by:

The Children's Legal Centre
University of Essex
Wivenhoe Park
Colchester
Essex CO4 3SQ
Tel: 0120 687 3820, Fax: 0120 687 4026
Email: clc@essex.ac.uk, Website: www2.essex.ac.uk/clc/

An independent panel of special education experts is also available at this address and will assist parents who seek a second opinion.

The Independent Panel for Special Educational Advice (IPSEA) also offers advice on the duties LEAs have towards children with special SENs and can provide a professional second opinion on those in need of such. Contact IPSEA at:

Independent Panel for Special Educational Advice (IPSEA)
6 Carlow Mews
Woodbridge
Suffolk IP12 1DH
Tel: 0800 018 4016 (for advice); 020 8682 0442 (re tribunals)
Fax: 01390 438 0518
Email: ipsea.org.uk, Website: www.ipsea.org.uk
Note: If you live in Scotland ring 0131 454 0082; if you live in Northern Ireland ring 0123 270 5654

A free information service and a range of publications is available from the National Children's Bureau (NCB) at:
The National Children's Bureau
8 Wakley Street
London EC1V 7QE
Tel: 020 7843 6000, Fax: 020 7278 9512
Email: nhilliard@ncb.org.uk (enquiries), Website: www.ncb.org.uk

Note: You may at some time need to consult an Ombudsman. The address will depend on where you live as there are three to cover the country.

London boroughs north of the River Thames (including Richmond), Essex, Kent, Surrey, Suffolk, East and West Sussex:

Local Government Ombudsman
21 Queen Anne's Gate
London SW1H 9BU
Tel: 020 7915 3210, Fax: 020 7233 0396
Email: complaints.london@lgo, Website: www.open.gov.uk.lgo

The West Midlands (except Coventry City), Shropshire, Staffordshire, Cheshire, Derbyshire, Nottinghamshire, Lincolnshire, and the North of England (except the cities of York and Lancaster):

Local Government Ombudsman
Beverley House
17 Shipton Road
York YO30 5FZ
Tel: 0190 466 3200, Fax: 0190 466 3269
Email: complaints.York@lgo.org.uk, Website: www.lgo.org.uk

London boroughs south of the River Thames (except Richmond), the cities of York, Lancaster and Coventry, and the rest of England not included in the two above:

Local Government Ombudsman
The Oaks No 2
Westwood Way
Westwood Business Park
Coventry CV4 8JB
Tel: 0247 669 5999, Fax: 0247 669 5902
Email: complaints.coventry@lgo.org.uk, Website: www.open.gov.uk/lgo

There is also an Advice line - 0845 602 1983. There are separate Local Government Ombudsmen for:

Scotland (tel: 0131 225 5300) and Wales (tel: 0165 666 1325)

The British Education Communications and Technology Agency (BECTA), which was set up in 1988, promotes the use of new technologies in education generally. Special needs feature, of course, and dyslexia is included in this:

British Education Communications and Technology Agency (BECTA)
Milburn Hill Road
University of Warwick Science Park
Coventry CV4 7JJ
Tel: 0247 641 6994, Fax: 0247 641 1418
Email: becta@becta.org.uk, Website: www.becta.org.uk

The National Federation of Access centres is a nationwide group of further education (FE) establishments which assess adult students, and recommend suitable software and aids. They undertake assessments for the Open University (OU) and LEAs. They also help students with specific learning difficulties:

National Federation of Access Centres
Hereward College of Further Education
Branston Crescent
Tile Hill Lane
Coventry CV4 9SW
Tel: 0247 642 6146, Fax: 0247 669 4303
Email: donnajackson@hereward.ac.uk, Website: www.hereward.ac.uk

Network '81 is a national network of parents of children with special educational needs, who work towards achieving properly resourced inclusive education. Contact them at:

Network '81
1-7 Woodfield Terrace
Stansted
Essex CM24 8AJ
Tel: 0127 964 7415, Fax: 0127 981 4908
Email: network81@tesco.net, Website: www.network81.co.uk

The helpline is open Monday to Friday from 10am to 2pm.

Independent bodies (concerned with dyslexia)

Much of the work in relation to children with dyslexia who are resident in the British Isles is carried out by the British Dyslexia

Association (BDA) and the Dyslexia Institute (DI), with other bodies and organizations providing additional and much-valued contributions. Taking them in order, we have:

British Dyslexia Association
98 London Road
Reading
Berkshire RG1 5AN
Tel: 0118 966 8271, Fax: 0118 935 1927
Email: info@dyslexiahelp-bda.demon.co.uk, Website:www.bda/dyslexia.org.uk

The BDA provides advice and information on resources, workshops, clubs, LEA initiatives and regional networks. A magazine - *Dyslexia Contact* - is published three times a year, and much other literature is available.

The helpline is open Monday to Friday, from 9am to 5pm. Remember that there is likely to be a local branch near to where you live.

You may also wish to contact the BDA Computer Resource Centre, which is now located at the same address as the BDA (above).

The Dyslexic Institute has a number of centres throughout the UK to provide educational and psychological assessment of children and adults, special tuition, teacher training and information:

The Dyslexia Institute
133 Gresham Road
Staines
Middlesex TW18 2AJ
Tel: 0178 446 3851, Fax: 0178 446 0747
Email: staines@dyslexia-inst.org.uk, Website: www.dyslexia-inst.org.uk

There could be one of the DI's centres located close to you.

The Professional Association of Teachers of Students with Specific Learning Difficulties (PATOSS) is a professional body representing those who hold the nationally recognized RSA Diploma in Specific Learning Difficulties. Its aim is to raise the standard of debate at a national level, as well as to influence decision makers. There are local PATOSS groups, an annual conference and a professional journal (*The PATOSS Bulletin*), as well as newsletters. Contact:

PATOSS
PO Box 10
Evesham
Worcestershire WR11 6ZW
Tel: 0138 671 2650 (manned most office hours), Fax: 0138 671 2716
E-mail: patoss@evesham.ac.uk, Website: www.patoss-dyslexia.org/

The Helen Arkell Dyslexia Centre arranges consultations and assessments by educational psychologists, teachers and speech therapists; and provides tuition, speech and language therapy, counselling and training of various types (e.g. keyboarding skills). Contact:

The Helen Arkell Dyslexia Centre
Frensham
Farnham
Surrey GU10 3DW
Tel: 0125 279 2400, Fax: 0125 279 5669
Email: arkellcentre@org.uk, Website: www.arkellcentre.org.uk

The Council for the Registration of Schools Teaching Dyslexic Pupils (CreSTeD) provides information about schools that cater for the needs of dyslexic children, and aims to help parents and those who advise them to choose a suitable school for their dyslexic child:

Council for the Registration of Schools Teaching Dyslexic Pupils (CreSTeD)
Greygarth
Littleworth
Winchcombe
Cheltenham
Gloucestershire GL54 5BT
Tel: 0124 260 2689, Fax: 0124 260 2689
Email: admin@crested.org.uk, Website: www.crested.org.uk

The Arts Dyslexia Trust operates an advisory service for all dyslexics who are concerned with arts and education, particularly dyslexic adults intending to make a career in the arts. Contact:

Susan Parkinson, ARCA (General Secretary)
Arts Dyslexia Trust
c/o Lodge Cottage, Brabourne Lees
Ashford
Kent TN25 6QZ
Tel: 0130 381 3221, Fax: 0130 381 3221
Email: sp@artsdysx.demon.co.uk, Website: www.rmplc.co.uk/orgs/nellalex

The enquiry/helpline is open between 7pm and midnight.

The Adult Dyslexia Organisation (ADO) runs a helpline, and also produces a quarterly magazine:

Adult Dyslexia Organisation
336 Brixton Road
London SW9 7AA
Tel: 020 7924 9559, Fax: 020 7207 7796
Email: dyslexia.hq@dial.pipex.com
Website: www.futurenet.co.uk/charity/ado/index.htm

In recent years websites have emerged, and no doubt they are bound to increase in number as the Internet continues to grow. The two listed below are well established.

Dyslexia A2Z aims to enable anyone with an interest in dyslexia to find people or information quickly and easily. This relates to books, tests, teachers and psychologists:

Dyslexia A2Z
Swindon Dyslexia Centre
134 Morrison Street
Swindon
Wiltshire SN2 2DH
Tel: 0179 343 3967, Fax: 0179 343-3967
Email: info@dyslexiaa2z.com, Website: www.dyslexiaa2z.com

DYXI
Alan Walford (Founder)
Tel: 0800 970 6732, Fax: 0127 181 5593
Email: info@dyxi.co.uk, Website: www.dyxi.co.uk

For readers resident in Scotland or Ireland, it might be of interest to know that each of these countries has its own Dyslexia Association:

Dyslexia in Scotland
Stirling Business Centre
Wellgreen
Stirling
Scotland FK8 2DZ
Tel: 0178 644 6650, Fax: 0178 647 1235
Email: info@dyslexia-in-scotland.org, Website: www.dyslexia-in-scotland.org

Dyslexia Association of Ireland
1 Suffolk Chambers
Suffolk Street
Dublin 2
Eire
Tel: (01) 679 0276 (from within Ireland), Fax: (01) 679 0273 (from within Ireland)
Email: acld@iol.ie, Website: www.acld-dyslexia.com

The Association now has 30 branches throughout the Republic of Ireland and continues to grow.

Chapter 16
A brief history of dyslexia

What follows is a summary of the key events in the story of how dyslexia came to be recognized, described and to grow in the awareness of people worldwide until it has achieved the status it enjoys today. Most of the details given relate to Britain, but some developments in other parts of the world are also included.

Before the year 1500 people considered that thoughts and feelings originated in the heart

1500   After 1500 it slowly became realized that the brain was the organ involved

1800   About 1800 scientists realized that the faculty of language was located within the cerebral hemispheres and that loss of speech was due to a malfunction of the brain and not the tongue

1861   The connection was established between the frontal lobes of the brain and the impairment of speech

1865   *Elsewhere*   Broca concluded that speech was located in the left half of the brain only and not both sides

Later it was realized that this does not apply to all people but is true in the case of the great majority

The name *aphasia* was applied to those cases of people who had lost the power of speech

Eventually it was realized that a number of aphasias existed - some in which reading and writing was affected as well as speech, others in which reading and writing were seriously affected but speech only to a lesser extent. This latter group were then described as 'word blind' but today could be called 'alexic'

1870   The Forster Education Act granted an elementary level of education to all children. Large numbers of children could be observed by teachers and others over a lengthy period of time. Reading difficulties came to be studied more widely

1877   *Elsewhere*   Kussmaul described alexia which he called 'word blindness'

1879   Wundt in Leipzig set up the first psychology laboratory and thereby
                       instituted the modern scientific approach to the subject

1887   Professor Berlin first used the word 'dyslexia' to describe 'alexia'

1896   Kerr and Pringle-Morgan described 'dyslexia' in children, calling it 'congenital
        word blindness'

Late   Throughout this period the early psychologists pioneered psychologically
19th   based methods of helping children with reading difficulties
century

1913   First educational psychologist in the British Isles (Cyril Burt - later knighted for
        his service to education) appointed by the London County Council

1920s   Much work carried out in relation to reading difficulties by Burt and Schonell

1920s   *Elsewhere*   (USA) Orton noted that an immensely high proportion of children
onwards   with specific reading disability were producing mirror writing and
                       had orientation difficulties

1938   (Denmark) Edith Norrie founded the first organization in the world
                       devoted to diagnosing and teaching dyslexics, The Word Blind
                       Instutute in Copenhagen

1949   (USA) The Orton Society was founded but later was called the
                       Orton Dyslexia Society. It produced *The Bulletin of the Orton Society*,
                       which was later renamed *Annals of Dyslexia*

1950s   St Bartholomew's Hospital (London) became involved in the diagnosis and the
(early) treatment of dyslexic children. Other Hospitals also showed an interest and
        carried out work

1950s   *Elsewhere*   (South Africa) Rebecca Oistrowick started work and was one of the
                       pioneers who used multisensory methods

1960   Maisie Holt, a psychologist, started teaching dyslexic children at the instigation of
        Dr Franklin White, a paediatrician, who afterwards became Chairman of the
        Invalid Children's Aid Association (ICAA). A clinic was set up to give free help to
        large numbers of children and adults, paid for by the NHS. The Hornsby
        Centre in Wandsworth and the Hornsby School were offshoots of this

1963   The ICAA established the Word Blind Centre for Dyslexic Children in London.
        (It closed in 1972 having been intended only as a short-term measure.) However,
        the establishment of the Centre was probably the point at which dyslexia started
        to become known to the public at large and generated a great deal of interest

1960s   The Dyslexia Unit was set up at the University College of North Wales, Bangor,
(mid) by Professor T Miles, in order to undertake assessments and carry out research
1965–   Eight voluntary dyslexia associations were started
72

1967 *Elsewhere* (Australia) SPELD (which stands for *Specific Learning Difficulties*) was set up in New South Wales. The movement grew, spreading throughout Australia, Tasmania and New Zealand

1970 The Chronically Sick and Disabled Persons Act passed. The word 'dyslexia' was first mentioned by the legal system

1971 The Helen Arkell Dyslexia Centre was set up. (It is now located at Frensham, Surrey)

1972 The Dyslexia Institute was set up by the North Surrey Dyslexia Association. It now has many institutes, outposts and schools throughout England, Scotland and Guernsey.
The British Dyslexia Association (BDA) was founded by Marion Welchman. It is the national organization and the parent body to which local associations are affiliated. At present there are a hundred of these. The BDA is based in Reading.
The Tizard Report was published. It recommended the use of the term 'specific reading difficulties'

1973 The first meetings between the BDA and the Department of Education were set up

1974 The BDA was invited to give evidence to the Warnock Committee of Enquiry into Special Educational Needs

1975 *Alpha to Omega* published

1977 The BDA established formal links with the DES (now DfES)

1978 The Warnock Report *Special Educational Needs* published

1980 The British Medical Association advised its members that dyslexia is not a medical problem

1981 Education Act passed. It became possible for a dyslexic child to have his or her special educational needs protected by the issuing of a formal 'Statement of Special Education Needs'. Tansley and Panckhurst published *Children with Specific Learning Difficulties*

1982 The Watford Dyslexia Unit was set up by Violet Brand.
The City of London Dyslexia Institute training unit was opened.
First edition of 'Dyslexia Contact' published

1983 The 1981 Education Act was enacted as from 1 April

1984 Pilot courses were conducted for the BDA Diploma for teachers of dyslexic pupils

1987 *Elsewhere* The European Dyslexia Association (EDA) was formed
1988 *Elsewhere* The European Dyslexia Association was given the Belgian Royal Assent

1989   The BDA organized the first international conference on dyslexia which was very successful

1988/ 89   A survey of 882 educational psychologists in relation to specific learning difficulties/dyslexia was organized by Professor Pumfrey and Ms Reason (Sen Ed Psych) based at the School of Education, Manchester University

1991   The BDA organized the second International Conference on dyslexia. *Specific Learning Difficulties (Dyslexia): challenges and responses* published. A legal precedent was set when the existence of dyslexia was recognized in law

1992   Dyslexia Institute Week (2-8 March) organized by the Dyslexia Institute

1993   Education Act 1993

1994   *Elsewhere*   26-27 March in Brussels representatives from all the European Union countries met for the very first time to discuss specialist teaching for dyslexia.
The DFE published the Code of Practice on the identification of special needs, in which clear guidelines are given to LEAs and governing bodies of all maintained schools, about their responsibilities to children with specific learning difficulties (for example, dyslexia). The Code came into effect on 1 September 1994

1995   The Booksellers Association (the trade association representing the interests of all book retailers) adopts the British Dyslexia Association for 1995 (the Booksellers Association's Centenary year) The Joint Council for the GCSE's special arrangements and special considerations, which includes children with specific learning difficulties, became effective in and from summer 1995. Schools must publish information on their SEN policies by 1 August 1995

1996   Professor Pumfrey advocates the use of the exact term 'specific developmental dyslexia' (SDD). The centenary of the first mention of dyslexia is celebrated

1997   The Green Paper 'Excellence for all Children' published (DfEE). The Association of Educational Psychologists (AEP) publishes its 'Statement on Dyslexia'

1998   Guidance for educational psychologists statutory assessments published (AEP). 'Year of Reading' commenced (September). First UK Masters Degree course in dyslexia studies inaugurated at De Montfort University, Lincoln. The National Literacy Strategy (NLS) inaugurated (DfEE). The BDA's 'Dyslexia-Friendly Schools' campaign launched

1999   Guidance for educational psychologists assessments published (DECP). *Dyslexia, Literacy and Psychological Assessment* published by the DECP

2000   The Human Rights Act comes into force (October). The right of access to education is included. The BDA has 100 local associations and 113 corporate members

2001 The BDA-organized 5th International Conference is held at York. A total of 35 countries were represented

2002 The new Code of Practice on special educational needs comes into effect January.

Appendix 1

The definitions used in Chapter 6 are given here in full.

A *Dyslexia* 'A disorder in children who, despite conventional class-room experience, fail to attain the language skills of reading, writing and spelling commensurate with their intellectual abilities' (World Federation of Neurology, 1968).

B *Dyslexia* 'We define dyslexia as a specific difficulty in learning, constitutional in origin, in one or more of reading, spelling and written language which may be accompanied by difficulty in number work. It is particularly related to mastering and using written language (alphabetic, numerical and musical notation) although often affecting oral language to some degree' (British Dyslexia Association, 1989).

C *Specific developmental dyslexia* 'A disorder manifested by difficulty in learning to read despite conventional instruction, adequate intelligence, and socio-cultural opportunity. It depends on fundamental cognitive disabilities which are frequently of constitutional origin' (World Federation of Neurology, 1968).

D *Specific reading retardation* '...an attainment on either reading accuracy or reading comprehension which was 28 months or more below the level predicted on the basis of each child's age and short WISC IQ' (Rutter, Tizard and Whitmore, 1970).

E *Specific learning difficulties* 'Children with specific learning difficulties are those who in the absence of sensory defect or overt organic damage, have an intractable learning problem in one or more of reading, writing, spelling and mathematics, and who do not respond to normal teaching. For these children, early identification, sensitive encouragement and specific remedial arrangements are necessary' (Tansley and Panckhurst, 1981).

F *Specific learning difficulties* These 'are defined as organising or learning deficiencies which restrict the student's competencies in information processing, in motor skills and working memory, so causing limitations in some or all of the skills of speech, reading, writing, essay writing, numeracy and behaviour' (Dyslexia Institute, 1989).

G *Specific reading difficulties* A descriptive term used to indicate the problems of the relatively small proportion of pupils 'whose reading (and perhaps writing, spelling and number) abilities are significantly below the standards which their abilities in other spheres would lead one to expect' (DES, 1972).

H *Dyslexia* is present when the automatization of word identification (reading) and/or word spelling does not develop or does so very incompletely or with great difficulty (Committee of the Health Council of the Netherlands, 1997).

I *Dyslexia* is evident when accurate and fluent word reading and/or spelling develops very incompletely or with great difficulty. This focuses on literacy learning at the 'word level' and implies that the problem is severe and persistent despite appropriate learning opportunities. It provides the basis for a staged process of assessment through teaching (DECP, 1999).

Appendix 2

Survey of 25 reports - intellectual abilities featured on just *one* occasion

1   attention difficulties
2   auditory processing
3   classical sequential dyslexia
4   common sense reasoning
5   concentration
6   cursive handwriting patterns
7   days of the week (ability to recite)
8   decoding skills
9   dotting speed
10 factual data (long-term retention of)
11 fine motor skills processing (speed of)
12 general knowledge
13 grapheme-phoneme relationships
14 information processing (speed of)
15 language in thinking (use of)
16 linguistic reasoning ability
17 logical thinking
18 motor co-ordination
19 motor planning/control
20 organizational difficulties
21 organizing and sequencing information
22 potential (not fulfilling)
23 problem-solving ability
24 problem-solving (non-verbal)
25 reversals
26 reversed digits
27 rote memory (long-term)

28 sequential dyslexia
29 social judgement
30 spatial ability
31 spatial reasoning
32 symbolic information (processing of)
33 T-score differences
34 verbal comprehension
35 verbal reasoning ability
36 verbal-visual IQ differences
37 visual memory
38 visual memory (short-term)
39 visual processing
40 visual retention
41 visual scanning
42 vocabulary
43 word processing
44 word retrieval
45 written information (processing of)

Appendix 3

Books and other resource material recommended by the psychologists in the survey

Books (25)

1 *Easy Type* (Kinloch) (12%)
2 *Spelling Made Easy* (Brand) (8%)
3 *The Mind Map Book* (Buzan) (8%)
   (All others = 4%)
4 *Alpha to Omega* (Hornsby)
5 *Dyslexia and Mathematics* (Miles & Miles)
6 *Dyslexia at College* (Miles)
7 *Enterprise Skills for Students* (Guirdham & Tyler)
8 *Handwriting Helpline* (Alston)
9 *Help for the Dyslexic Adolescent* (Stirling)
10 *How To get Things Done* (Hardingham)
11 *Individualised Reading* (Moon)
12 *Mathematics for Dyslexics* (Chinn & Ashcroft)
13 *Maths and Dyslexics* (Anderson)
14 *Maths For Life* (Collins Educational)
15 *Maximising Examination Performance* (Daniel)
16 *National Writing Project Guidelines*
17 *Radical Thinking* (Buzan)
18 *Solving Language Difficulties* (Steere, Peck & Kahn)
19 *Spelling in Context* (Peters & Smith)
20 *Study!* (Barrass)
21 *Taking Action* (Wright & Poynter)
22 *The SENCo Guide* (DfEE)
23 *Use Your Head* (Buzan)
24 *Use Your Memory* (Buzan)
25 *Visualising and Verbalising* (Bell)

Other resources (7)

1   Ann Arbour Materials
2   Bangor Dyslexia Teaching System (Miles)
3   BDA's Computer Users Bulletin
4   Dyslexia: a language training system for teachers (Hickey)
5   Get Ahead (video) (Buzan)
6   Naxos Audio Books
7   The Dyslexia Handbook (BDA)

Appendix 4

Computer programmes recommended in the survey (19)

Note: (?) after a title indicates that the publisher is not stated in the report.

1   Advanced Folio (BBC/Archimedes)
2   An Eye for Spelling (BBC/Nimbus)
3   BBC Write Plus (BBC/PC/Apple)
4   Better Spelling (BBC/CECC)
5   Crossword Call up (BBC/Nimbus)
6   Desktop Folio (Archimedes)
7   Dyspel (Amiga/Sally Systems)
8   Festive Folio (Archimedes)
9   Hi-Spell (Xavier)
10   Logical Spelling (?)
11   Mind Reader (Brown Bag Software)
12   Predictype (Scetlander Ltd)
13   Spelling It Out (?)
14   Spelling Patterns (?)
15   Starspell (Fisher-Marriott)
16   Stylus (MAPE)
17   The Complete Speller (BBC/Archimedes)
18   Unscrambling Spelling (?)
19   Wordshark 2 (?)

Glossary

ACE Advisory Centre for Education.

ACID (test) An expression used in relation to the results obtained from a dyslexic child when given the WISC. Low scores on the Arithmetic, Coding, Information and Digit span subtests are claimed by some researchers to result often, and the four initials of these subtests when combined together produce ACID.

acquired dyslexia Also known as alexia, this is one of the two main types of dyslexia and is the form found in adults. It refers to the loss of the ability to read by a person who was previously able to do so.

actual reading age The reading age a person achieves when given a reading test.

acute dyslexia A misleading term, as dyslexia cannot be acute in the medical sense of 'coming sharply to a crisis'. The term was used in the Chronically Sick and Disabled Persons Act of 1970 and its use caused some confusion. It is presumed that 'acute' means 'severe'.

ADO Adult Dyslexia Organization.

ADT Arts Dyslexia Trust.

Advice (to an LEA) A piece of information in the form of a written report provided to an LEA on request by a professional or parent in relation to a child undergoing a statutory assessment of his special educational needs. Advice must be provided by a teacher, a doctor and a psychologist (usually an educational psychologist) in each case. Advice may be provided by a parent or other agency. Should the statutory assessment result in the production of a Statement of Special Educational Needs, then each piece of Advice will be attached to the Statement and redesignated as an Appendix with an alphabetic letter tag, i.e. Appendix A, Appendix B, etc.

agnosia The ability to recognize familiar sounds, images, etc. There are various forms such as visual agnosia, auditory agnosia and tactile agnosia. (See also *finger agnosia*.)

AHA Area health authority.

alexia Also known as acquired dyslexia, this is one of the two main types of dyslexia and is the form in adults. A person with alexia has lost the ability to read, usually as a result of head injury, brain tumour or the effect of drugs, etc.

algorithm A sequence of instructions for carrying out an operation using the smallest number of steps.

alliteration A number of words occurring together and beginning with the same sound, e.g. slithery, slippery, slimy snake; long-legged, lanky Liz.

alphabetic principle The fact that the phonemes (small speech sounds) of a word can be represented by letters of the alphabet.

alphabetic phase The middle of three stages of reading development (as proposed by Uta Frith); it is preceded by the logographic phase and followed by the orthographic phase.

aphasia Loss of, or impairment to, the ability to use language because of damage to the brain. Expressive aphasia is the inability to produce a required word even though the word is known to the person affected. Receptive aphasia involves the understanding of speech. There are other aphasias. Any person affected is described as aphasic

Appendix 'F' The designation given to the Advice (in the form of a report) provided to an LEA by a psychologist (usually an educational psychologist) after a Statement of Special Educational Needs has been produced. (See **Advice**.) Redesignated **Appendix 'D'** from January 2002.

aqueous humour The clear, watery liquid that fills the front part of the eye between the cornea and the lens.

ARROW Aural-Read-Response-Oral-Written.

attentional dyslexia A subtype of alexia (acquired dyslexia) claimed to exist by at least one researcher.

auditory dyslexia A subtype of developmental dyslexia such that the child cannot associate the printed image of the word with the sound the word makes. Such children respond best to a whole-word 'look-and-say' approach during the initial stages of reading, as they are unable to break down a word into the smaller sounds (phonemes) of which the word is composed.

BAS British Abilities Scales.

BDA British Dyslexia Association.

BECTA British Education, Communication and Technology Agency.

blending The process of taking the individual speech sounds (phonemes) of a word and combining them - either in the mind or aloud - correctly and smoothly to produce the word itself.

Broca's area That part of the brain (about 4 cm^2 in area) which enables a person to speak.

CA Chronological age.

CAL Computer-assisted learning.

capital letter The large form of a letter of the alphabet used at the start of proper names and to begin a sentence. Also known as *upper-case* (derived from the printing trade). (Compare with *small letter*.)

CASE Campaign for the Advancement of State Education.

CAT Cognitive Abilities Test.

CAT (scan) Computerized axial tomography, also referred to as computerized tomography (CT).

cerebellar Related to the cerebellum.

cerebellum Sometimes referred to as the subsidiary brain or hind brain and located underneath the back of the main brain (cerebrum). It is concerned mainly with unconscious and automatic functions such as balance and the control and co-ordination of voluntary movements.

cerebral cortex The grey surface of the brain, a layer only 3 mm thick and composed of more than one million million nerve cells, each with connections to many thousands of others. Underneath the cerebral cortex is the brain's white matter.

cerebral hemisphere One half of the brain, there being a left and a right cerebral hemisphere separated by the deep longitudinal fissure, which runs from front to back.

Certificate of Secondary Education (CSE) An examination designed to be taken by school leavers as an alternative to GCE O-level examination. It was introduced in 1965 but discontinued after 1987, when it was replaced by the GCSE

chronological age A person's age in the everyday meaning of the word - the amount of time that has elapsed since he or she was born. Often abbreviated to CA. A child can be described in terms of other ages as well, e.g. developmental age, reading age, mental age.

Cloze procedure A method designed to measure how readable a book is. A child attempts to read a passage from which some words have been removed. How easily he is able to give the words that should occupy the blank spaces is taken as a measure of the passage's readability.

clumsiness A lack of co-ordination of bodily movements. Sometimes referred to as dyspraxia or developmental co-ordination disorder (DCD).

CMO Clinical medical officer. Formerly known as SMO (school medical officer) or, simply, school doctor.

Cognitive Profiling System (CoPS) An interactive computer program to produce a profile of a child's cognitive weaknesses.

computerized axial tomography (CAT) A medical scanning of part or all of the body by an advanced form of X-ray machine.

concrete operations A stage of intellectual development described by Piaget.

cones Highly specialized cells in the retina (the light-sensitive layer at the back of the eyeball). The cones respond to different colours and there are six million of them in each eye. They work in close association with the *rods*.

congenital Literally this means 'appearing with birth' but has unfortunately become confused in the minds of many people with 'hereditary' and this is incorrect. Anything hereditary is handed on from parent to child, whereas something congenital (e.g. a disease) can arise after conception but before birth. Hereditary diseases are congenital but congenital diseases are not necessarily hereditary.

congenital dyslexia One of a number of terms used to describe developmental dyslexia.

congenital word blindness One of the many terms used to describe developmental dyslexia. It was first used by Kerr (a medical officer of health) and Pringle-Morgan (a general practitioner) in 1896.

conjunctiva The thin transparent sheet of membrane which covers the front of the eye.

control group/controls A group of individuals that matches, as closely as possible, another group that is being experimented on in some way. As the controls are treated the same way in all respects except any relating to the experiment, any differences that result in the second group must be as a result of the experimental treatment they have been given. A control group is a reference.

CoPS Cognitive Profiling System.

cornea A clear, transparent layer at the front of the eyeball, which is the window of the eye. The thin *conjunctiva* is on the outside surface and the inside surface is in contact with the *aqueous humour*.

Light rays pass through it, permitting us to see.

corpus callosum A large bundle of fibres in the brain which lies immediately below the longitudinal fissure. It bridges the two halves of the brain (cerebral hemispheres) and so allows 'signals' to pass from one half to the other.

correlation The manner in which two sets of measures vary together, e.g. shops sell more ice-cream when the weather is hot, taller people buy larger shoes, young children tend to weigh little and older children much more. Correlation can be measured mathematically and correlations can vary between very positive and very negative. (The three examples given are all positive, as an increase in one leads to an increase in the other.)

CreSTeD Council for the Registration of Schools Teaching Dyslexic Pupils.

cross-lateral A description of a person who prefers to use different sides of his body for different purposes, e.g. the right eye for sighting something but the left hand for throwing a ball.

CSE Certificate of Secondary Education.

CSIE Centre for Studies on Integration in Education.

cumulative The sum of two or more numbers, items or quantities.

DAST Dyslexia Adult Screening Test.

DATAPAC Daily Teaching and Assessment (Primary Aged Children).

DCD developmental co-ordination disorder.

DECP Division of Education and Child Psychology (of the British Dyslexia Association - BDA).

deep dyslexia A subtype of alexia. People who have deep dyslexia cannot connect a word they see in print with the sound of the word. Familiar words are read more easily than unfamiliar ones and abstract words are particularly difficult for them. Meaningful substitutions are made for difficult words.

deficit The amount by which something is less than or smaller than it ought to be.

deletion The removal or striking-out of something, e.g. phoneme deletion in which one of the speech sounds (phonemes) that go to make up a word is removed from the word and so produces either a new word or a non-word, e.g. 'smell' without the /m/ phoneme produces 'sell'.

Department for Education and Skills (DfES) Since June 2001 - after the Labour Party's second general election victory - the new name of the former Department for Education and Employment (DfEE).

DES Department of Education and Science (changed in June 1995 to the Department for Education and Employment (DfEE).

DEST Dyslexia Early Screening Test.

developmental aphasia Term used in the literature to describe dyslexia (according to Miles).

developmental co-ordination disorder (DCD) Also referred to as either clumsiness or dyspraxia.

developmental dyslexia The type of dyslexia found in children and called by many names. It is different from *acquired dyslexia*, which occurs in adults.

DFE Department for Education.

DfES Department for Education and Skills. In existence since June 2001 (replacing the DfEE).

DI Dyslexia Institute.

direct dyslexia Also called *hyperlexia*, and one of the subtypes of *acquired dyslexia*, which is found in adults. Individuals are able to read quite accurately but the meaning of what they have read is understood quite poorly. While phonological and whole-word strategies are competent, their semantic analysis skills are deficient.

discrepancy A difference or inconsistency.

dominance (1) The fact that one half of the brain exercises more power over the body than does the other. This is cerebral dominance. (2) The preferred use of one side of the body. If right eye, right hand and right leg are preferred by a person s/he is right-side dominant and if the others are preferred s/he is left-side dominant. If a person uses both the left and the right of a pair of limbs with equal ease (as does someone ambidextrous), then s/he is described as having mixed dominance. (Dominance in this second sense is similar to laterality.)

dominant hemisphere (1) The half of the brain on the opposite side of the body to the preferred hand. The left hemisphere is the dominant one for most people. (2) In relation to a particular activity or function (such as language), the half of the brain which controls it. In the case of language, the left hemisphere controls 90% of right-handed people but only 30% of left-handed people.

DORRS Development of Reading and Related Skills with Pupils of Secondary Age.

DST Dyslexia Screening Test.

dyseidetic dyslexia A subgroup of dyslexic children (according to Boder). The word is of Greek origin and indicates a difficulty with images or what is being looked at. A dyseidetic child is described as one who has difficulties with visuospatial aspects.

More simply, there is difficulty experienced in the ability to perceive letters and whole words as belonging together. See *dysphonetic dyslexia* and *mixed (dyseidetic/dysphonetic) dyslexia*.

dyslexia There are two forms of dyslexia. In the case of children, dyslexia is a difficulty in learning to read, which is often associated with other difficulties (such as spelling and writing), and for which there is no obvious explanation such as low intelligence, visual defects, lack of adequate and consistent schooling, etc. The other form of dyslexia relates to adults who had previously been able to read and have lost their ability to do so (*alexia*). Both forms have been given a variety of names in the century or more that has elapsed since the condition was first described. Both types have been described as being composed of subgroupings and many names describing these subgroups have been given. Dyslexia in children is a highly controversial topic, with every aspect of the subject, even its very existence, being strongly debated. *Specific learning difficulties* is the name preferred by many.

dysphonetic dyslexia A subgroup of dyslexic children (according to Boder). The word is of Greek origin and indicates a difficulty with sounds. A dysphonetic child is described as having difficulties with sound-symbol relations. More simply, the child is unable to look at the printed word, analyse it into its basic sounds and then synthesize (or blend) them together in order to say the word (correctly). See *dyseidetic dyslexia* and *mixed (dyseidetic/dysphonetic) dyslexia*.

dyspraxia Also referred to as clumsiness or *development co-ordination disorder* (DCD).

EAL English as an Additional Language.

EASE European Association for Special Education.

educational psychologist (EP) A person who has (1) a first degree in psychology (usually an Honours), (2) a postgraduate qualification in educational psychology (usually a Masters degree), (3) a teaching qualification, (4) a minimum of two years' teaching experience. EPs are usually employed by local education authorities (LEAs), although some work for other bodies and yet more are in private practice. EPs are responsible for carrying out assessments on children suspected of having special educational needs and for giving appropriate advice as to how those needs would be best met. Other types of work are also undertaken by them in their involvement with children, parents and teachers.

EEG Electroencephalogram.

electroencephalogram A record of the electrical activity of the brain. Different types of brain activity produce regular wave patterns (rhythms) and these are called alpha, beta, delta, theta. The patient's scalp is wired to an electroencephalograph machine which records the patterns on a continuous sheet of paper. Irregular patterns can be a clue to brain damage, epilepsy, etc., and up to 16 'channels' may be recorded.

EP Educational psychologist.

EPS Educational Psychology Service.

EWO Education welfare officer.

expected reading age See *reading age*.

eye dominance A term used to describe the fact that most people have one eye which they prefer over the other when sighting (e.g. in using a telescope). About two thirds of the population prefer to use their right eye. Several theories suggest that eye dominance is important in relation to dyslexia.

eye tracking The movement of the eye when scanning something. In reading, most people 'track' or follow the line of print from left to right. There are reports of a high incidence of tracking from right to left among dyslexic people which, if accurate, could account for some reading difficulties.

factor An influence or force. Something that affects the outcome of an event. For example, the length of a rectangle is one factor in deciding its area; soil richness is a factor involved in how high a tree will grow.

filter A sheet of material, usually in the form of spectacle lenses or a page overlay that is tinted and removes certain light wavelengths.

finger agnosia The inability of a person to know, when blindfolded, how many of his fingers have been touched. (At one time this was employed by Professor Miles as part of a battery of tests aimed at detecting dyslexic children but eventually he did not feel justified in continuing with it.)

fissure A deep cleft or separation in the surface of the brain, a shallow cleft being termed a *sulcus*.

flash card A large card on which a word is printed, used by teachers in the teaching of reading. The flash card is shown to the class for a very brief period of time to increase the speed at which they can recognize the word. Flash cards complement the whole-word 'look-and-say' method and are often used in remedial work.

frontal lobe The lobe on each cerebral hemisphere that lies to the front of the brain and is separated from the lobes behind by the central fissure.

GCA General cognitive ability.

GCE General Certificate of Education.

GCSE General Certificate of Secondary Education.

General Certificate of Education (GCE) The O-level and A-level examinations taken up until 1987, which were then replaced by GCSEs.

General Certificate of Secondary Education (GCSE) In 1988, the GCSE examination replaced the GCE and the CSE O-level examinations.

grapheme A letter or combination of letters used to represent a basic speech sound (*phoneme*). The sound at beginning of the spoken word 'cat' is represented in the written version of that word by the letter *c* (but by *k* in 'kit' by *ck* in 'lock' and by *ch* in 'choir'). There are six other graphemes that can be used to represent this same sound or phoneme (/k/ in the International Phonetic Alphabet).

grapheme-phoneme correspondence The manner in which letters of the alphabet, used singly or in combination, can represent the speech sounds of a language.

graphemic processor dyslexia Another name for visual processor dyslexia.

grey matter The name given to the thin outer layer (cerebral cortex) of the brain. Underneath is the white matter. In the spine, the grey and white matters are reversed, with the grey matter being on the inside.

gyrus A ridge of the brain's surface.

'hard' signs (of brain damage) Usually the actual injury, wound or scar.

homograph A word that is spelled the same as another word but happens to be pronounce differently as it has a different meaning, e.g. 'I can hear the *wind* in the trees', but 'Now I will *wind* the clock'. (See also *homonym* and *homophone*.)

homonym A word that has at least two completely different senses, e.g. Bank: (i) a building, (ii) a piece of land; Pole: (i) a piece of wood, (ii) a native of Poland, (iii) an old-fashioned measure of length. (See also *homophone* and *homograph*.)

homophone A word that sounds the same as another word of different meaning, e.g. sale - sail, horse - hoarse, saw - sore - soar. (See also *homonym* and *homograph*.)

hyperlexia See *direct dyslexia*.

hypothesis A supposition made as a starting point for an investigation.

ICAA Invalid Children's Aid Association.

ICT Information and communications technology.

IEP Individual education plan.

incidence The frequency with which an event occurs. The incidence of cystic fibrosis is 1 in every 2000-2500. The incidence of dyslexia has varied a great deal between one claim and another but 4 in 100 appears to be the most commonly agreed figure.

inorganic books Traditional reading books that are designed to teach reading in a formal manner. There is much repetition and often a rather artificial style of language. They are to be contrasted with *organic books*.

International Phonetic Alphabet (IPA) An alphabet produced by the International Phonetic Association to provide symbols for the sounds of any language. It has been revised on a number of occasions since the first version, the latest being in 1989. A total of 98 symbols are employed, 44 of which apply to ordinary English (received pronunciation).

intuitive (substage) A stage of intellectual development in a young person as described by Piaget.

IPA International Phonetic Alphabet; International Phonetic Association.

IPSEA Independent Panel for Special Educational Advice.

IQ Intelligence quotient.

ITA Initial Teaching Alphabet.

kinaesthetic The kinaesthetic sense, or kinaesthesis, is that which enables us to appreciate the positions and movements of our limbs. It depends on specialized receptor cells in muscles, tendons and joints.

lateral geniculate nucleus There is a lateral geniculate nucleus in each cerebral hemisphere. They are involved with the visual process and are an important part of the visual pathway. The vision 'signals' from the two eyes are passed to the lateral geniculate nucleus and are transferred to the nerves that pass back through the optic radiations to the rear of the brain.

laterality The preference for using the right or left side of the body. The development of laterality is of assistance to the child in acquiring a full sense of bodily awareness and general co-ordination. See *dominance*.

LEA Local education authority.

learning difficulty A child has a learning difficulty if he requires something additional to, or different from, the majority of other children of the same age in order to pursue the National School Curriculum within his LEA. Note that this is a different meaning from that of everyday usage. (A child in a wheelchair is considered to have a learning difficulty by this description yet that child could be a high achiever and display no difficulties in the ordinary learning process.)

legasthenia One of the many terms for dyslexia used in the past.

lens (1) The part of the eye that focuses the incoming light rays on to the retina at the rear. (2) Specially shaped pieces of glass or plastic in spectacles that correct vision defects.

lexical system That which relates to the words of a language.

linguistic dyslexia Usually referred to as L-type dyslexia. One of two subgroups of dyslexia (as claimed by Bakker). Children in this group are described as reading in a hurried fashion and producing many errors. The other subgroup is described as P-type (*perceptual dyslexia*).

logographic phase (of reading) The first of three phases (or stages) of reading development as proposed by Uta Frith. The others are the alphabetic and the orthographic phases.

look-and-say (method of teaching reading) Also called the whole-word method. The child is encouraged to recognize a word (or group of words) by shape when this method is used. It is most commonly employed in the early stages of reading in order to build up the child's sight vocabulary and is rarely used entirely on its own. It is to be contrasted with the *phonic* method.

lower-case letter The 'small' form of the letters of the alphabet, as opposed to the 'capitals'. (The term 'lower case' is one associated with the printing trade.)

LSS Learning Support Service. Referred to by the DfES in the draft version of the new Code of Practice (page 21).

L-type dyslexia See *linguistic dyslexia*.

MA Mental age.

magnocells A system of large neurones (nerve cells) in the brain that is responsible for timing sensory and motor events, the proper development of which is thought to be essential for being able to learn to read.

masking effect The fact that one condition in a person may be strong enough to hide another entirely different condition that is also present. In children, a low level of basic ability may mask dyslexic difficulties.

mental age (MA) An attempt to measure the amount of learning experiences a person has had in life. A calculation is made using both the person's chronological age (CA) and their intelligence level (IQ) in order to get as exact an age as possible.

mental lexicon The number of words a person can recognize and understand; the words of the language at their disposal.

metacognition Internal language; the questioning of ones own plans and intentions; 'thinking about thinking'.

mind blindness A term used by Morgan at the end of the 19th century to describe dyslexia.

mixed (dyseidetic/dysphonetic) dyslexia A subgroup of dyslexic children described by Boder. Children in this group show symptoms that are a mixture of the *dyseidetic* and the *dysphonetic* groups.

morpheme A letter pattern that forms a meaningful unit and which occurs in many words. Some common morphemes are: un-, im-, tri-, -ly, -less, -ness, -ous and -ic.

morphemic dyslexia Another term for the surface dyslexia found in children, being one of two types described by Snowling. (The other subgroup is *phonological dyslexia*.)

MRS Magnetic resonance spectroscopy.

multisensory A method of teaching that employs as many of the senses as possible. When learning letters children can listen to its sound (hearing), look at it in print (vision), handle a plywood cut-out shape of it (touch) and also trace the outline with a finger (kinaesthetic).

NAS/UWT National Association of School Masters/Union of Women Teachers.

National Curriculum In 1988, the Education Reform Act introduced a National Curriculum to be used in all county, voluntary-maintained, special and grant-maintained schools. This was the first time any such action had been taken in the history of British Education. It began to be phased in over a number of years, commencing in 1989. There are core subjects (Maths, English, Science) and foundation subjects (History, Geography, Technology, Art, Music, Physical Education and a Modern Foreign Language). The National Curriculum is delivered over a 12-year period in four key stages: (1) = 5-7 yrs, (2) = 8-11 yrs, (3) = 12-14 yrs and (4) = 15-16 yrs. The years are called, in order, R, 1, 2 and so on up to year 11. Assessments are carried out close to the end of each key stage and compared with the attainment targets expected to be achieved at that key stage. Reports are supplied to parents.

NCB National Children's Bureau.

NCET National Council for Educational Technology.

nerve cell The basic unit or building block of the body's nervous system, the medical term for such a cell being a neurone. They vary in size from as small as 3 μm to over 1 m and have three parts (cell body, dendrites, axon). The basic purpose is to convey 'messages' from one part of the body to another. (See also *nerve fibre*.)

nerve fibre The axon of a nerve cell (neurone), together with its surrounding membrane, is known as a nerve fibre.

neurologist One who studies neurology, which is concerned with the structure and function of the nervous system.

neuropsychology The study of the interrelationship between behaviour and the nervous system.

NFER National Foundation for Educational Research.

normal curve The shape of a graph which results when the distribution of some property (or aspect) of a population is plotted. The shape is derived from probability theory, with most scores being clustered about an average (mean) value and scores very different from the mean occurring far less often. Height and weight are examples of what yield a normal curve, as are speeds of running or swimming.

occipital lobe Each hemisphere of the brain has an occipital lobe, which is the rearmost of the four lobes.

onset The sound (or sounds) within the first part of a word up to the first vowel. The onset of 'horse' is 'h-', that of 'trick' is 'tr-' and of 'splash' is 'spl-'. (If a word begins with a vowel, e.g. ape, egg, ink, etc., then it can have no onset.)

optic chiasma Located in the brain and part of the visual pathway, it is the place where the two inside bundles of optic nerve fibres from the back of the eye cross over. In front of the optic chiasma are the optic nerves and behind them are the *optic tracts*.

optic radiations Part of the visual pathway of the brain and located between the *lateral geniculate nucleus* and the *occipital lobes*, each of the two optic radiations transmits visual information from the former to the latter. The nerves of the optic radiations form a distinct pattern.

optic tracts Part of the visual pathway of the brain and located immediately behind the *optic chiasma*. Each of the two optic tracts (one in each half of the brain) consists of nerves from the outside half of the eye on the same side of the brain as itself, together with those from the inside half of the other eye.

organic books Also called *real books*, they are written in a different style from *inorganic books* (which are the ones that have traditionally been used to teach reading). The aim of organic books is to tell a story in a way which will attract children and encourage them to learn to read. They sound well when read aloud, the language being more natural and with a more natural 'flow' to it than that in inorganic books.

orthographic (stage) A stage or phase in reading development. The last stage of three (as proposed by Uta Frith). The others are, in order, the alphabetic and the logographic phases.

orthography The correct, acceptable or commonly agreed way of spelling the words of a language.

parietal lobe One of the four lobes which make up each half of the brain. Its location is above the temporal lobe and between the frontal and occipital lobes.

PAT Phonological Abilities Test; Phonological Awareness Training.

PATOSS Professional Association of Teachers of Students with Specific Learning Difficulties.

PDD Pervasive developmental disorder.

PEP Principal educational psychologist.

perceptual dyslexia Usually referred to as P-type dyslexia. One of two subgroups of dyslexia (as claimed by Bakker). The other subgroup is described as L-type (*linguistic dyslexia*). Bakker claims that 60-70% of dyslexic children fall into one or other of these subgroups. A P-type dyslexic child is described as reading relatively slowly and in a fragmented fashion, albeit rather accurately as they remain sensitive to the perceptual features of text.

PET (scan) Positron emission tomography.

PhAB Phonological Assessment Battery.

phoneme The smallest unit of sound that can distinguish one word from another, e.g. pan-ban or cat-cot. Normal English makes use of 44 phonemes: 24 consonants and 20 vowels. When English is written down, the fact that there are only 26 letters in the alphabet to represent 44 different sounds, means that some letters, used singly or in pairs, need to represent more than one sound. This is a complication that children have to overcome in learning to read.

phonemic analysis The process of analysing the sound of a word into the smaller sounds (phonemes) from which it is formed.

phonemic awareness The realization that a word is not a single 'block' of sound but is made up of a collection of smaller sounds (phonemes). When learning to read, a child must be able to analyse a word into its component sounds and then synthesize (or blend) them together to produce the spoken word. See *phonemic analysis, phonemic synthesis.*

phonemic segmentation Another name for *phonemic analysis.*

phonemic synthesis The process of building up a word from the smaller sounds (phonemes) from which it is composed.

phonetics The scientific study of the sounds involved in speech production generally (compare with *phonology*).

phonics (1) A method of teaching reading and spelling. It is based on the sounding out of each letter (or grouping of letters) in a word. It is to be contrasted with the *look-and-say* method. (2) An obsolete term for *phonetics* (used in the 17th century).

phonological dyslexia (1) A subgrouping of the *acquired dyslexia* found in adults. It is described as being similar to *deep dyslexia* but less pronounced in intensity. A person who is a phonological dyslexic has difficulty with nonwords and the sounding out of words generally. Visual errors are quite likely to occur but there is less chance of errors related to word meanings. (2) A subgrouping of the *developmental dyslexia* found in children. It was one of two types proposed by Snowling in 1987, the other being *surface* (or *morphemic*) *dyslexia*. Children who are phonological dyslexics are described as resembling phonologically dyslexic adults in their reading and spelling.

phonological processor dyslexia A subgrouping of the developmental dyslexia found in children; one of three subgroups proposed by Seymour (1986). He found evidence of phonological weakness in all his dyslexic subjects. The other two subgroupings he proposed are *semantic processor* and *visual processor dyslexics*.

phonological system The particular skills an individual needs in order to be able to comprehend and use language. The system is still not yet fully defined nor are the exact interrelationships of the relevant skills fully understood.

phonology The study of the speech sounds of a particular language (compare with *phonetics*).

pictogram (often referred to as pictograph) A symbol used in picture writing, e.g. a set of wavy lines might represent the sea or a river.

pilot study A study carried out before the main study is undertaken and which is intended as a trial run in order to identify any possible future difficulties while there is still time to carry out improvements to the design of the main study.

pre-conceptual (substage) A stage in the young person's intellectual development, as described by Piaget.

pre-operations (stage) A stage in the young person's intellectual development, as described by Piaget.

pre-reading skills Those skills considered beneficial to a child when about to be taught reading, e.g. the ability to listen to stories, to distinguish between one sound and another, or one shape and another, to compare and contrast, to order and arrange, to draw and paint, etc.

pro forma A document with blanks to be filled in.

PSP Parental Support Project.

P-type dyslexia See *perceptual dyslexia*.

RA Reading age.

raw score A number that shows how many questions/tasks/items a child got correct in a test. It is simply a quantity that has little if any meaning, as it needs to be converted into a *scaled score*. This will give an indication of the quality of the test results obtained by comparing them with those from many other children of the same age.

Reading Recovery A programme produced in New Zealand by Professor Marie Clay and established 1988. It operates in all New Zealand primary schools as well as in many Australian and US schools. Introduced into the UK in Surrey. It requires 1:1 teaching for half an hour every day for 12-20 weeks. The method is known as 'Pause, Prompt and Praise' and relies on catching difficulties early.

real books Another name for *organic books*.

rebus A picture or symbol that represents a word or phrase. Many road signs consist of a rebus, e.g. a red and black car side by side within a red circle means 'no overtaking', a human figure holding a spade means 'road works ahead', etc. (A child with reading difficulties might respond to a scheme that employs rebuses.)

received pronunciation (RP) Pronunciation that is regarded as correct or proper. RP should be understood by all who use the language and should also be the pronunciation taught to foreigners who are learning the language.

retina The light-sensitive layer at the back of the eye, which is composed of the highly specialised *rod* and *cone* cells and on to which images of the outside world are focused by the *lens*.

rime The sound (or sounds) within the end part of a word, starting at the first vowel. The rime of 'horse' is '-orse', of 'trick' is '-ick' and of 'splash' is '-ash'. Some words begin with a vowel and hence the rime consists of the entire word, e.g. ape, egg, ink, on, up. Two words sharing the same rime will rhyme with one another, e.g. 'bell' and 'sell'. (Some rhyming words will not always have rimes that are spelled the same, e.g. 'few' and 'through'.)

rods One of the two specialized cells in the retina of the eye, the other being the *cones*. There are 120 million rods in each eye and they respond to differences in light and shade.

RP Received pronunciation.

SALVA See-And-Learn-Visual-Aid.

scaled score The meaningful score into which the *raw score* of a test is converted. It is meaningful as it produces a figure that can be compared with that produced by large numbers of other children of the same age and so can give an insight into whether a child has a particular difficulty and, if so, how serious it is likely to be.

School Action The action undertaken by a school in relation to a pupil when it is first suspected that the pupil might have *special educadional needs (SENs)*.

School Action Plus The further action undertaken by a school when the initial action (see *School Action*) is deemed not to have been successful.

segmentation The process of dividing up something into smaller pieces or segments. In the case of learning to read, it is the process of looking at a printed word and breaking it down (segmenting) into the smaller phonemes (speech sound) that go to make up the word.

semantic processor dyslexia A subgrouping of the developmental dyslexia found in children; one of three subgroups proposed by Seymour (1986). However, he found that his data could not 'easily be put into a coherent scheme of subtypes'.

SEN Special educational need.

SENCO Special educational needs co-ordinator.

sensorimotor (stage) A stage of intellectual development in the young person, as described by Piaget.

sequencing The arranging of items into the correct order.

sequential dyslexia A term used by a clinical psychologist in a report but unfortunately not explained.

short-term memory The part of the memory process involved in remembering something for a relatively brief period of time. It is used a great deal in most mental activities and is sometimes referred to as working memory. Being able to remember a telephone number accurately for a sufficiently long enough time to be able to write it down or dial it is a good example of short-term memory in use.

small letter Also known as *lower-case* to distinguish from *capital* or *upper-case*.

SNAP Special Needs Action Programme.

'soft' signs (of brain damage) Features such as co-ordination difficulties, abnormal reflex actions or an unusual EEG pattern. There could also be a mild degree of speech impairment or a difficulty with balance.

SOS Simultaneous oral spelling.

specific developmental dyslexia One of the many terms used to describe the form of dyslexia found in children. (It was defined by the World Federation of Neurology in 1968.)

specific dyslexia A short form of *specific developmental dyslexia*.

specific learning difficulties (SpLD) The term preferred by many educational psychologists, teachers and researchers to describe *dyslexia* in children. (It was defined by Tansley and Panckhurst in 1981 and by the Dyslexia Institute in 1989.)

specific reading difficulties One of the many terms used to describe *dyslexia* in children. It was used by the DES in 1972 in one of its reports which had resulted from the formation of the Advisory Committee for Handicapped Children (Chairman Professor J Tizard). The report was entitled *Children with Specific Reading Difficulties*.

specific reading disabilities One of the many terms used to describe *dyslexia* in children.

specific reading retardation One of the many terms used to describe *dyslexia* in children. (It was defined by Rutter, Tizard and Whitmore in 1970.)

SPELD *Specific Learning Difficulties*, which stands for a movement set up in New South Wales in 1967 and must not be confused with SpLD.

SpLD Specific learning difficulties. (This should not be confused with SLD, which stands for severe learning difficulties.)

spoonerism A slip of the tongue in which the beginning part of one word replaces that of another and vice versa, e.g. intending to say 'Silly boy!' but actually saying 'Billy soy'.

SPS Schools Psychological Service.

SS Social services.

SSS Scotopic sensitivity syndrome.

standardize This refers to the process of transforming the rough (or raw) results of testing into units of measurement which are meaningful. The outcome is that the standardized scores can be compared in a meaningful way with scores from a different test, e.g. a score of 48 out of 100 on one test can be compared with 37 out of 60 on another, even if one was marked more severely than another.

strephosymbolia Literally, 'the twisting of symbols'. An early term to describe *dyslexia*.

sulcus A shallow cleft on the brain's surface. Being of Latin origin, the plural form is sulci.

surface dyslexia (1) A subgroup of the acquired dyslexia found in adults. Surface dyslexics are able to read phonetically regular words and nonwords. However, they have difficulties with irregular words and cannot make use of visual analysis to recognize whole words. The surface dyslexic over-relies on phonological methods, slowly sounding out the words as he reads. (2) Also known as *morphemic dyslexia*, surface dyslexics are a subgrouping of children described by Snowling in 1987. (The other subgrouping is *phonological dyslexia*.) Children who are surface dyslexics are described as being similar to adults with surface dyslexia.

SW Social worker.

syllabification The process of breaking down a word into its syllables.

syllable A part of a word, distinguishable from the other part(s) by the sounds of speech. Each syllable must either have one, two or more vowels in combination, or contain the letter y. There may be consonants in addition, but the foregoing is essential. There is one syllable in: dog, soup, sky; two syllables in: wa-ter, mon-key, wel-come; and three syllables in: hap-pi-ness, won-der-ful, ti-di-ly. Syllables are themselves made up of *phonemes*.

syntax The way in which words are arranged grammatically to show relationships and meaning within a sentence.

TEACH (method) The Treatment and Education of Autistic and related Communication-Handicapped Children.

temporal lobe One of the four lobes of each cerebral hemisphere. It is at the side of the head, in the region of the temple (hence the name) and lies below the lateral fissure.

traumatic dyslexia Another name for *acquired dyslexia* in adults.

UKRA United Kingdom Reading Association.

upper-case letter A printer's term for a *capital letter*, as opposed to a *small* (or *lower-case*) *letter*.

ventricle A small cavity in the brain filled with cerebrospinal fluid. There are four in all.

verbal-imagery (dimension) A characteristic of learning which all people are considered to possess to some degree.

visual dyslexia Claimed to be a subtype of both *alexia* and *developmental dyslexia* and, together with auditory dyslexia, one of the earliest subtypes to be identified. A visual dyslexic has difficulty in recognizing the appearance of a word on the basis of how the word sounds. 'Auditory methods' of teaching are claimed to produce the best results. Many make comparisons between visual dyslexia, dyseidetic dyslexia and the visualgrapheme processor dyslexia.

visual pathway The route taken by nerve impulses as they travel from the rear of the eyes to the visual cortex at the back of the brain. The parts involved are, in order: the *retinas*, the *optic nerves*, the *optic chiasma*, the *optic tracts*, the *lateral geniculate nuclei*, the *optic radiations* and the *occipital lobes*.

visual processor dyslexia A subgrouping of the developmental dyslexia found in children, one of three proposed by Seymour in 1986. (The other two subgroups he proposed are *semantic processor* and *phonological processor* dyslexics. After carrying out his study he felt that the results could not 'easily be fitted into a coherent scheme of subtypes'.

vitreous humour The clear, jelly-like substance that fills most of the eyeball and which lies between the lens and the retina.

WAIS Wechsler Adult Intelligence Scale.

white matter The bulk of the material which goes to make up the brain. It lies beneath the 3 mm thick *grey matter* or *cerebral cortex* but in the spine is on the outside of the grey matter. It is mainly composed of nerve fibres.

whole-word (method of teaching reading) Another name for the *look-and-say* method.

wholist-analytic (dimension) A characteristic of learning which all people are considered to possess to some degree.

WISC Wechsler Intelligence Scale for Children.

WORD Wechsler Objective Reading Dimensions.

word blindness One of the first names given to dyslexia and, despite the passage of more than a century, one that is still quite popular in the public mind.

WPPSI Wechsler Pre-School and Primary Scale of Intelligence.

Y A letter of the alphabet that is unique insofar as it sometimes acts as a vowel and sometimes as a consonant. Vowels and consonants are sounds, not letters, and our alphabet letters in many cases only approximate to the sounds intended, e.g. Y acts as a consonant in some words (yacht, yellow), but as a vowel in others (happy, easy). We also say/write 'a youth', not 'an youth', but say/write 'an' in front of every other word beginning with a vowel, e.g. 'an apple', 'an egg', etc.

Bibliography

The information presented in this book is based on a wide range of sources assembled over a period of more than a decade, from 1990 to mid-2001. Some of the sources drawn upon originated decades earlier.

The bulk of the information comes from books. Some of these are general reference books, for the most part of the medical type, and there is no point in listing them here. The other, more academic and specialized books ought to be obtainable from any academic bookseller.

Some of the information comes from other sources and the average parent or teacher will, unfortunately, find this less easy to obtain. These sources include articles in journals and newspapers, the contents of television programmes, notes taken in lectures, discussions with educational psychologist colleagues (and other professionals) and information imparted - sometimes by means of private correspondence - by university-based researchers.

The journals referred to are likely to be found, in many cases, only in the libraries of universities: departments such as Education and Psychology in particular. Some of my other sources, such as the manuals of 'closed' psychological tests, are accessible only to registered psychologists.

The books listed are those I believe will be of greatest assistance to the concerned parent or teacher who wishes to learn more about dyslexia.

Books

Bradley L, Bryant P (1985) Rhyme and Reason in Reading and Spelling. Ann Arbor: University of Michigan Press.
British Psychological Society (1999) Dyslexia, Literacy and Psychological Assessment. Leicester: BPS.

Bryant P, Bradley L (1987) Children's Reading Problems. Oxford: Blackwell.

Department for Education and Employment (1997) Excellence for all Children: meeting special educational needs. London: DfEE.

Department for Education and Employment (1997) The SENCo Guide. London: DfEE.

Department for Education and Employment (1998) Meeting Special Educational Needs: A Programme of Action. London: DfEE.

Department for Education and Employment (1998) The National Literacy Strategy: Framework for Teaching. London: DfEE.

Department for Education and Employment (2000) Educational Psychology Services (England): current role, good practice and future directions. Report of the Working Group. London: DfEE.

Department for Education and Employment (2000) Educational Psychology Services (England): current role, good practice and future directions. The Research Report. London: DfEE.

Department for Education and Employment (2000) SEN Code of Practice on the Assessment of Pupils with Special Educational Needs. (Draft Code and Guidance). London: DfEE.

Elliot CD (1996) British Ability Scales, 2nd edn (BAS II) (Manual). Windsor: NFER-Nelson.

Fawcett A (ed) (2001) Dyslexia Theory and Good Practice. London: Whurr.

Franklin AW, Naidoo S (eds) (1970) Assessment and Teaching of Dyslexic Children. London: Invalid Children's Aid Association.

Goswami U, Bryant P (1990) Phonological Skills and Learning to Read. East Sussex: Lawrence Erlbaum Associates.

Hornsby B (1984/88) Overcoming Dyslexia. London: Macdonald.

Hornsby B, Shear F (1982) Alpha to Omega: the A-Z of teaching writing and spelling. London: Heinemann.

Miles TR (1983) Dyslexia: the pattern of difficulties. London/Toronto/Sydney/ New York: Granada.

Miles TR, Miles E (1990) Dyslexia: a hundred years on. Milton Keynes: Open University Press.

Pumfrey P, Reason R (1991) Specific Learning Difficulties (Dyslexia): challenges and responses. London: Routledge.

Quin V, Macauslan A (1986) Dyslexia: what parents ought to know. Harmondsworth: Penguin.

Reason R, Boote R (1989) Learning Difficulties in Reading and Writing: a teacher's manual. Windsor: NFER-Nelson.

Snowling M (1987) Dyslexia: a cognitive developmental perspective. Oxford/New York: Blackwell.

Young P, Tyre C (1983) Dyslexia or illiteracy? Realising the Right to Read. Milton Keynes: Open University Press.

Journals

British Journal of Educational Psychology
British Journal of Pschology
Child Development
DECP Newsletter
Dyslexia (The Journal of the British Dyslexia Association)
Educational Psychology in Practice
International Reading Association
Journal of Learning Disabilities
Reading Research Quarterly
Science
Special Children
Support for Learning
The Psychologist

Index

Aarons reading test 130
absenteeism 16, 18, 20, 21, 24
Academic and Developmental Learning
     Disabilities 184
ACE Special Education Handbook 226
'acid' tests 39, 40
acquisition components (of intelligence)
     27
Activity Literacy Kit 184
Adult Dyslexia Organisation (ADO) 231
'Advice' to LEA/Appendix to Statement
     of SENS 127
Advisory Centre for Education (ACE)
     225, 226
Advisory Committee on Handicapped
     Children 213
age 16, 17, 18, 21
alexia 83, 85, 86, 90, 215, 216, 233
alliteration 126, 132, 165, 173, 174
alphabet 54, 62
alphabetic method 59
alphabetic phase (of reading) 73
Alphabetic Phonics 184
Alphabetic principle 173,175
Alpha to Omega 184, 235
amnesia visualis verbalis 83
analfabeta partialis 83
Andy Pandy 165
Annals of Dyslexia 234
answers (in note form) 135
aphasia 233
apprenticeship approach 64–66, 68
aqueous humour 152, 153
area health authority (AHA) 23, 24
arithmetic (WISC Sub-test) 35, 36, 38,
     118, 128

arithmetic/number skills 133, 137
ARROW 182, 189
art and craft 107
articulation 150
Arts Dyslexia Trust 230
Assistant Masters and Mistresses
     Association (AMMA) 190
Association of Educational Psychologists
     (AEP) 236
Aston Index (Revised) 125, 132, 184, 188
Aston Portfolio (Checklist) 184,188
Attack-a-Track 189
attention 56
auditory long-term memory (BAS-
     related) 129
auditory memory 75
auditory perception 75, 157
auditory short-term memory (BAS Sub-
     test) 129, 137, 138

Bakker 90
balance 75
'b' and 'd' confusion 104
Bangor Dyslexia Screening Test 133
Bangor Dyslexia Teaching System 184
Bangor Teaching Programme 184
Bannatynes's Colour Phonics 184
Barking Reading Project 188
basic number skills (BAS Sub-test) 128
basic reading 130
BAS reading sub-test 130
BAS spelling sub-test 130
BDA Computer Resource Centre 229
BDA Diploma 235
Beat Dyslexia 184
bell ringing 107

Bender (motor gestalt) test 132
Benton test 132
Berlin (Professor) 216, 234
Billy Bunter 165
blackboard, copying from 106
Bleak House 215
blending 165,166
block design (BAS or WISC Sub-test) 35, 36, 119, 128, 129, 137, 138
Bob the Builder 165
Boder 89, 91
Booksellers Association 236
Bottomley 104
Bradley, Lynette 86, 87, 107, 167
bradylexia 83
Brand, Violet 235
Bristol Social Adjustment Guide 132
British Abilities Scales (BAS) 40, 41, 128, 133
British Dyslexia Association 92, 189, 190, 212, 228, 235–7
British Education Communications and Technology Agency (BECTA) 228
British Medical Association 213, 217, 235
British Psychological Society 94
Broca's language area 149, 233
Bromley Screening Pack 188
Bryant, Peter 86, 87, 107, 167
Bulletin of the Orton Society 234
Burt, Cyril (Sir) 216, 217, 234

Campaign for the Advancement of State Education (CASE) 225
capital letter 55
central fissure 142, 143
Centre for Studies on Inclusive Education (CSIE) 226
cerebellar deficit hypothesis 148, 150, 151
cerebellum 147–151, 157, 158
cerebral cortex 144
cerebral hemisphere 142–7, 163
Checking Individual Progress in Phonics (ChIPPs 184
chess 107
Children's Legal Centre, The 226
Children's Written Language Difficulties 184
Children with Specific Learning Difficulties 235
chromosome 6 220

chromosome 15 220
Chronically Sick and Disabled Person's Act 235
City of London Dyslexia Institute 235
Classroom Observation Procedure 188
clinical medical officer (CMO) 24, 98
clinical psychologist 126
Cloze procedure 134
Cloze Procedures and the Teaching of Reading 188
Code of Practice (relating to SENS) 117, 134, 195–9, 202, 204, 221, 236–7
coding (WISC Sub-test) 35, 36, 39, 118, 128, 137, 138
cognitive control model 79–81
cognitive history 79, 80
Cognitive Profiling System (CoPS) 188
coloured filters/overlays/papers/spectacles 134, 137, 162
comprehension (WISC Sub-test) 35, 36, 118, 128, 137, 138
comprehension of continuous prose 130
computer-assisted learning (CAL) 187
Computer-Assisted Learning Programmes with Speech Enhancement 188
computerised axial tomography (CAT) 141
concrete operations (stage of development) 72
cones 154, 157
congenital symbol amblyopia 83
congenital typholexia 83
congenital word blindness 83, 216, 217
conjunctiva 152, 153
Connexions Service 210
control groups/controls 176
copying ability 114, 132
cornea 152, 153
corpus callosum 143, 146, 148, 154, 163
Council for the Registration of Schools Teaching Dyslexic Pupils (CReSTeD) 230
Council on Tribunals 224
creative writing 107
cross-lateral 161, 221
CSE Board 213
cued spelling 135
cursive script 189

Dale, Nellie 59, 60
Dame Schools 55

Davidson, Helen 57
DATAPAC 188
Dealing with Dyslexia 184
decoding skills 130
De Montfort University 236
Dennis the Menace 165
Department of Education 235
DES 94, 190, 235
Desperate Dan 165
developmental aphasia 83
Development of Reading and Related
    Skills with Pupils of Secondary Age
    (DORRS) 188
DFE 236
DfEE 67, 236
DfES 6, 67, 186, 195, 197, 199, 200, 221,
    223, 236
diacritical marks 59
Diagnostic Spelling Dictation Test 130
Dickens, Charles 215
dictation 114
Differential Ability Scales (DAS) 41
digit span (WISC Sub-test) 35, 39, 118,
    128, 137, 138
digraphs 130
Diploma in Special Education 183
Direct Instruction 188
directionality 132
Director of Education LEA) 207
discrimination 62
Division of Educational and Child
    Psychology (of the BPS) 214
dominance 148, 160, 161, 163
dominant hemisphere 146
driving a car 107
dual route process 159
dyslexia, acquired 82, 83, 85–92, 216
  acute 83
  attentional 83, 87, 91
  auditory 83, 89, 91
  classical sequential 83
  congenital 83, 85, 91
  constitutional 83
  deep 83, 88, 91
  developmental 83, 85, 89–92, 216, 217
  direct 83, 87, 89, 91
  dyseidetic 83, 89, 91
  dysphonetic 83, 89, 91
  familial 83
  graphemic processor 83, 89, 91
  'L' -type 83, 90, 91

  mixed 83, 89, 91
  morphemic 83, 91
  phonological 83, 87–91
  phonological processor 83, 90, 91
  'P'-type 83, 90, 91
  'R'-type 83
  secondary 83
  semantic processor 83, 90, 91
  sequential 83
  specific 83
  specific developmental 83, 85, 93, 94,
    236
  surface 82, 83, 87, 89–91
  traumatic 83, 85, 86
  visual 83, 87, 89, 91
  visual processor 83, 90
Dyslexia Adult Screening Test 131, 133
Dyslexia Association of Ireland (DAI) 232
Dyslexia: A Teaching Handbook 184
Dyslexia A2Z (website) 231
Dyslexia Contact 229, 235
Dyslexia Early Screening Test (DEST)
    125
Dyslexia-Friendly Schools 236
Dyslexia in Scotland 232
Dyslexia Institute 92, 126, 190, 212, 229,
    235–6
Dyslexia Institute Adult Questionnaire
    133
Dyslexia Institute Skills Development
    Programme 134
Dyslexia Institute Week 236
Dyslexia, Literacy and Psychological Assessment
    (DECP) 236
dyslexia screening 127, 137
Dyslexia Screening Test 125
Dyslexia Unit (Univ of Bangor) 190, 234
DYXI (website) 231

Early Detection of Reading Difficulties
    188
Early Identification of Special Needs 188
'early years' battery (BAS Sub-tests) 41
east-west confusion 103
'Easy Type' 136
Eden 160
Edgeworth, Richard and Maria 59
Edith Norrie Letter Case 184, 191
Education Act 1981 84, 235
Education Act 1983 197, 236

Education Act 1996 196, 197
Educational Applications of the WISC - R 188
educational psychologist (EP) 24, 38, 52, 97, 110–13, 115–6, 123, 126, 138–9, 200, 207, 217
Educational Psychology Service (EPS) 96, 116, 200
education welfare officer (EWO) 24, 98
electroencephalogram (EEG) 86
embedded pictures 189
emotional difficulties 16, 20, 21, 24
English as an additional/second language 16, 21, 24, 68
English Colour Code Programmed Reading Course, The 189
essays 135
European Dyslexia Association (EDA) 235
examination concessions 135, 136, 138
eye dominance 115
eye test, specialist 134

family life 16, 21, 24
Famous Five, The 165
Fernand and Kelly 58
Fernand Multi-Sensory Approach 184
fine motor control 115
finger agnosia 221
finger spelling 189
fissure 142
fixation 132, 157
flash card 57, 61, 64
foreign language, learning of 106
formal operations (stage of development) 72
Forster Education Act (1870) 55, 233
Framework for Teaching 67, 68
freedom from distractibility (WISC factor) 40, 128
free writing 115, 120
Frith 71, 73, 74, 166
frontal lobe 142, 143
full-scale/general IQ 35–8, 119, 123–4, 128, 138

Gates 57
Gattegno 59
GCE Board 213
gender 15
General conceptual ability (GCA) (BAS-related) 41, 128

general learning difficulty 49, 100
Gillingham-Stillman Alphabetic Method 184
Ginn 360 56
grafting-on process 57
grammar 115
grapheme 68, 75, 125, 160
Green Paper (1997) 197, 236
Guidance for Educational Psychologists' Assessments (DECP) 236
Guidance for Educational Psychologists' Statutory Assessments (AEP) 236
Guilford 27, 33
gyrus 142

handedness (left- or right-) 115, 131
handwriting 1, 67, 119, 122–3, 130–1, 135, 137, 138, 150–1, 222
'hard' signs (of brain damage/dyslexia) 86, 92, 221
Health Council of the Netherlands 94
hearing difficulties 16, 21, 24, 50
Helen Arkell Dyslexia Centre 230, 235
Hickey Method 184
Hinshelwood 175, 216
Holt, Maisie 234
homophones 88
Hornsby Centre 234
Hornsby School 234
Human Rights Act 236
hyperlexia 83, 87, 89, 91, 95

Icon Approach 184
illiteracy 16, 21, 24
immigration 16, 21, 24
Independent Panel for Special Educational Advice (IPSEA) 226
individual education plan (IEP) 117, 122, 123, 201
information (WISC Sub-test) 35, 36, 39, 118, 128
information and computer technology (ICT) 199
initial teaching alphabet (ITA) 59
inorganic books 65
Institute of Cognitive Neuroscience 160
intelligence/intellectual ability 16–18, 20–1, 26–47, 49, 53, 79, 100, 113, 122
intelligence quotient (IQ) 30, 32–3, 41, 44–52, 85, 93–4, 100, 113
intelligence scales/tests 29, 30, 32–3, 44

International Phonetic Alphabet (IPA) 170–1
intuitive sub-stage (of development) 72
Invalid Children's Aid Association (ICAA) 234
invented words 68
Irlen, Helen 162
Irlen Institute (USA) 162

Jagger 58
Johnson and Mykelbust 89, 91
Joint Council for GCSE 236
Jolly Phonics 184

Kerr, James (Dr) 216, 234
Keyboard Skills 135
Keywords 62–3
Kinaesthetic Method 58
Kirklees reading test 130
Kussmaul 215–6, 234

Ladybird reading scheme 56
language 53
language learning disorder 83
LASS (Junior) 188
LASS (Secondary) 188
lateral fissure 142–3
lateral geniculate nucleus 155–6
laterality 115, 132, 137
LEA person 201, 205
Learning Difficulties in Reading and Writing: A Teacher's Manual 188
learning style 76–8, 80
left-right awareness/confusion 103, 115, 121, 138
legasthenia 83
lens (of the eye) 152
letter reversals 221–2
lexical (visual) route 159
Lexicon (the game) 191
lexicon 159
light sensitivity 132
Lincoln-Oseretsky Hand Function Test 132
Linguistic Awareness in Reading Readiness 188
listening 75
Literacy Hour 67–8
local college 24
local education authority (LEA) 23–4, 96, 111, 126, 140, 183, 185–6, 196–7, 199–201, 203–10, 212, 223–4, 229

Local Government Ombudsman 227–8
logographic phase (of reading) 73
London County Council 217, 234
longitudinal fissure 142–3
longitudinal study 177
look and say approach/method 56–7, 60, 64, 66, 68
lower case letters 55, 62
Lucid Cognitive Profiling System (CoPS) 125

Macauslan, Alan 86
magnetic resonance imaging (MRI) 141
magnification facilities 134
magnocells 157–8
magnocellular system 157–8
Making Sense of It (Miscue Analysis) 188
map reading 132
Marsh 71–4
'masking' effect 101
matched control group 100
matrixes (BAS Sub-test) 129
mazes (WISC Sub-test) 35
McDonald Critchley 217
McMullen reading test 130
mechanical reading skills 130
Meeting Special Educational Needs: a programme of action 197
memory 56, 115, 157, 196
memory for sentences 106
mental age 43–52, 113, 176–7
mental arithmetic (BAS Sub-test) 129
Meredith, (Professor) 213
metacognition 75, 77–9, 191
metacomponents (of intelligence) 27
Miles, Elaine 86–7
Miles, Tim (Professor) 86–7, 99–100, 102–9, 234
Milly Molly Mandy 165
mind blindness 83
Mind Map Book, The 136
mirror writing 221–2
mnemonic drawings 189
Monroe-Sherman handwriting test 131
Monroe-Sherman reading test 130
months of the year (recall of) 104, 132
Motion detection 75
motivation 16, 21, 24, 56
motor control/skills 75, 121, 132, 147, 150
motor gestalt 132
Muffin the Mule 165

Multi-Sensory Learning 184
Multi-Sensory Teaching System for Reading (MTSR) 184
music 107

naming memory 75
naming speed 75, 126, 132
National Adult Reading Test 130
National Association for Remedial Education (NARE) 190
National Association of School Masters and Union of Women Teachers (NAS-UWT) 190
National Children's Bureau 227
National Curriculum 198
National Federation of Access Centres 228
National Literacy Project 67
National Literacy Strategy 67, 198, 236
National Numeracy Strategy 198
Neale reading test 129, 130
nerve cells 144
Network '81 228–9
neuropsychology 54
Nicholson (Professor) 148–9
non-verbal reasoning ability (BAS-related) 41
nonword(s) 126, 137, 138
Non-word Repetition Test 132
normal curve 45
Norrie, Edith 234
'Note in Lieu' (of Statement of SENS) 201, 205

object assembly (WISC Sub-test) 35–6, 118, 128, 137
occipital lobe 142–3, 156
occupational therapist 123
Oistrowick, Rebecca 234
One-Minute Addition Test 133
One-Minute Reading Test 130
One-Minute Subtraction Test 133
Onset 151, 164–5, 167–8
optic chiasma 154, 156
optic nerve 153–4, 156
optic radiations 155–6
optic tract 154, 156
optometric intervention 126
organic books 65
orthographic patterns 173
orthographic phase (of reading) 73
orthographic skills 158

Orton 216–7, 234
Orton Dyslexia Society 234
Orton - Gillingham Method 184
Orton Society 234

paired reading 134, 187, 191
Panel of Independent Experts on Special Educational Needs 209
parental support project 24
parietal lobe 142–3
PATOSS Bulletin, The 230
pattern construction 129
Patterns of Sound 189
Paulesu 160
Pause - prompt - praise 134
payment by results 55
Peabody Rebus Reading Programme 184
pen grip 115, 131
perceptual difficulties 16, 21, 22, 24
perceptual organisation (WISC factor) 40, 128
performance components (of intelligence) 28
performance/non-verbal IQ 35–8, 113, 119, 123–4, 128, 138
performance scale (of the WISC) 35, 36, 119, 123
performance sub-tests (of the WISC) 34, 36
phonemes 60, 68, 75, 125, 130, 160, 167–73, 175, 178, 180
phoneme addition 166, 173
phoneme blending 159
phoneme deletion 126, 132, 166, 173
phoneme segmentation 132, 159–60, 178
phonemic awareness/skills 169, 174, 178, 180, 187
phonetics 169
phonic approach/method 56–7, 59–60, 64, 66–8, 130
phonic drill 57
Phono-Graphix 184
phonological abilities/skills 75, 88, 125–7, 132, 137–8, 158–9, 164–5, 167, 172, 174, 187, 196, 199, 219
Phonological Abilities Test (PAT) 125–6
phonological analysis 158
Phonological Approach to Teaching 184
Phonological Assessment Battery (PhAB) 125–6
phonological awareness 68, 75, 125–6, 132, 150, 164–5, 167–8, 172, 174, 178–80, 197, 199

phonological deficits 75, 151, 157
phonological fluency 132
phonological memory 174
phonological processing 76, 125, 172, 174
phonological production 173–4
phonological structures 173
phonological system 172–4
phonology 164–5, 169, 172–5
phrase 168
Piaget 72–3
Pictogram System 189
picture arrangement (WISC Sub-test) 35–6, 118, 128
picture completion (WISC Sub-test) 35–6, 118, 128, 137–8
pictures 57
pilot study 4–5, 31
plastic letters 189
position emission tomography (PET) 141, 150, 160
Postman Pat 165
posture 132
preconceptual sub-stage (of development) 72
preferred hand 161
pre-operations stage (of development) 72
preparatory cards 135
Preventing Classroom Failure 188
Primary Language Record, The 188
primary reading retardation 83
Principal Educational Psychologist (PEP) 207
Pringle-Morgan (Dr) 216, 234
processing speed (WISC factor) 40
Professional Association of Teachers of Students with Specific Learning Difficulties (PATOSS) 229–30)
proof reading 132
psychomotor programmes 189
Pumfrey, Peter (Professor) 87, 236
punctuation 115, 120

quantitative reasoning (BAS Sub-test) 129
QUEST Screening, Diagnosis and Remediation Kit 188
Quin, Vera 86–7

reading accuracy 130
reading age 9, 43–52, 113, 122, 130, 137, 177

reading alone 134
reading books 56
reading 'code' 60
reading comprehension 75, 114
reading programme 135
Reading Recovery 189
reading schemes 56
reading speed 114, 130
reading tests 2–13, 114
reading together 134
'real books' (method) 64–6, 68
Reason, Rea 87, 236
recall 62
recall of designs (BAS Sub-test) 128
recall of digits (backwards) (BAS Sub-test) 129
recall of digits (forward) (BAS Sub-test) 105, 128
received pronunciation (RP) 169
reciprocal teaching 79, 134
reciting tables 105
recognition 62
recording equipment 135
retention components (of intelligence) 27
retina 152–4, 156, 157
rhyme 68, 106, 126, 132, 160, 165–6, 171, 173–4, 179
rhyming patterns 68
Riding 79, 80
rime 151, 164–8
rods 154, 157
RSA Diploma (in specific learning difficulties) 230
Rutter, Tizard and Whitmore 92

Salford reading test 130
scanning techniques/facilities 134, 135, 138
Schonell graded word spelling test 130
Schonell reading test 3, 130, 234
school (location of) 15
School Action 196, 201, 205
School Action Plus 196, 201, 205
'school age' battery (BAS Sub-tests) 41
School Board Officers 55
School Situation Questionnaire 132
schooling 16, 21, 22, 24
Schools Council 213
Schools Psychological Service (SPS) 96, 97
scotopic sensitivity syndrome (SSS) 162
Scottish Committee, The 225

Scrabble 62, 191
See-And-Learn-Visual-Aid (SALVA)
    machine 192
segmentation 165–6 219
self-esteem enhancement 189
semantic/semantic system 159, 180
SEN Appeals Tribunal 225
sensori-motor stage (of development) 72
sentence method 58, 60
Sentence Method of Teaching Reading
    58
SEN Toolkit 197
sequencing 115, 130, 221
Seymour 90–1
sight vocabulary 60
Signposts to Spelling 189
similarities (BAS Sub-test) 129
similarities (WISC Sub-test) 35, 36, 118,
    128
simultaneous oral spelling (S-O-S) 135,
    138, 189
single-word recognition 130
Slingerland Approach 184
slow learner 25, 49, 50, 52
Snakes and Ladders 191
Snider 77
Snowling 90, 158, 160, 167
sociability 16, 21–2, 24
social class 15
Social Services (SS) 23–4
social worker 24
'soft' signs (of brain damage/dyslexia) 86,
    92, 221
software 135
'sounding out' approach 56
Sound Linkage Programme 188
spatial ability (general part of BAS) 41
Spearman 27
special educational needs co-ordinator
    (SENCo) 201, 207
special learning difficulties 196
Special Needs Action Programme
    (SNAP) 188
Special Needs in the Primary School:
    Identification and Intervention 188
specialist teacher 24, 135, 207
specific difficulties (children with) 25, 51
specific language disability 83
specific learning difficulty 49–50, 52,
    82–3, 85, 93–4, 196–8
*Specific Learning Difficulties/Dyslexia: Chal-
    lenges and Responses* 236

specific reading difficulties 83, 85, 93–4,
    216
specific reading disabilities 83, 85
specific reading retardation 82–3, 93–4
speech 16, 21–2, 24, 53, 93, 118, 147
speech and language therapist (SpALT)
    24, 98
speed of information processing (BAS
    subtest) 129
speed reading 135
SPELD 235
spellchecker 135, 138
spelling 1, 67–8, 75, 93–4, 103, 108,
    114–5, 122, 125, 130, 137–8,
    150–1
spelling (BAS subtest) 130
Spelling Made Easy 136, 184
spelling programme 135
spelling rules 135
Spooner 166
spoonerism 126, 132, 166–7, 173
standardization 5
Stanovich 167
Statement of SENs 186, 200–2, 204–5,
    209, 235
Statement on Dyslexia (AEP) 236
St Bartholomew's Hospital 234
Stein, (Professor) 157–8, 220
stimulation 16, 21–2, 24
story method 57
strephosymbolia 83, 217
sub-lexical (phonological) route 159, 160
subtraction and addition 104
sulcus 142
syllabification 168, 189
syllable 168
syllable counting 132
symbol search (WISC Sub-test) 35, 128
syntax 115, 131, 180

Tactics for Teaching Dyslexic Students
    184
Tansley and Panckhurst 92, 235
tape recording (use of) 135, 189, 191
taped reading 135
teaching difficulties 16, 21–2, 24
teaching styles 76
Teaching with Precision 188
Teletubbies 165
temporal lobe 142–3
Thomas the Tank Engine 165
three Rs 55, 56, 108

Thurstone 27
times and dates confusion 104
time estimation 75
Tizard Report 213, 235
Toe-by-Toe reading programme 135, 184
Touchstones 188
tracking 161
transfer components (of intelligence) 27
transition plan 210
trauma 16, 21, 23–4
Tribunal for Special Educational Needs 201, 205, 207, 211
Two-Minute spelling (sub) test 131
typing skills 135
Tyre, Colin 86–7

United Kingdom Reading Association (UKRA) 190
unpunctuality 16, 21, 23
Vellutino 167
ventricle 144
verbal ability (general part of BAS) 41
verbal comprehension (WISC factor) 40, 128
verbal-imagery dimension 78
verbal IQ 34, 36–8, 113, 119, 123–4, 128, 138
verbal reasoning skills (BAS Sub-test) 129
verbal scale (of the WISC) 35–6, 118, 124
verbal similarities (BAS Sub-test) 41
verbal sub-tests (of the WISC) 34
Vernon 27
Vernon graded spelling test 130
Vernon reading test 130
Vernon-Ward reading test 130
visual cortex 153, 156–7
visual difficulties 16, 18, 21, 23–4, 50
visual memory processing speed (BAS) 129
visual motor co-ordination (BAS-related) 129
visual pathway 153–4, 156
visual perception 75
visual recall, delayed (BAS-related) 129
visual recall, immediate (BAS-related) 129
visual retention 132
visual sequencing (BAS Sub-test) 129

visual thinking competence (BAS) 129
vitreous humour 152–3
vocabulary (WISC Sub-test) 35–6, 118, 128
vowel sounds 130

Warnock Committee 235
Warnock Report 235
Watford Dyslexia Unit 235
Wechsler Adult Intelligence Scale (WAIS) 34, 128
Wechsler Intelligence Scale for Children (WISC) 34–41, 113, 118, 119, 123–5, 128, 133
Wechsler Objective Reading Dimensions (WORD) 119, 124, 129, 130, 133
Wechsler Pre-school and Primary Scale of Intelligence (WPPSI) 34
Welchman, Marion 235
Wepman Test 132
White, Franklin (Dr) 234
Whittaker 217
'whole' method 56–7
wholist - analytic dimension 78
WIAT 133
Wide Range Activity Test (WRAT) 132
Wide Range Spelling (Sub-test) 130
Wilkins Rate of Reading Test 126
word-attack skills 130
Word Blind Centre for Dyslexic Children 234
Word Blind Institute (Copenhagen) 234
word blind(ness) 83, 86, 215–6, 233
word definitions (BAS Sub-test) 41, 128
word envelope 57–8
word patterns 57
word processing 135, 191
word reading (BAS Sub-test) 129
Words in Colour 59
World Federation of Neurology 92
WRAT (arithmetic sub-test) 133
WRAT (reading sub-test) 129
writing 114, 120, 147
writing speed 115, 120, 138
Wundt 234

Year of Reading 236
Young, Peter 86, 87